MW01104170

THE SIMON & SCHUSTER POCKET GUIDE TO

CHARDONNAY WINES

ROGER VOSS

A Fireside Book
Published by Simon & Schuster Inc.
New York London Toronto
Sydney Tokyo Singapore

The Simon & Schuster Pocket Guide to Chardonnay Wines Edited and designed by Mitchell Beazley International Limited, Artists House, 14-15 Manette Street, London W1V 5LB

Fireside
Simon & Schuster Building
Rockefeller Center
1230 Avenue of the Americas
New York, New York 10020

10 9 8 7 6 5 4 3 2 1

ISBN 0-671-72894-6

Library of Congress catalogue information available upon request.

The author and publishers will be grateful for any information that will assist them in keeping future editions up to date. Although all reasonable care has been taken in the preparation of this book, neither the publishers nor the author can accept any liability for any consequences arising from the use thereof or from the information contained therein.

Editor	Stephanie Horner
Assistant Editor	Alessandra Perotto
Art Editor	Gaye Allen
Production	Barbara Hind
Maps	John Hutchinson
Co-ordinating Editor	Alison Franks
Managing Editor	Chris Foulkes

Typeset by Servis Filmsetting Ltd, Manchester, England
Produced by Mandarin Offset
Printed and bound in Malaysia

THE SIMON & SCHUSTER POCKET GUIDE TO

CHARDONNAY WINES

ROGER VOSS

A Fireside Book
Published by Simon & Schuster Inc.
New York London Toronto
Sydney Tokyo Singapore

The Simon & Schuster Pocket Guide to Chardonnay Wines Edited and
designed by Mitchell Beazley International Limited, Artists
House, 14-15 Manette Street, London W1V 5LB

Fireside
Simon & Schuster Building
Rockefeller Center
1230 Avenue of the Americas
New York, New York 10020

10 9 8 7 6 5 4 3 2 1

ISBN 0-671-72894-6

Library of Congress catalogue information available upon
request.

The author and publishers will be grateful for any information
that will assist them in keeping future editions up to date.
Although all reasonable care has been taken in the
preparation of this book, neither the publishers nor the
author can accept any liability for any consequences arising
from the use thereof or from the information contained
therein.

Editor	Stephanie Horner
Assistant Editor	Alessandra Perotto
Art Editor	Gaye Allen
Production	Barbara Hind
Maps	John Hutchinson
Co-ordinating Editor	Alison Franks
Managing Editor	Chris Foulkes

Typeset by Servis Filmsetting Ltd, Manchester, England
Produced by Mandarin Offset
Printed and bound in Malaysia

Contents

Acknowledgments

I have received a marvellous amount of help during my research for this book from wineproducers around the world, from their representatives in the United Kingdom, and from the representatives of national or state wineproducers' associations in London. To them all, a big thank you. But in particular, I must mention a few generous people without whom I could never have hoped to finish this study.

For French wines, and Burgundy in particular: Bernard Repolt, of the négociant house of Jaffelin; David Prentice of the négociants La Reine Pédauque; Anthony Hanson of wine merchants Haynes Hanson & Clark in London; Catherine Manac'h of Food & Wine from France in London.

For wines from California: Sam Folsom of the California Wine Institute in San Francisco; Gus Fertado of Fetzer Wines; Manfred Essler of Cuvaison Wines; Clarke Swanson and Chris Anstee of Swanson Vineyards; Fritz Draeger of Flora Springs.

For wines from Australia: Hazel Murphy of the Australian Wine Bureau in London; Stephen Walker of Gullin & Company, South Australia.

For wines from New Zealand: Terry Dunleavy MBE and Philip Greegan of the Wine Institute of New Zealand; Philip Atkinson of the New Zealand High Commission, London; John Hancock of Morton Estate; Rose Delegat of Delegat's Wines; the Giesen family of Giesen Wine Estate, Canterbury; the wineproducers of Martinborough; Hermann Seifried of Weingut Seifried in Nelson; Michael Brajkovich MW of Kumeu River Wines.

For wines from South Africa: Tim Hamilton-Russell and Hamilton-Russell Vineyards; Peter Devereux, wine consultant and journalist; John Platter, author of the 1990 *South African Wine Guide* (1990 Cape Town) and wineproducer. I am grateful to them all.

Foreword

This book is the study of one grape variety, how it is grown and turned into wine around the world. There are two sections: the first is a general survey of the history of the Chardonnay from its earliest recorded days, a study of how it is treated in the vineyard and in the winery, and what styles of wine it makes, ending with a personal selection of the best Chardonnays around; and the second section is a directory of the best producers of Chardonnay wines in the different areas of the world in which the grape is planted. Within the directory, the listings are preceded by a short introduction to each country or wine region.

Chardonnay producers in the directory section are rated, according to the general quality of the Chardonnays they produce. I should emphasize that the rating is based on Chardonnays alone: some producers with low ratings in this book make star wines from other grape varieties – and vice versa. The rating system works as follows:

*	Below average quality
**	Average quality
***	Good in their class and category
****	Supreme examples
→	Represents finer gradations within this framework

Introduction

In an enclosed valley in the heart of the Burgundian countryside lies the tiny village of Chardonnay. It is nothing much to look at: a huddle of houses around a church, vineyards on the slopes above and below, a main road bypassing the village centre, few shops. Its wine goes to the local winemakers' coopérative to make Mâcon Blanc or Rouge. Chardonnay's wine is highly unlikely to be seen dignified with a separate identity or label.

Did the Chardonnay vine come from that nondescript Burgundian village? It seems so improbable, given the obscurity of the place. Certainly no records mention the village when witnessing the history of the vine. Or did the village take its name from the vine – and if so why *this* village when there are so many more important sources of Chardonnay? We will probably never know. But it is pleasing to imagine, looking at this tiny village basking in the warm Burgundian sun, that this is where the world's most famous white vine was first identified – and that this is the starting point for a viticultural and vinous career that has swept the world in a way no other vine variety has done.

During the 1980s, the Chardonnay was the cult white grape variety. Every winemaker worth his oenology degree – whether in Italy, in California, in Australia or in New Zealand – had to make a Chardonnay. Anyone without it was regarded as almost eccentric, certainly out of fashion. It had everything: popularity with consumers, who liked to drink it, popularity with wine-makers, who could impose their own style on its comparatively neutral taste. Chardonnays were the priciest, smartest, most sought-after white wines in the world.

But why Chardonnay? Why not Viura, or Malvasia, or Chenin Blanc? Why not, indeed, the outrageously neglected Riesling? What made Chardonnay the Gucci of wine? The taste, certainly. The quality of some of the wines produced, equally surely. But also the quality of the prototype Chardonnay wine white: burgundy. If France produces the world's most famous wines, white burgundy at its best is without doubt her greatest dry white. The names of Meursault, Corton-Charlemagne and Montrachet are just as much the object of admiration, reverence and indeed emulation as Château Margaux, Château Lafite or Château Latour are amongst red wines.

Throughout the ever-expanding wine world during the 1970s and early 1980s, producers wanted to make their own version of one of those white burgundian prototypes. New World producers set out to prove that Montrachet could be made just about anywhere, given the magic ingredients: Chardonnay grapes and a clever winemaker. And in the world of sparkling wine, Chardonnay's major role in champagne led to emulation in a hundred scattered cellars.

As the 1980s passed, producers, gaining in confidence, made Chardonnay in, say, an Australian or a Californian way, rather than harking back to Burgundy. And in Burgundy wine-producers realized that there was much of interest happening outside their borders: they went overseas to look, learn and taste. Before long an interaction developed, and also a realization that the Chardonnay can inspire a wide range of wine styles, from light, fresh and early-drinking to full, buttery and heavily oaked, with every permutation in between.

THE TASTE OF CHARDONNAY

The Chardonnay grape has been described as a blank canvas on which a producer can draw any picture. In its natural, raw state it does not make wines of the intense, instantly recognizable character of, say, the Muscat or the Sauvignon Blanc. It is more muted. The Chardonnay taste is of a rounded, smooth wine, not too dry because it does not have very high acid levels, quite high in alcohol, pleasantly rather than overtly green, perhaps slightly nutty like walnuts – and always easy to drink and refreshing.

From this comparatively neutral base, good producers can unleash a wide palate of flavours. They can get greater intensity by starting fermentation with whole bunches of grapes in the must. They can get more or less acidity by encouraging or discouraging the malolactic fermentation (which changes the malic acid in a wine into the softer lactic acid). They can decide whether to ferment in oak barrels or in tanks and whether to give the wine a stronger taste of wood by leaving it in oak to mature. The permutations are almost endless.

The one thing producers probably will not contemplate is blending Chardonnay with anything else. Unlike its nearest rival in the wine world's popularity stakes – the red Cabernet Sauvignon – Chardonnay is almost always (with a few exceptions in the Antipodes) made as an unblended wine. This is probably because of its roots back in Burgundy where, since the middle of the 19th century if not before, the greatest white burgundies have been – in theory at least – pure Chardonnay by custom and by law.

Chardonnay's adaptability in the winery has meant that it is the number one favourite with wineproducers the world over. They can impose their interpretation on the grapes coming from the vineyard. And in the vineyard where, as the French will always point out, a wine is primarily made – the Chardonnay is equally rewarding. It is an extremely tolerant variety, giving few problems apart from a susceptibility to grey rot, and often giving excellent and, importantly, regular yields of grapes which have a high potential alcohol.

The popularity of Chardonnay with wineproducers – as with the drinking public – is very clear anywhere in New World vineyards - and, to a lesser extent, in Europe's. From 1988 to 1990, the world's vineyard area under Chardonnay has increased by a staggering 50 percent. Prices of the grapes – and therefore the wines – are expected to fall, or at least stabilize.

So now is the time to take advantage of the Chardonnay boom. There will probably never be a greater range of wines, at better prices and from a wider variety of countries than there is today. So drink now, while the going's good, and perhaps even raise a glass to that small village in Burgundy.

History

The history of the Chardonnay grape is effectively linked to the history of three French wine regions until well after World War II: Burgundy, which has most of the limelight, Auxerre (or Chablis) and Champagne.

One of the obvious problems with tracing the history of any vine variety is lack of information. Until certainly the 16th century – and really not until the late 18th – wineproducers were fairly relaxed about the vines that were planted in their vineyards. The vines were there, they had always been there – and that was about as far as the reasoning went. What was growing was much less important than the wine they made.

So it is with Chardonnay. Indeed, in Burgundy until well into the 17th century, white and red grapes were often planted, picked and vinified together. And even as late as the 19th century, according to the mouth-filling 1831 *Statistique de la Vigne dans le Département de la Côte d'Or* of Dr Morelot, the only one properly documented areas of Chardonnay in Burgundy were the three famous white wine villages of Meursault, Chassagne-Montrachet and Puligny-Montrachet. Elsewhere in the region there was a hotchpotch of grapes: the Melon de Bourgogne (also known as the Muscadet and now planted nowhere in France except on the Loire), Aligoté (still grown in Burgundy for lesser white wines), Gamay Blanc and Pinot Blanc (the last of these now more often seen in Alsace).

To this day there remains confusion about the relationship between Pinot Blanc (or Pineau Blanc as it is sometimes spelt) and Chardonnay. In the Mâconnais region there is still an appellation called Pinot Chardonnay. Some of the "Chardonnay" vines in the region may really be Pinot Blanc. And the firm belief that the Chardonnay was part of the Pinot family (and hence to be properly called Pinot Chardonnay) has only just been laid to rest in California.

This identity problem makes it difficult to pinpoint the exact arrival of Chardonnay in the Burgundy region. The timing of the arrival of the grape vine itself is easier, and it is now generally agreed to have been carried by Greek traders from Masilia (now Marseille) who travelled up the Rhône and the Saône rivers well before the time of Christ. The *Vitis vinifera* is believed to have come from the Lebanon.

Those traders must have recognized a good vineyard slope when they saw it, because from the earliest records of the Burgundy vineyards the slope of the Côte d'Or, that fabled and priceless strip of land that still holds all the finest Burgundy vineyards, had the greatest reputation for its vines. Along with this reputation, a little later, went the Auxerre region to the north and the Mâconnais to the south. Under the Romans, it is believed, villas – presumably with vineyards – were built at what are now the villages of Aloxe-Corton, Volnay and possibly Meursault, while Beaune was a major crossroads for trade.

But it was the Church, not commerce, which established

viticulture in Burgundy on a large-scale basis, and which retained, throughout the Dark Ages, some vestiges of civilized winemaking while all around culture disintegrated. The famous Clos de Vougeot, formerly the property of the Cistercians, is only one of many walled vineyards that were part of the estates of the great abbeys of the region – Cluny (founded in 910) in the hills behind Mâcon and Citeaux (founded in 1098) in the Saône valley to the east of Nuits-St-Georges.

The Church kept winemaking alive primarily because of its essential role in the liturgy. But since much of our picture of rollicking monks derives from the monastic orders which were first established in Burgundy, it is unsurprising to learn that consumption beyond the call of duty was a part of daily life, and that, through the international connections of the senior churchmen, the wines of the Burgundian abbeys travelled far and gained a high reputation. They are recorded variously in Paris and in southern France, in England and in Italy.

It was the monks who first marked out what are now accepted as the best vineyards in Burgundy. While the Clos de Vougeot, with its surviving medieval wall, is the most obvious relic of these times, this vineyard was merely typical of the monks as viticulteurs, not unique. They marked out the *clos* (or enclosed walled vineyard under one ownership) which produced the finest wines, the *climats* (or named vineyards), and observed which were more suited to white wines, which to red.

Burgundian wine labels still tell the tale of these medieval viticulturalists: Clos de Tart, Clos de Beze, Clos St Denis, Clos Prieur, Clos du Chapitre. And even today, there is a much stronger religious link with wine in Burgundy – through such events as the Hospices de Beaune auction, still linked with the famous charitable and semi-religious hospital in Beaune – than there is in Bordeaux, where the interest of the Church in the vineyards was much less strong.

In medieval times, Burgundy and especially Chablis were better known for their white wine than their red. The white wines of Auxerre, west of Chablis proper, achieved considerable fame. In *White Burgundy* (London 1988), Christopher Fielden records that Anseric, High Steward of Burgundy in the 12th century, left his vineyard in Chablis to the Church with the comment that it gave a good white wine ''that one can keep for a long time''.

Yet by the 14th and 15th centuries, when Burgundy was divided by the powerful Valois Dukes, things had changed. As any wineproducer knows, red wine is much easier to make and transport than white. And so it proved in the Middle Ages, aided, according to Hugh Johnson in *The Story of Wine* (London 1989), by a level of political salesmanship of the red wines of Beaune by the Dukes of Burgundy which would make any modern-day Champagne house gasp in admiration.

So while Chablis continued to be an important centre for white wines, the major wines from further south, and from Beaune in particular, were increasingly red. It is not until the 17th century that we get some firm idea of what was actually planted in the vineyards of Burgundy. In *Les Délices de la Campagne* written in 1654, the best white grapes of Chablis are recorded as being Meslier, Beaunois and Fromentier. Learned speculation about the Meslier suggests it was the Petit Meslier which still grows in small quantities in the Aube region of Champagne. The Fromentier lends itself to two possibilities. One that it is the same as the Pinot Gris of Alsace (still called the Fromentot in Champagne); the other – less widely accepted – that it is the same as the Savagnin of the Jura where it is also called the Fromente (and in Hungary it is called the Formentin or Furmint). Whatever its present-day character, back in the 17th century, it was regarded as making the best white wine of Burgundy.

Much more is known about the third member of that 17th century trio, the Beaunois. This was most certainly the Chardonnay, which in fact is known as the Beaunois in Chablis to this day – a strong suggestion that the Chardonnay reached Auxerre from the vineyards of the Côte d'Or or around Beaune.

There are records of other white wine grapes grown in smaller quantities in the Burgundy vineyards in the 17th century. These were: the Bourguignon Blanc (probably the Sylvaner), the Gray, the Beaunier (now unidentifiable, but possibly a synonym for Beaunois), Muscat and Malaga (which may have had some link with the Pedro Ximénez grown in Malaga in Spain). The Juillet was also grown as a table grape. With so many varieties it is apparent that the Chardonnay was not alone in the bid to become the dominant white grape of Burgundy. It was, even at the beginning of the 19th century, one among many. Chardonnay was however also planted in other winegrowing regions of France. The Jura, eastern neighbour of the Burgundy vineyards, has long had plantings which, blended with Savagnin have been used to make sherry-like wines rather than light wines. There were even Chardonnay vineyards in Paris – at least until the beginning of the 18th century. But its spread into regions such as the Loire, Haut-Poitou and the Ardèche is much more recent.

By the turn of the 19th century, Burgundy proper was still overwhelmingly devoted to red wine grapes. In Dr Morelot's *Statistique de la Vigne*, the hectares under white vines do not even rate a mention. Despite the tiny amounts grown, in the same book we learn of the pre-eminence of the vineyards of Le Montrachet, Meursault and Puligny-Montrachet as producers of white wine, with Le Montrachet "so superior to the others that it must be placed alone". According to Dr Morelot, it was the Chardonnay (or Pineau Blanc with which he continued to confuse it) which made the wines from these vineyards so fine.

"The stalk of the Pineau Blanc is fragile and thin: it bears all the traits of delicacy. Two or three small branches grow out of the main trunk. When they reach maturity, they have a yellow colour with some red striations. The bunches are made up of small grapes, not very numerous, coloured yellow, very pleasing to the eye. The taste of the mature grapes is exquisite: it has a very special aroma which it is difficult to put into words. The wine which comes from the grapes has very superior qualities which allows it to command a high price, starting at 500 Francs for a *pièce* [a barrel of 228 litres]. In addition, the harvest is normally of a small quantity."

It was, Dr Morelot concluded, by far the best white wine in

Burgundy, and contrasted favourably with wines "of mediocre quality" which were the norm in other parts of the *département* of the Côte d'Or, and which presumably came from vineyards (now no longer in existence) on the flat floor of the Saône valley.

Some 20 years later, Cyrus Redding in *A History and Description of Modern Wines* (1833) echoed Dr Morelot's praise for the wines of "Mont-Rachet": "it is deemed one of the most perfect white wines in Burgundy, and even of France, being the French Tokay in the opinion of many connoisseurs". Redding gives prices: Le Montrachet at 1,200 francs per hectolitre, Chevalier Montrachet at 600 francs per hectolitre and Bâtard-Montrachet at 400 francs.

Redding classifies wines into three categories. Le Montrachet achieves first-class status, Meursault and other white burgundies reach the second class, while Chablis Grand Cru merely reaches the third class and is dismissed as being "in considerable esteem in Paris as a wine of the table". The other white wines of the Yonne *département* (those not made with the Pineau Blanc/Chardonnay) come nowhere at all.

Redding also gives us some clue as to the problems in his day of making what we would regard as clean, fresh white wines:

"In making they endeavour to keep it [the white must] with as little colour as possible, no doubt for the purpose of preserving that lightness of hue which white wines rarely possess, being yellowed, probably by the absorption of oxygen which incorporates with them while in contact with the atmosphere."

Redding was writing 20 years before the advent of the phylloxera beetle which arrived in Meursault in 1875, beginning its devastation with a Chardonnay vine. It was also Meursault which produced the first wines to be made in Burgundy from vines grafted on to American rootstocks (still the only way to prevent further attacks of the louse). But, typically, it required 20 years before a vineyard that had been destroyed by phylloxera could be restored to full production which, for many growers, meant the time and costs were too great, and they turned to other crops.

The vineyards of Auxerre in the Yonne departement were the worst affected by the loss of vines. While the total vineyard area in Burgundy halved between 1875 and 1900, that of Auxerre almost disappeared. Only since the 1970s has the Chablis vineyard begun to approach the size it was in the 1860s. In terms of quality, there was one advantage to be gained out of the phylloxera epidemic. Those vineyards that were replanted were inevitably those which could command the highest prices for their wines – those that make what are now the *appellation contrôlée* (AC) wines, as distinct from the basic *vins de table*. And it was from this point in the history of the region that Chardonnay came to dominate the white wine production of Burgundy (while Pinot Noir was consolidating its hold on the reds).

But Chardonnay still had some competition. Not until the 1950s were Pinot Blanc and Chardonnay finally distinguished from one another and it was only then that Pinot Blanc began to lose its status and disappear from the main Burgundian vineyards. As the white wines of Burgundy (and Chablis) have increased in price and prestige since World War II, so has the planting of its most prestigious white wine grape, Chardonnay, proceeded apace. The size of the Chablis vineyard has increased fourfold in 40 years, while in Burgundy proper, there have been extensive new plantings of new vineyards in the Côte Chalonnaise and in the Mâconnais, as well as in the vineyards behind the main Côte d'Or.

CHAMPAGNE AND CHARDONNAY

While the high esteem of Chardonnay in Burgundy and Chablis was being established at the turn of the century, further north in Champagne, it was having a more difficult time. As Hugh Johnson points out in *The Story of Wine*, (London 1989) Champagne "had deliberately set out to compete with Burgundy as far back as the days of the Valois Dukes" (in the 14th and 15th centuries). And, clearly, successful competition meant producing red wines, made from a range of grapes, of which, by the 17th century, Pinot Noir (or Noirien) was proving to be the finest. At the beginning of the 18th century, when the first attempts at controlling the fermentation of the naturally explosive wines of the Champagne region were being made by Dom Perignon and his fellow cellar-masters at other abbeys in Champagne, it was to black-skinned grapes that they turned – to make white wines. Chardonnay and other white-skinned grapes were frowned upon, partly because they had a greater tendency to oxidize, and partly because their higher sugar levels meant they were more likely to re-ferment.

Surprisingly considering the incredible future success story of sparkling champagne, Dom Perignon's initial attempts were intended, first of all to make white wine with black skinned grapes and then to stop the wine fermenting once it was bottled. Secondary fermentation (and hence the bubbles) in the bottle was the result of popular demand (probably created by the only partial success of Dom Perignon's efforts) for sparkling wine, and it was only then that white grapes began to be used for their extra fizziness. This increased demand heralded the rise to fame of such white-wine villages such as Cramant, Le Mesnil-sur-Oger and Avize on what is now called the Côte des Blancs.

None the less, throughout the 19th century, the black-skinned grapes were considered to be the most important in champagne. Weight and richness – as well as sweetness – were the virtues sought by the great champagne houses of the day. Thomas George Shaw – author of *Wine, the Vine and the Cellar* in 1863, is quoted by Serena Sutcliffe in *A Celebration of Champagne* (London 1988) as saying that the average blend was two-thirds black grapes, one-third Chardonnay. It was the house of Pommery in the 1870s which first developed the dry, or Brut, champagnes we know today, and which included a higher percentage of Chardonnay, to give lightness and greater shape to wines that could not rely on sweetness to hide their faults.

With the current popularity of *blanc de blancs*-style of champagne, Chardonnay's time as the most fashionable Champagne grape seems to have really come. While Chardonnay occupies

26 percent of the total Champagne vineyard area, it occupies a massive 45 percent of all Grand Cru and Premier Cru vineyards.

CHARDONNAY OUTSIDE FRANCE

Chardonnay is a relative newcomer to vineyards beyond France. Its spread has been rapid and dramatic, fuelled by the demand for wines that could emulate the aristocratic white burgundy and Chablis. With a few exceptions, it has been almost entirely concentrated into the decades since 1960.

EUROPE

Although Chardonnay has been planted in parts of Italy for over a century, for example in Frescobaldi's vineyards in Tuscany, it was not until the 1970s that there was any attempt at serious production. Since then, it has spread to many of the other major northern Italian wineproducing areas: to Friuli, to Trentino (which some regard as potentially the best area of all for Italian Chardonnay), to Piedmont, and, to a lesser extent to Lombardy and Emilia Romagna. Initially often confused with the Pinot Bianco (Pinot Blanc) as it was in Burgundy, Chardonnay is now being cultivated and vinified separately as a prestige variety (see page 146).

Elsewhere in Europe, its spread has been more patchy, with small but significant plantings in Spain (see page 154), in Portugal, in Austria and in England. There is continuing confusion in Germany between the Pinot Blanc (Weissburgunder) and Chardonnay. Much more recently, it has played a major part of the astonishing success of Bulgarian wines. It also appears in Slovenia, Romania, the USSR and Hungary and its establishment in all of these countries testifies to the adaptability of the grape.

THE NEW WORLD

Chardonnay's position as cult status grape of the 1980s was reached mainly outside Europe and nowhere more so than on the west coast of the United States. Remarkably, it seems to have reached that position from almost a standing start in less than 40 years.

European vine varieties reached California as long ago as the 1840s when a native of Bordeaux, the appropriately named Jean-Louis Vignes, arrived with cuttings of (presumably) Bordeaux vine varieties. But there is no mention of Chardonnay either from him, or from the influential figure of the Hungarian Agoston Haraszthy (who in 1861 was commissioned by the California State Governor to go to Europe to select high quality European vine cuttings for planting in California). Pinot Noir, yes, Chardonnay no.

The first appearance of Chardonnay in California is not until 1948. James Zellerbach, a retired US diplomat, had decided that his lifelong ambition was not to serve the State Department but to produce wines that would match those of Burgundy as far as possible. He planted Chardonnay as well as Pinot Noir in Sonoma and produced grapes that Hugh Johnson describes as having "the buttery, half-smoked aromas and flavours that up to then had spelt only Meursault, Le Montrachet and Corton-Charlemagne."

When Zellerbach died in 1961, his cellarfull of wines was bought – and sold with much acclaim – by Joe Heitz, a Napa Valley wineproducer, best known for his Martha's Vineyard Cabernet Sauvignon. Plantings of Chardonnay increased from 4,100ha (10,000 acres) in 1975 to 12,100ha (30,000 acres) in 1987, making it third most popular white grape in the state. Chardonnay vineyards are set to increase still further as plantings in the late 1980s come on stream.

Further north, in Washington State and Oregon Chardonnay has likewise spread. Production here is of comparatively small quantities of wines with delicate flavours that contrast the richer taste of California Chardonnay.

The story in Australia is much the same, if even more recent. A clone of Chardonnay was planted in the Mudgee area of New South Wales for many years, but because of a general confusion with Australian grape names its provenance went undetected.

It was really the plantings of Dr Max Lake (one of the many Australian medical men who decided to make wine) in the 1960s at his Lake's Folly Vineyard in the Hunter Valley which made Australians realize the potential for high-quality Chardonnay. Lake was aiming for a soft, rich style of wine, Meursault in character, which set the standard for Australia's Chardonnay producers right into the 1980s. But the success of his wines, and those of other Hunter producers such as Tyrrells, launched the Chardonnay craze in Australia which has spread right across the continent. Such is the demand that Chardonnay has been planted on new land, has replaced old red vines and, in a country where most things are allowed, has been grafted onto red vines in the vineyard. So rapid is the pace of change that the 1986 production of 17,000 tonnes (16,700 tons) of Chardonnay was half as much again in 1990.

Likewise, in New Zealand, the Chardonnay cult has spread fast. As in all the New World wine countries the grape was a poor second to Cabernet Sauvignon, at least until the demand for white wines – and for the Chardonnay style in particular – mushroomed in the 1980s.

According to Michael Cooper in his book *The Wines and Vineyards of New Zealand* (Auckland 1988), the first clones were imported from Europe in the 1920s. They suffered from the leaf-roll virus, still a problem with Chardonnay even in Burgundy, and there was the common confusion between Chardonnay and Pinot Blanc. However some fine "Pinot Chardonnays" were apparently being made in small quantities (at a time when three-quarters of New Zealand's vineyards were not actually planted with classic *Vitis vinifera* varieties but with hybrids): those made by the Auckland-based Western Vineyards in the 1960s were especially praised.

Better, virus-free clones have really only appeared in New Zealand in the 1980s, with the most widely planted new clone coming from California. The area under Chardonnay has – as in Australia – shot up: from 384ha (950 acres) in 1986 to 689ha (1,702 acres) in 1990 today.

For many years, Chardonnay production in South Africa was inhibited by poor clonal material. It suffered from fan leaf disease, poor yields and the hot climate. They have resolved many of these problems with better clones and planting conditions and since 1980 production of fine Chardonnays has increased.

In Chile, the other source of potentially high-quality Chardonnay, progress has been much slower since the focus of attention has been on red wine. Around 100 hectares (247 acres) are planted with Chardonnay, and the figure remains fairly static.

OLD WORLD V NEW WORLD

The June 1988 issue of the British magazine *Decanter* carried an article called "The Great Chardonnay Challenge". In it 85 Chardonnays from around the world were pitted against an impressive panel of tasters to see which, in their opinion, was the finest. There were 10 wines from France, 17 from Australia, 20 from California, nine from New Zealand, 11 from South Africa, 12 from Italy and six from other countries.

The results were, to a Burgundian, predictable. A Californian wine (Robert Mondavi's Reserve Chardonnay 1985) came top, Australia had the highest number of winners in the top ten, and there was one South African and one New Zealand wine. France and Italy – the Old World representatives – came nowhere.

The French would shrug off this result. They would argue that the more subtle taste of a great burgundy cannot compete in directness and oomph with most of the New World Chardonnays – certainly not in comparative tastings. This is not mere casuistry on the part of the French. The cooler climate of Burgundy compared with the warmth of California's Napa Valley or Australia's Padthaway or Margaret River regions certainly produces wines with higher acidity, less overt "up-front" flavour, and the need for longer maturation before reaching its peak.

But in an international tasting, professionals take all these factors into account. And still the judges came up with a negative result for France. What they were saying, in effect, is that while Burgundy makes the prototype Chardonnays, it no longer has the monopoly on premium quality. They also commented that Burgundy does seem to have a monopoly on top prices for its wines.

But does a tasting like the *Decanter* challenge really confirm who produces the greatest Chardonnay? The answer is no, not completely. Despite the excellent quality and lower prices of New World Chardonnay, Burgundy can, when it tries, still come up with the finest white wines in the world. The point is that when we are talking about the great wines it is becoming less and less possible to compare Old World and New World Chardonnay, fun though that may be for wine tasters. The stylistic differences between Oregon Chardonnay and Chablis, or Marlborough Chardonnay and Puligny-Montrachet are now becoming so great that the wines are no longer directly comparable. We can, of course, continue to say which wine we enjoy more. But to say one is better than the other is no longer feasible.

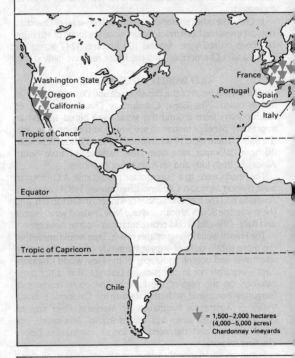

World-wide distribution of Chardonnay vineyards

Washington State
Oregon
California

Tropic of Cancer

Equator

Tropic of Capricorn

France
Portugal Spain
Italy

Chile

▼ = 1,500–2,000 hectares
(4,000–5,000 acres)
Chardonnay vineyards

Areas under Chardonnay in major producing			
		hectares	acres
France	1979:	13,062	32,300
Italy	1982:	5,000	12,000
California	1979:	5,949	15,000
Pacific States, USA	1979:	353	872
Australia	1981:	1,159	2,900
New Zealand	1980:	175	432
Chile	1980:	100	247
South Africa	1979:	8	20
Bulgaria	1979:	1,843	4,500

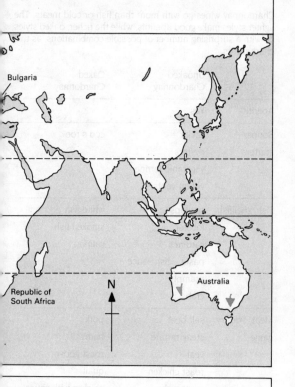

Bulgaria

Republic of
South Africa

N

Australia

countries			
	hectares	acres	% increase
1988:	19,870	49,000	52
1989:	10,000	25,000	100
1988:	17,445	43,000	193
1989:	1,102	30,000	212
1988:	2,978	7,400	156
1989:	487	1,200	178
1985:	1,000	2,470	900
1989:	1,000	2,470	12,400
1989:	2,792	7,000	51

Chardonnay and food

Chardonnay wines go with more than fish or cold meats. The lighter styles make good aperitifs, while the richer, oaked styles go with a surprising number of possible combinations, as this chart shows.

	Unoaked Chardonnay	Oaked Chardonnay
Aperitif	Yes	
Soups/ starters	caviar	cod's roe
	oysters	
	vegetable terrine	
	vol-au-vents	
Fish/shellfish	scallops	white fish
	lobster	smoked fish
	sardines	salmon
	pasta – fish sauce	
	scampi	
	crab	
Meat, Poultry, game	salt beef	pork
	steak tartare	ham
	veal	roast goose
	roast chicken	quail
	roast turkey	chicken with sauce
	chicken risotto	spaghetti carbonara
		quiche lorraine
Cheeses		Mild hard cheeses

The grape in the vineyard

Like many well-travelled grape varieties, Chardonnay is astonishingly tolerant. After all, there is a world of difference between conditions in the Napa Valley in California and in the Côte d'Or in Burgundy, or between the Mâconnais and the Sudtirol of Italy. But Chardonnay flourishes in all these places – and, of course, in many more.

Are there any basic conditions that Chardonnay insists on, before it decides it likes its new patch of vineyard? It makes sense to start with Burgundy, "homeland" of the Chardonnay, to look at the demands it makes there, before seeing if any of these are satisfied elsewhere in the world.

Burgundy is toward the northern limit of reliable vinegrowing. (Champagne, of course, is further north, which is why its rather thin wines are much more suited to become sparkling wine.) In Burgundy, the best vineyards are on south-east facing slopes, halfway up to avoid frosts, and sheltered from the wet winds by the hills of the Morvan to the west. The climate is normally characterized by very cold winters, late springs, a wet early summer and dry autumns. Because of its northerly latitude, Burgundy has the advantage of longer sunshine hours in summer than, say, the vineyards of the south of France or Italy, but without the intense heat. Thus the ripening period is prolonged: normally a benefit to fine white winemaking.

White vines need comparatively cool climates in which to give their best. Their wines need to preserve some acidity as a balance to any sweetness, while too much alcohol can throw a white wine much more out of balance than a red. In fact, it is generally agreed that Burgundy is a more reliable area for producing white wines than red, simply because of the comparative overall coolness of its climate, untempered (unlike Bordeaux on a similar latitude) by the warming effect of the sea.

So, despite these natural advantages, why is so little white wine produced in Burgundy? At present, only about 15 percent of all vineyards are planted with Chardonnay, and that is mostly confined to parts of the southern Côte d'Or (the Côte de Beaune), to the Côte Chalonnais and to the Mâconnais. The great wine villages of the Côte de Nuits are almost entirely given over to red wines. Tradition is one reason. But soil is a deciding factor here.

SOIL FOR THE CHARDONNAY

The vineyards of the Côte d'Or are made up of a limestone base on which outcrops of richer marl and alluvial deposits occur. The accepted rule is that Chardonnay is planted where the limestone predominates and where the ground is stonier – both these conditions are met in villages in the southern Côte de Beaune such as Meursault, and on the hill of Corton. Limestone is also an essential component of the soil in Chablis further north, where it is known as Kimmeridgian (after the village of Kimmeridge in Dorset in the UK where it was first identified.)

And, of course, in the Champagne region chalk is the predominant feature.

So in France limestone/chalk soil is seen as a vital component in the makeup of Chardonnay wines. And yet around the world we find Chardonnay being planted on many types of soil in varying climates. However, I think it is possible to draw out some common elements from this diversity. They are: poor-quality soil, good drainage, plenty of stones, and possibly a sloping site. Are these elements common to Chardonnay vineyards throughout the world?

In cool-climate Marlborough, New Zealand, the source of some of the best Chardonnay outside France, most of these elements are found. The name of Corbans' Stoneleigh Vineyard says it all: fist-sized stones scattered over poor-quality alluvial loam, sitting on a bed of well-drained gravel. The slope is not there, but the good drainage compensates.

Next, a change in continent, to Los Carneros, at the southern end of Napa and Sonoma in California. Here are sloping vineyards in contrast to the valley-floor vineyards of Napa proper, on stony, well-drained ground of the final reaches of the Mayacamas Mountains. This is now generally regarded as the best area for Chardonnay (as well as Pinot Noir) certainly in Napa, possibly in Sonoma. As with Marlborough and with Burgundy, these vineyards enjoy cool-climate conditions, with a growing season that is rarely too hot because of the effect of the San Francisco Bay fogs.

Moving continents again, the third example is in South Africa. One of the most highly regarded of the few Chardonnays to be produced in the Cape vineyards comes from Hamilton-Russell Vineyards in the coolest growing region right on the southern coast at Hermanus. Here the soil is poor quality well-drained shale, which previously was covered only with scrub. The vineyards are on steep slopes, with the cooling ocean breezes compensating for the fact that even here, at the southern end of Africa, the latitude is still only 34 degrees (Beaune in Burgundy is at 47 degrees).

These three examples are all vineyard areas producing highly regarded Chardonnay. The climate is right, the soil is right: winemaking I will discuss later. But elsewhere there are what would appear at first sight to be complete contrasts.

What could seem more different from cool-climate Marlborough in New Zealand than the Upper Hunter Valley in New South Wales, Australia? Yet even here, through careful choice of vineyard sites, we find similarities. The Roxburgh vineyard, part of Rosemount Estates, produces a much respected single-vineyard Chardonnay. The vineyard is on volcanic soil with a limestone base (a characteristic of Burgundy here), on slopes which face north-east into the morning sun (a repeat of the south-east facing slopes of Côte d'Or in the northern hemisphere). Drainage is good, and the best blocks of Chardonnay are grown at mid-slope where the vines can dry off quickly after rain. Even the climate which could be expected to be hot this far north of Sydney is tempered by the height of the vineyards (around 400m, 300ft) and, critically, by the relatively high amount of cloud cover. These factors have a cooling effect on the vineyards, especially during harvest time.

CHARDONNAY IN THE VINEYARD

In a well-maintained vineyard, Chardonnay is a naturally vigorous vine, whose yields need to be controlled rather than encouraged. This has not always been the case: in the 19th century it was described as having poor yields, even though the quality was high. In many wine-regions of the world today, Chardonnay is still regarded as a low yielding variety, with only the high prices it commands making up for the low quantity.

Why this discrepancy? The yield clearly reflects the health of the vineyard and the right clonal material (see page 24). Although the Chardonnay is a tolerant vine, it does suffer from two diseases which can drastically affect its yields. The first is one that is particularly prevalent in cooler, wetter vinegrowing areas: grey rot. In a benign form it can produce the great noble rot wines of Sauternes. But when and where it is not wanted – as in a wet summer in Burgundy or New Zealand – it becomes a menace, needing expensive treatment with antirot sprays. Its effect is to destroy the colour cells in the skin of the grapes, so it is more of a problem for vines where colour is an essential element of the wine such as red Pinot Noir, than for Chardonnay where the skins are normally discarded.

Much more serious for Chardonnay is *court-noué*, which is known in English as fan leaf. The visible symptom is a change in leaf colour from green to yellow. The effect of the disease is to reduce the strength of the vine and consequently its yield. It also shortens the life of the vine to 10-15 years from planting. Fan leaf is caused by a virus carried by a root-sucking worm, rejoicing in the name of *Xiphenima index*, and although chemicals can be applied to the soil, reinfection is easy and likely.

During the three decades from the late 1940s to the mid 1970s, fan leaf was a major problem in Meursault and Montrachet. It has also occurred in South Africa and New Zealand which has also suffered from an air-borne viral disease called leaf roll. This was found in much of the clonal material imported before the late 1970s. Indeed in those two countries, it was widely believed that the Chardonnay they were planting could not be of Burgundian origin, because of the poor quality of yields due to the leaf roll disease.

Modern clonal selection has proved to be a real step toward preventing the outbreak and spread of the disease. Since 1980, 28ha (70 acres) of vineyard on the Côte d'Or in Burgundy have been replanted with a virus-resistant Chardonnay clone. In the New World, too, new Chardonnay clones are being planted which should see a reduction in – even an end to – losses through this disease.

Grey rot and fan leaf are the two principal diseases from which the Chardonnay can suffer. But in cooler vineyards, where there is the risk of frost in spring – mainly Burgundy, especially Chablis, and Champagne, but also in parts of the Pacific North-west of the United States – the grape has one other important disadvantage: it buds early. At the beginning of

May each year, the vignerons of Chablis are up every night on a rota basis, watching the thermometer, ready to spring into action the moment the mercury drops below zero. There are two ways of combating the risk of frost. One is to light fires in the vineyard using small portable paraffin stoves which stand in rows between the vines, to bring the night temperature up by those few precious degrees. The second system might seem quite crazy: to spray the vines with water. This has the effect of surrounding the buds with a film of ice which, just as snow cover protects the ground from frost, actually keeps the buds tightly cocooned and therefore protected from any risk of frost damage. Antifrost measures are being refined, particularly in California, to reduce the need for night-time vigils.

Of course, early budding does mean early ripening. Normally Chardonnay is picked just after Pinot Noir. In Burgundy and California the harvest will be in mid-September, in Australia and Chile in early March, and in New Zealand in late March, thereby reducing the amount of rot caused by autumn rains.

GETTING THE QUALITY

In an ideal year (the sort that never occurs), the Chardonnay – given its head – would be able to yield anything between 50 to 100hl/ha in Burgundy and Chablis, or 2.5 to 5 tons/acre in California. High yields *and* high prices for Chardonnay growers – what could be better?

The reality is quite different. The pressure is there all the time to control yield, because – other things being equal – high yields mean low quality. The soil only has so much nutrient to give to the vine. Spread between a large number of bunches, the grapes will lack flavour; restricted to fewer bunches and they will have intensity, richness, high sugar – exactly what a good grower is looking for.

There are a host of ways to control yields. The classic way, practised by quality-conscious growers from the best Chardonnay estates in Corton-Charlemagne to the vineyards of Pomino in Tuscany, is to reduce the number of bunches on a vine. After flowering, the grapes begin to form as tiny bunches, rather like small green pin heads. In Burgundy, this takes place towards the end of June and the beginning of July. By the end of July the conscientious grower will be out in the vineyard cutting off any bunches that look malformed, or are too near the ground or too far from it. The ideal place for bunches is right in the middle of the vine. To ensure those selected bunches have the best chance of ripening successfully, growers practise what is called in modern parlance canopy management: clearing the leaves away from the bunches, either mechanically or by hand, rather like trimming the sides of a hedge. This is especially important with the vigorous Chardonnay, which would otherwise put all its energies into growing new leaves rather than ripening the fruit.

While some form of canopy management has probably been practised in Burgundy for years, it has taken a New World country to develop the technique to suit its own grape-growing conditions. In New Zealand where vines positively explode in all directions in the cool and relatively wet climate, some form of growth control is essential. It fell to an Australian working for the New Zealand Government, Dr Richard Smart, to formalize canopy management, and the practice has already shown its worth in the greatly improved yields and quality of fruit coming out of that country.

Canopy management according to Dr Smart means rather more than plucking leaves if they shade the bunches of grapes (too much pruning can be as harmful as too little), it also entails training the shoots of the vine to allow the grapes just the right amount of exposure to the sun, removing secondary shoots from the vine to prevent the plant's reserves being wasted, and positioning the remaining branches so that they will not excessively shade each other.

The net effect on the Chardonnay is to maximize the exposure of the grapes, increasing the sugar levels (and therefore alcohol) with the extra ripening. It could, of course, encourage high yields of grapes but with careful management good producers in New Zealand are finding they can achieve medium quantities and high quality – the grapegrowers' dream.

The number of plants per unit area also affects the quality of the fruit. It might be reasonable to assume that more vines equals more fruit per unit. But that is not necessarily so. More vines per unit means that the soil has to feed more plants and therefore each individual plant gets less nourishment. In this competitive situation, the plant is more stressed, the quantity of grapes diminishes, and those that are left have more concentration of sugar. The French have always maintained that, up to a point, a stressed vine is a positive factor resulting in better wine coming from a particular vineyard. Some of the finest wines in the world are produced in France which would seem to endorse the French tradition of dense planting (developed in the days before mechanical harvesting imposed the need for wider spaces between rows of vines).

PRUNING

Apart from the winemaking itself, pruning is the most important and skilful task of the grower. It marks the beginning of the viticultural year and takes place in February/March in the northern hemisphere, in June/July in the southern. The usual technique for Chardonnay in Burgundy and Chablis is known as the Guyot pruning. In his book *Burgundy* (London 1982), Anthony Hanson describes the system:

"A long fruit-bearing cane, called the *baguette*, is attached to the lowest of the three levels of wire installed to support the shoots and foliage. In addition a short cane, the *courson*, is left to produce some fruit but particularly the shoots which will become the following year's *baguette* and *courson*."

Other countries have different training systems, although the Guyot (or a variation called the Double Guyot) is found around the world. In the United States, there is no specific system, the soil and climate being the deciding factors in trellising but generally, heavy soil needs a divided trellis to curtail vine-growth while vines in weaker soil are more closely spaced and vertically trained for extra strength.

In Australia, where labour costs are high and pruners are in short supply, mechanical pruning has become the norm. Unlike the Burgundian vineyards the vines have been planted in widely spaced rows to permit mechanical harvesting, so introducing another machine presents no problem. However, because the mechanized pruner is less selective it does mean that there are more canes produced on a vine, and in drier areas of the continent they have to follow mechanical pruning with some form of hand pruning, even though the implement used may be a mechanical saw rather than secateurs. It is, of course, particularly important to prune Chardonnay hard, in order to restrict the yield.

New Zealand has adopted two systems of pruning: cane pruning which leaves two or four canes on the plant to take the new season's growth; and spur pruning which reduces one-year old wood to a number of spurs. The latter has been shown to give similar yields without loss in quality and cuts down on costs. In Chile, the vines are trained according to the Bordeaux method brought from France in the 19th century. The system, called here *espalderas*, trains two, four or more shoots on wines supported by posts, normally 80cm (almost 3 ft) high, but sometimes up to two m (6 ft 6 in) high from the ground.

Whatever the method of training and pruning, this treatment is a vital moment in the viticultural year. It will help determine the yield of the vines in the following harvest, and subsequently the quality of the wine.

HARVESTING

Chardonnay tends to ripen early in the sequence of grape varieties. Burgundy it is normally picked around the beginning of October, just after the Pinot Noir harvest. In hot years, the harvest can be earlier, say mid-September, as it is in California. In the southern hemisphere, the Australian Chardonnay harvest will usually take place in March, while in South Africa it can take place at the end of February. In New Zealand harvesting is later, normally the end of March or beginning of April.

The skill of the grapegrower is judging the right balance between acidity and sugar content. In cooler climate vineyards, such as Burgundy and Chablis, the main problem is rarely acidity, more often sugar – hence the need to chaptalize by adding sugar (see the section on winemaking on page 27). In the warmer climates the opposite is true: the need is to preserve some acidity, which tends to disappear with ripeness – hence, in Australia, the practice of adding some acidity, usually in the form of citric acid, to the wine during the winemaking process.

CLONES

As with any plants, vines can be bred to enhance certain desirable characteristics, and to minimize those that are not required. The importance of clones in producing good-quality wine has only recently been recognized.

Until well into this century, the selection of clones was essentially empirical: in effect when vinegrowers wanted to propagate, they would take cuttings from vines which had made good wine, and ignore those which were poor producers, or which were prone to disease. In the established regions of Burgundy or Chablis the practice would work well enough. With the spread of Chardonnay to regions of the world with different climatic or soil conditions, growers began to recognize the need to plant the most suitable variety of the Chardonnay.

Research has been most intense at the University of California in Davis, which has a research centre specializing in viticulture and winemaking. In fact, when clonal development started, in Germany in the 1920s, increasing the yield was the principal aim. The scientists at Davis have been developing a range of Chardonnay clones to suit different conditions. There are now other wine research stations working on developing clones. In Australia, Roseworthy College has developed strains, as has the wine school of Lausanne in Switzerland. And in Burgundy the University of Dijon is experimenting with a range of clones. One of the biggest problems in clonal development, as Raymond Bernard of the University of Dijon has said is that ''a delay of about 15 years is required before the material can be safely released to the vigneron''. Only over this period of time can the careful process of identifying the characteristics of each clone be plotted, and the performance of the resultant wine be evaluated.

Although an increase in quantity remains one desirable characteristic of any new clone, more sophisticated aims have replaced the single quest for bigger yields. There is greater emphasis on trying to eliminate the diseases to which Chardonnay is prone – mildew, fan leaf, *coulure* (the poor set of the flowers) and so on. In addition much effort has been concentrated on what many wine authorities would now consider the most important requirement of all – the need to improve quality.

Research at Dijon University has shown that high yields tend to reduce the ageing ability of a Chardonnay wine quite dramatically. High yields affect the potential alcohol content of the grapes. But yields can be much higher with Chardonnay than with some other varieties – that other staple of Burgundy the Pinot Noir, for example, suffers much more quickly from high yields than Chardonnay.

The result of modern research is that there are now many hundreds of different clones of Chardonnay in circulation. A list of some of those now being recommended in Burgundy shows the wide range of character combinations possible.

Clones now available for Chardonnay plantings in Burgundy:

Type number 75. Developed in Montpellier, France, after trials in Meursault. This gives a high yield when young, but has a short life. Not recommended as the sole clone in any vineyard.

Type number 76. Developed in the Mâconnais. Gives a good and regular yield of an above-average quality. Below average sugar levels. Over-vigorous in rich soils.

Type number 78. Developed in Meursault. High yielding, but with below-average quality. Of limited use for wines in Burgundy, and not to be used as the sole clone in a vineyard.

Type number 95. Developed in Meursault. A vigorous yielder, with good quality, but susceptible to mildew and frosts. Only plant in well-favoured vineyards.

Type number 277. Also developed in Meursault. Highly vigorous vine, producing good quality fruit, provided yields do not go above 70hl/ha. Not to be used in fertile soils.

Type number 96. Again developed in Meursault. Another high-yielding vine, which should not be used in rich soils. Very susceptible to mildew.

To take a second example, from the New World, the clones in New Zealand derive from all around the world. As so often in New World vineyards, the original clone planted has not proved to be the best. Some of those now being grown include:

Mendoza. The first NZ Chardonnay clone. An Australian development, widely planted, which suffers from "milleran-dage", the problem of uneven-sized grapes on one bunch.

UCD4/UCD5. Two clones developed at Davis in California. Both ripen well and evenly, but are felt to produce wines which lack character.

2/23. A clone developed in Lausanne, Switzerland. Moderate and even crop, with good quality. Only just being planted, but recommended.

RUA1. A local New Zealand clone, which is heat treated (to destroy any viruses). Another moderate and even yielder.

UCD6. Another Californian development, popular in Australia (where it is called IIOV1). Medium yields, high quality. Better in drier vineyard areas of New Zealand.

In addition to these, in early 1990, there were a further five clones (including two from Burgundy – numbers 95 and 96) held by the New Zealand health authorities in quarantine before test planting could begin.

The grape in the winery

There has been a revolution in the cellars and wineries of the world. While the techniques of viticulture in the vineyard have remained relatively unchanged, once the grapes have been picked they are now treated in ways our forebears could never have imagined.

This is especially true of white wines. Cyrus Redding was complaining in 1833 of the fact that white wines were normally yellow in colour – meaning they were oxidized. There were two reasons for that: one was too much air getting to the must and the wine while it was fermenting; and the second was poor hygiene in the cellar. While both factors must have adversely affected all wines, their effect on whites was much more serious, and might well explain the comparative neglect of white wines in Burgundy after the middle of the Middle Ages. It would certainly explain the long-standing preference for sweeter champagne that really only disappeared during the 19th century, since sweetness can hide a multitude of sins.

Today things are very different. A cellar in Burgundy may still look ancient with cobwebs and white fungus hanging above rows of wooden barrels, but the actual press houses, fermentation rooms and other areas where the wine is prepared before it goes into the wooden barrels will be scrupulously clean. Tanks, whether cement with a glass lining or the more modern stainless steel models, control the fermentation without the slightest risk of air getting to the must. In wineries in the New World the transformation of cellar techniques has been almost total. At least until the last few years, there has been the widespread belief that a wine was made in a winery, and not – as the French have always maintained – in the vineyards. Any problems with the grapes could be resolved once they reached the safety of the hands of scientists. More recently, though, there has been a move back to accepting that nature, too, has a role in the creation of a wine; that subtle variations in soil, aspect, and climate contribute in no small way to the taste of the grapes; and a willingness to let the grapes speak rather than overwhelming them with scientific techniques.

The growing popularity of Chardonnay in recent years means that by charting the changing tastes in Chardonnay wines, the change from the path of exclusive technology to one of nature-plus-technology becomes apparent. And the fact that Chardonnay producers from both schools of thought can make fine wines illustrates the grape's versatility.

The fairly neutral taste of Chardonnay makes it amenable to straightforward fermentation in stainless steel-tanks and almost instant bottling. Equally, excellent results are obtained if it is barrel-fermented, aged in casks and then laid down for some years in bottle. And it lends itself to virtually any permutation in between. It can form the base of great sparkling wines and champagne, just as it can produce rich, fat, buttery wines from a winery in Australia.

THE GRAPES REACH THE PRESSES

In many parts of the world, mechanical harvesting is taking over from hand picking. Arguments continue to rage about whether the action of the mechanical harvester, which literally shakes the grapes from the vines, damages the grapes and the roots of the vines. For Chardonnay, the argument is less important than with some white grapes. Its thick skins prevent too much damage to the fruit, although care has to be taken to separate out, by hand, any bunches suffering from Chardonnay's principal disease, grey rot. However, there is a school of thought even in the pro-mechanical harvesting countries such as New Zealand and Australia which believes that a portion of the Chardonnay crop should be pressed with hand-picked whole bunches, stalks and all. The idea is to give greater delicacy, with lower solids and purer flavours in the juice, all of which means the fermentation process is cleaner.

In the hope of increasing the extract from the grapes a series of tests in Burgundy with the 1987 vintage of some white Hautes Côtes de Beaune was carried out by the Ecole Nationale d'Ingènieurs des Travaux Agricoles in Dijon. It suggested that the juice resulting from whole bunch maceration was richer and with greater extract, provided the grapes were in good condition. Other Burgundian experiments have involved freezing grapes before pressing, a process rejoicing in the name of cryoextraction (the word *kruos* in Greek means frost). This has the effect of concentrating the flavour, giving greater intensity to the fruit.

Once the crop reaches the press house, the normal practice with Chardonnay – as with other white wine varietals – is to press the grapes quickly to extract the juice. Often the weight of grapes will allow a certain portion of the juice to be "free-run" - juice which comes out without pressing. This is generally regarded as the best form of juice, and is often described as "*tête de cuvée*".

The importance of the quality of free-run juice is less important than it used to be, since modern presses operate more gently than the old-fashioned style using a huge mechanical screw. Every well-equipped winery now needs a pneumatic Willmes press, or its equivalent: a huge rubber bag which squeezes the grapes gently and evenly, producing very clean juice. Being enclosed, this press also reduces the risk of oxidization inherent in the old open-screw presses.

Many champagne press houses still display the old-fashioned, highly traditional vertical press, which gives a similar gentle, even pressure and allows the first pressing (which releases the richest juice from the centre of the grape) to be used for the highest quality wines. Even in Champagne, where wineproduction is controlled by a maze of regulations which specify the amount of juice to be taken from the presses, modern pneumatic presses are making an appearance.

THE FERMENTING WINE AND THE SUGAR BAGS

The fermenting process is another subject about which wineproducers love to argue. On one side are those who want to have the control that a stainless steel tank guarantees, full of gauges and gadgets to ensure the fermentation temperature is right. On the other, equally convinced, are those who believe that wood fermentation is better, giving greater depth of flavour, greater richness. Until the mid-1980s I would have said that the tank fermentation side had won. But now the fashion has swung partly the other way, with producers from anywhere between Burgundy and New Zealand saying they will always ferment at least some of the wine in wood. Even in Champagne there are stalwarts, such as Krug, who make great claims for the fact their wines are fermented in wood.

Fermentation temperature depends upon the process used. The New World winemakers have always been great advocates of low fermentation temperatures – down to as low as 12°C (53.6°F). But those who ferment in wood – and even those who ferment in tank - now agree that temperatures of around 20°C (68°F) are perfectly acceptable, provided the level can be kept constant.

All this fine-tuning of the fermentation process is a combination of a highly enjoyable (if financially risky) challenge to create a certain style and a desire to extract the maximum flavour out of the Chardonnay grape. It also relates to whether a wine is being made for rapid consumption – the cool temperature, tank-fermentation approach – or whether it is going into wooden barrels for ageing and then maturing in bottle for some years. Essentially, though, it is a legitimate search for a particular style on which to build a reputation.

What is much more dubious is the process of adding sugar to the fermenting must to increase the alcohol content of the final wine. The technique is called chaptalization after Jean Chaptal, Napoléon's Minister of Agriculture, who takes credit for the idea. In Burgundy, in poor vintages, judicious use of sugar (or, with changes in European rules, concentrated grape juice) can at least give a wine some chance of quality. The law states that chaptalization can only be used to raise the alcohol content by two degrees, but that is repeatedly broken, even in good years. It is often used to compensate for the fact that the yields from the vines have been much too high.

While chaptalization is practised more in Burgundy for red wines (those who have drunk a disappointing red Burgundy which was heavy and tasted more of burnt caramel than fruit will know the effect of too much chaptalization), producers – at least the less scrupulous ones – can get quite carried away with the sugar bags in preparing their white wines as well. The process is practised to a lesser extent throughout the world, especially in cooler climates. But to their credit, I know of no producers in the New World who abuse the system as they do in Burgundy. Perhaps that's because they care more for their reputations.

THE SECOND FERMENTATION

All wines go through a first fermentation which turns the sugar in the grapes into alcohol. But there is also a second fermentation which may or may not occur naturally, and which producers can either encourage or actively prevent. This is the malolactic fermentation, known in the wine world as the malo. Its effect is to change the sharp malic acid in the wine into gentler lactic acid, thereby reducing its tartness. All red wines go through this fermentation, because high acidity is considered a fault in reds. But with whites the situation is different.

It all depends on what a producer wants from his wine, and where the grapes were grown. The malo is usually encouraged in cooler wine regions but may need to be suppressed in hotter ones. A comparison between Australian and New Zealand Chardonnay producers illustrates the point. In Australia, the super-ripe Chardonnay grapes have one problem: they lack acidity, they are too sweet. Producers do everything they can to discourage a fermentation which further reduces the acidity. Indeed, they may actually add acidity (in the form of citric acid) to give their Chardonnay more shape and stop it being too flabby, a technique which, in the wrong hands can easily be the Australian equivalent of Burgundian over-chaptalization.

In cooler climate New Zealand, on the other hand, many producers (certainly in less warm years) find that their grapes have a high natural acidity and therefore want to encourage the malo. This is particularly true of areas like Marlborough or Canterbury on South Island. In warmer regions like Hawke's Bay or Gisborne on the North Island producers have more of a choice. They can put the wine through a malo if they are making wines for ageing in wood, and want to create a fatter, buttery style; or they can prevent the malo happening by filtering the wine off its sediment if they want to make a clean, early-drinking wine.

The same contrasts can be made between warm-climate California Chardonnay and cooler Washington or Oregon wines. In Burgundy and Chablis, the generally high acidity of the Chardonnay means that the malo is almost invariably encouraged. In Champagne likewise, depending on the vintage, the malo will be encouraged before the wine is blended and bottled for fermentation in the bottle, rather than in tanks.

Until recently the process of the malolactic fermentation was almost a black art. Few producers understood how it happened, how it started, or how to control it. They had to rely on the bacteria already in the wine, and on ensuring that the cellar was warm enough to start the fermentation. But the result could never be certain: often the fermentation did not happen, or it stuck, or it started months later in the spring. Sometimes nature needs a hand and scientists have developed what are called bacterial starter cultures which can be injected into the wine to start the malo. The normal practice is to start the malo as soon as the alcoholic fermentation is finished.

TO WOOD OR NOT TO WOOD?

This is the big question with Chardonnay producers. Traditional techniques in France used oak barrels for ageing the wine, simply because they were the only containers available. More likely than not, the barrels were old, and were certainly not giving off any taste of wood (which as most producers agree begins to tail off rapidly after three years' use). It was the New World which set off the craze for new wood ageing for Chardonnay. The weight and richness of the fruit in California lent itself immediately to the extra dimension given by the taste of oak. Out of virtually every grape variety, Chardonnay responds best to the oak treatment.

The need to balance the fruit of the wine with the extra complexity given by oak maturing is essential to all wines. But it is even more important with Chardonnay which so readily takes on oak flavours. It is very easy – and there have been numerous examples – for producers to ladle on the oak taste and in the process completely swamp the fruit.

Chardonnay can be aged in a wide variety of oaks. It is matured in American oak, in Spanish oak, in German oak. But most of all, throughout the world, barrels are made of French oak, for which there are at least two very strong reasons. One is because white burgundy is, naturally, put into French oak, and the desire to emulate white burgundy is still never far from the minds of most Chardonnay producers (most oak barrels anywhere in the world will be the standard Burgundian size of 225L). The other reason is more practical: the cool climate in which French oaks grow means they tend to grow more slowly than American oaks, and generally have tighter grains, which release a less obvious and overpowering taste of oak.

Within France, there are five major sources of oak. The forest of Limousin, in the west, is the source of oak for the red wines of Bordeaux as well as for cognac. It is wide grained, and gives off oak tastes quite quickly. The central forest of Nevers, west of Burgundy, produces medium-grained wood and provides oak for red Burgundy. For white wines, the forests of the Vosges (in Alsace) Allier and Tronçais (both from near Nevers) are now widely seen as producing the best, tightly-grained wood, which gives off its taste slowly and not too obviously. But in Burgundy a combination of all or any of these oaks are used for maturing white as well as red wines.

The same five forests provide the wood for nearly all of the world's Chardonnays. From the vast quantity of wooden barrels which are shipped around the world (and which must have made the fortunes of some French coopers), I can only assume that the forests are vast and that the management of the plantations is highly competent.

Every producer will have his favourite wood or woods as well as his favourite cooper. In two or three neighbouring wineries in the Napa Valley, you can get just as many views on the perfect wood for Chardonnay. The same is true in Australia or New Zealand. There is a form of consensus emerging – that Tronçais, Allier and Vosges are the most satisfactory in cooler climates, while Limousin and Nevers are more suitable for warmer climate wines in which the fruit tastes are stronger and therefore less likely to be overwhelmed by wood.

But there is a further permutation in the wood-ageing process which has been pioneered in California: the amount of toast a barrel should have. Coopering, the art of barrel making, is still very traditional. The staves are shaped over fires, which toast the inside of the new wood. The heavier the toast, the greater the taste that will be pass from the barrel into the wine, giving Chardonnay its characteristic smoky flavour.

In the late 1970s in the Napa Valley, the Robert Mondavi Winery ran a series of tests on barrel toast. They put Chardonnay and other wines in barrels which had been toasted to different degrees. Using Limousin and Nevers oak, they found that Chardonnay (and Pinot Noir) could take quite a high degree of toasting provided the wine did not stay in barrel too long, while Cabernet Sauvignon and Sauvignon Blanc needed more lightly toasted barrels. That was the result in the warm Napa Valley: in cooler New Zealand they find a medium toast is as much as Chardonnay can take.

How long the wine is left in the barrels is another decision the producer has to take. A period ranging from a few weeks to around 18 months will depend on the quality of the wine, the style the producer wants to create and the age of the barrels. During that time, the wine may be transferred from brand new barrels to barrels that are a year old, and therefore are giving off less wood taste. The aim, always, will be to ensure that the wood taste enhances the fruit and does not kill it.

BOTTLING

Finally, the wine will be ready for bottling, and here too Burgundy retains its influence. Almost anywhere in the world (I have seen a few exceptions in Italy), a Chardonnay will be put in a sloping shouldered bottle, the sort that has been used in Burgundy for several generations. The colour of the glass in Burgundy is yellow-green, called *feuilles mortes*, but elsewhere it can be anything from dark green to almost pale white. Some tinting is preferred to keep the light out and so prevent the wine from discolouring.

How the wine is bottled depends on the producer. There was a time a few years ago when a wine would be heavily filtered, cleaned up, even pasteurized – and some producers still do this. But with a return to more natural methods and traditional cellar techniques, many producers now believe that it is better to do as little as possible to a wine. So a gentle filtering will take place and no more. Then the wine will be bottled. Finer wines will be laid aside for a few months to recover from the shock of bottling (wine is after all a living product) before being labelled and sent out into the waiting world.

Chart-Busting Chardonnays

While researching this book, I have tasted innumerable Chardonnays from around the world, some great, some highly enjoyable, some which I would prefer to forget. As I tasted, I decided to work out a league table of Chardonnays, to try and place them in some kind of order. The results are in the lists below. They are not to be taken as tablets of stone: for a start they are my personal taste, and everybody with an interest in wine has different tastes at the elevated level under discussion. And, equally to the point, one producer's terrific Chardonnay one year is the same producer's disaster next year. So read the lists but — whether you agree or disagree, above all, keep sampling the incredible range and variety of Chardonnays currently available.

The 20 greatest Chardonnays in the world

These are the finest wines that I tasted in the course of my research for this book and which are from vintages currently available. I have included *blanc de blancs* champagne as a supreme expression of Chardonnay. The order is alphabetical, by producer, within country.

Australia
Gramp's 1987, Orlando,
  South Australia
Mamre Brook 1987, Saltram,
  South Australia
Tarrawarra 1987, Tarrawarra,
  Victoria
Coonawarra 1987, Wynns, South
  Australia

France – Burgundy
Corton-Charlemagne 1983,
  Bonneau du Martray
Meursault-Perrières 1986,
  J.-F. Coche-Dury
Montrachet 1986, Marquis de
  Laguiche, Joseph Drouhin
Chassagne-Montrachet 1er Cru
  Les Vergers 1988, Jaffelin
Chevalier Montrachet 1986,
  Domaine Leflaive

France – Chablis
Chablis 1er Cru Vaulorent 1985,
  Domaine de la Maladière,
  William Fèvre

France – Champagne
Krug, Clos du Mesnil 1981
Salon, Cuvée "S", 1979

New Zealand
Cloudy Bay, Marlborough 1988
Martinborough Vineyards 1988
Morton Estate Hawke's Bay
  Black Label 1986

United States – California
Ferrari-Carano 1987, Sonoma
Forman Winery 1986, Napa
Saintsbury 1988, Carneros
Les Pierres 1986, Sonoma-
  Cutrer, Sonoma

United States – Oregon
Ponzi Vineyards Reserve 1986

The 20 most famous Chardonnays in the world
This list differs from the first list: these are the Chardonnays that
have made the biggest waves, hit the most headlines. Some are
included in my list of the greatest, others are not – even though
they are all good. I have not included vintages: here it is the
wine's name that is important.

Australia
Petaluma, South Australia
Rothbury Estate, New South
  Wales
Roxburgh Estate, Rosemount,
  New South Wales

France – Burgundy
Chevalier Montrachet, Bouchard
  Père & Fils
Corton-Charlemagne, Louis
  Jadot
Meursault-Perrières, Domaine
  des Comtes Lafon
Corton-Charlemagne, Louis
  Latour
Chevalier Montrachet, Domaine
  Leflaive
Château Fuissé Vieilles Vignes,
  Pouilly Fuissé, Domaine Vincent

France – Chablis
Chablis Grand Cru Vaudésir,
  William Fèvre

France – Champagne
Krug, Clos du Mesnil
Ruinart, Dom Ruinart Blanc de
  Blancs

Italy
Gaia e Rey, Gaja (Piedmont)
Maculan (Veneto)

New Zealand
Cloudy Bay, Marlborough

Spain
Milmanda, Torres

United States – California
Acacia, Napa
Chalone Reserve, Monterey
Robert Mondavi Reserve, Napa
Sonoma-Cutrer Les Pierres,
  Sonoma

The 20 top Old World Chardonnay producers
This list is based on current track record. These are the
producers who seem, consistently, to be able to make fine
Chardonnays of world-class standard. There are others, of
course, but these are the very best.

France – Burgundy
Bonneau du Martray
Chartron & Trébuchet
J.-F. Coche-Dury
Domaine des Comtes Lafon
Domaine Vincent Leflaive
Louis Jadot
Jaffelin
Domaine Ramonet
Etienne Sauzet
Domaine Marcel Vincent

France – Chablis
René & Vincent Dauvissat
William Fèvre
Louis Michel
Domaine Raveneau

France – Champagne
Krug
Ruinart
Salon

Italy
Angelo Gaja, Piedmont
Pio Cesare, Piedmont
Vinattieri, Alto Adige

The 20 top New World Chardonnay producers
Again, this list is based on current track record.

Australia
Leeuwin Estate, Margaret River,
  Western Australia
Orlando, South Australia
Petaluma, Adelaide Hills,
  South Australia
Saltram, South Australia
Tarrawarra Vineyards, Yarra
  Valley, Victoria
Wynns, Coonawarra,
  South Australia

New Zealand
Cloudy Bay, Marlborough,
  South Island
Martinborough Vineyards,
  Martinborough, North Island
Morton Estate, Bay of Plenty,
  North Island

South Africa
Hamilton-Russell Vineyards,
  Hermanus
Klein Constantia, Constantia

United States – California
Chalone Vineyards, Monterey
Cuvaison, Napa
Ferrari-Carano, Dry Creek Valley,
  Sonoma
Forman Winery, Napa
Matanzas Creek, Sonoma
Robert Mondavi Winery, Napa
Sonoma-Cutrer Winery, Sonoma
ZD Wines, Napa

United States – Oregon
Ponzi Vineyards

The 20 best value Chardonnays
Chardonnay anywhere can be expensive, because it is in demand. But some producers manage to balance the magic equation of quality and value with at least one of their wines. The greatest wines do not come cheap, for their producers do not normally underestimate the price they can charge.

Australia
Berri Estates Chardonnay,
  Southeastern Australia
Hardy's Nottage Hill Chardonnay
Lindemans Bin 65 Chardonnay,
  Southeastern Australia
Orlando RF Chardonnay,
  Southeastern Australia
Seaview Chardonnay
Wynns Coonawarra Chardonnay,
  Coonawarra, South Australia

Chile
Miguel Torres Chilean
  Chardonnay

France – Burgundy
Georges Duboeuf, St Véran
Jaffelin, Chardonnay Bourgogne
  Blanc
Olivier Leflaive Chardonnay
  Bourgogne Blanc

Italy
Bollini, Chardonnay di
  Mezzocorona, Trentino
Pojer e Sandri Chardonnay,
  Trentino

New Zealand
Cooks Hawke's Bay Chardonnay
Montana Marlborough
  Chardonnay
Nobilo Gisborne Chardonnay

United States – California
Clos du Bois Chardonnay,
  Alexander Valley
Christian Brothers Chardonnay,
  Napa Valley
Hawks Crest Chardonnay,
  Sonoma
Hess Collection, Hess
  Chardonnay, California

**United States – Washington
State**
Covey Run, Yakima Valley
  Chardonnay

THE WINE DIRECTORY

Burgundy

The homeland of Chardonnay is also the most confusing, most misunderstood and downright infuriating wine region in France, and possibly in the world. The range of wines it can produce go from sublime Corton-Charlemagne from a top producer to the most mediocre offerings which are often paraded as Mâcon Blanc.

The division of the region into tiny appellations and even tinier vineyards is matched by the fact that one producer may have vines in 20 different places, sometimes with just a couple of rows in one vineyard. The price is often out of all proportion to the quality and yet, on occasion, it buys the most stunning white wine in the world that is worth every penny.

White burgundy's reputation is founded on an insoluble paradox. Demand has risen inexorably, but supply cannot keep pace. Unlike the lucky New World vineyards, where demand for more Chardonnay has been met by simply turning red vines into white by grafting, or new planting on virgin soil, in Burgundy, tradition, the law and simple geological fact make it almost impossible to change many vineyards from red to white, even allowing for the fact that red wine is in healthy demand as well.

With its great name, it is easy to forget that Burgundy is a small area. Its production is a fraction of that of Bordeaux, or of Champagne. And in that small area, white wine forms a tiny proportion of Burgundy's total production. In most years, white wine is only 21 percent of the total production of the region (including the prolific Mâconnais, but excluding Chablis). The production in 1985, for example, was 371,000 hectolitres – just about half the production of both sweet and dry white wine in Bordeaux in the same year.

One white wine appellation in Burgundy serves as an example. The proud hill of Corton is visible for miles around, its rounded top covered with trees, the slopes below crowded with vines. In one small patch is the vineyard of Corton-Charlemagne, home to one of the world's greatest white wines. Connoisseurs the world over crave the taste of this wine, and yet in one year, the total production may be 1.3 hectolitres – that's 169,000 bottles of wine, or 14,000 cases. That total has to be shared throughout the world, such is the demand for this special name. What makes matters worse is that the 14,000 cases are divided between upwards of 20 growers, some of whom bottle their own wine, some of whom sell it to négociants for maturing and bottling, some of whom do both. One producer may make merely a couple of hundred cases of Corton-Charlemagne, another, especially blessed, almost 1,000. And of course, all will taste different.

One of the results of this huge disparity between supply and demand is that producers have been able to push prices as high as (sometimes higher than) the market will bear. Good white burgundy is never cheap, great white burgundy demands the attentions of a friendly bank manager. Chardonnays from almost anywhere else in the world represent better value, even if, at the end of the day, the greatest white burgundies are beyond compare.

The huge diversity of white burgundies is what makes them both fascinating and frustrating. The golden rule, preached time and again, but always worth repetition is: buy wine by the producer's name, not by the wine's name. In other words, don't just buy Meursault (to take the largest white wine appellation of the Côte de Beaune), buy Monsieur X's, while avoiding Monsieur Y's like the plague.

Monsieur Y's wine, to sum up some of the faults from which white burgundy so frequently suffers, may taste dilute and watery because he has taken too many grapes from his vines rather than only the best – his yields, in effect, are too high. He may have used dirty old barrels in a filthy cellar which has definitely contaminated the fermenting must. He may then have added too much sulphur as an antidote, which means his wine will smell dirty and cause you to sneeze. He may have filtered the wine before bottling to get rid of all his problems, but have done it so thoroughly that any remaining flavour has been stripped away.

There are still enough producers in Burgundy who indulge in some or all of these practices to make it necessary to seek out the goodies and avoid the baddies. In the directory section that follows, I have put together a personal selection of those producers I feel are doing a good job – in some cases much, much more than that. With the thousands of producers in Burgundy, even in the tiny part of it that is white Burgundy, there will be others that readers will discover who are performing the miracles that produce the greatest white nectar in the wine world: let me know, so that they can be included in any updated editions.

CHARDONNAY VINEYARDS

The soil dictates where white wines are grown in Burgundy. As a generally observed rule, where chalk or limestone predominates, white wines are grown; where the reddish marl is found, red wines are produced.

This observation is the result of centuries of trial and error. And since most of the great Côte d'Or, the heartand slope of Burgundy, exposes more marl than limestone it follows that the bulk of the white wines are produced in only a few restricted areas.

So in the whole of Burgundy, five names take full credit for putting its white wine to the forefront of the wine world: Corton-Charlemagne, Chevalier-Montrachet, Le Montrachet, Meursault and Puligny-Montrachet. But these five make up only the minutest fraction of the different appellations and divisions of appellations that can grace the label of a bottle of white burgundy. And, of course, the bulk of white burgundy produced comes from further south in the Mâconnais.

There are five levels of appellation in Burgundy, which apply equally to white as well as red wines. They are:

GENERIC APPELLATIONS

REGIONAL APPELLATIONS

VILLAGE APPELLATIONS

PREMIER CRU APPELLATIONS

GRAND CRU APPELLATIONS

Generic appellations for white wines made from Chardonnay are: Bourgogne Blanc; Bourgogne Grand Ordinaire; Bourgogne Chardonnay.

Regional appellations are: Beaujolais Blanc; Beaujolais Supérieur; Beaujolais Villages; Hautes Côtes de Beaune; Hautes Côtes de Nuits; Côtes de Beaune; Mâcon; Mâcon Supérieur; Mâcon Villages.

Village appellations, many of which produce tiny amounts of white wine, are: Aloxe-Corton; Auxey-Duresses; Beaune; Blagny; Chassagne-Montrachet; Fixin; Givry; Ladoix; Maranges; Mercurey; Meursault; Montagny; Monthélie; Morey-St-Denis; Musigny; Nuits-St-Georges; Pernand-Vergelesses; Pouilly-Fuissé; Pouilly-Loche; Pouilly-Vinzelles; Puligny-Montrachet; Rully; St-Aubin; St-Romain; St-Veran; Santenay; Savigny-lès-Beaune; Vougeot.

Premiers Crus, arranged by village, are: Chassagne-Montrachet: Morgeot (part for red wine); Abbaye de Morgeot (part for red wine); La Boudriotte; La Maltroie; Clos St-Jean; Les Chenevottes; Les Champs Gain; Grandes Ruchottes; La Romanée; Les Brussonnes; Les Vergers; Les Macherelles; En Cailleret.

Meursault, for white and red wines: Les Bouchères; Les Cras; Les Caillerets; Les Charmes; Les Chaumes de Narvaux; Les Chaumes des Perrières; Les Genevrières; Les Gouttes d'Or; Les Perrières; Le Poruzot. For white wines only: La Jeunelotte; Meursault-Santenots; La Pièce sous le Bois; Les Plures; Sous le Dos d'Ane; Sous Blagny. Many of these vineyards are divided into upper (Dessus) and lower (Dessous) portions, the division being a small road that runs toward Chassagne-Montrachet.

Puligny-Montrachet: Le Cailleret; Le Chalumeaux; Le Champ Canet; Clavoillon; Les Combettes; Les Folatières; La Garenne; Hameau de Blagny; Les Pucelles; Les Referts; Sous le Puits.

Grands Crus stand alone as separate appellations, without reference to the village in which they are situated. They are:

Corton-Charlemagne, shared between the communes of Aloxe-Corton and Pernand-Vergelesses

Bâtard-Montrachet, shared between Puligny-Montrachet and Chassagne-Montrachet

Bienvenues Bâtard-Montrachet, solely in Puligny-Montrachet

Chevalier Montrachet, solely in Puligny-Montrachet

Criots Bâtard Montrachet, solely in Chassagne-Montrachet

Le Montrachet, shared between Puligny-Montrachet and Chassagne-Montrachet

The Grand Cru of Charlemagne is currently in disuse, the wines going under the Corton-Charlemagne name.

VINTAGES IN BURGUNDY

Vintages matter in Burgundy more than even in Bordeaux, certainly more than any other Chardonnay areas of the world. Burgundy is marginal country for the vine, almost at the northern extremity of reliable red winegrowing. That is why vintages, especially for red wines, can vary so much according to weather. With white burgundy, as the grapes need fewer hours of sunshine than the reds, the vagaries of the climate are less critical. But the climatic risks are there, and it is worth considering the vintage when purchasing white burgundy. As always a good producer will perform his usual miracles even in a poor year, so the question of vintage does not override the primary rule when buying burgundy – check the name of the producer first.

Here is a personal arrangement of the vintages of the 1980s in descending order of quality for white wines (ie the best vintages first). Be warned: this arrangement does not apply to red Burgundy.

86, 89, 85, 82, 88, 87, 83, 81, 84, 80.

MAKING CHARDONNAY

In the vineyards, grapes are still largely harvested by hand in Burgundy. There are three reasons for this: one, the belief on the part of many producers that mechanical harvesting damages the fruit; two, that the vineyards are too densely planted for mechanical harvesting to be feasible; and three, that an individual producer's parcels of land are so small and so geographically separated one from the other that anything but hand harvesting would be quite impractical. A few of the larger estates are experimenting with mechanical harvesting, but it is no more than that at the moment.

Once inside the *chai* – the cellar – it is fascinating to see that Burgundy's white winemaking is undergoing a series of transitions. There is the centuries-old traditional way of making the wine, the high-tech way, and the new tradition, which employs the philosophy of the high-tech but without ignoring the traditional cellar practises.

Tradition first. Picked grapes are pressed quickly, often with a first separation of the all important free-run juice. To clarify the must it is left to stand, before being transferred to large wooden casks or vats to ferment. Often fermentation takes place at quite high temperatures – around 18-20° C (64-68° F) and any subsequent cooling, if necessary, is carried out by the simple expedient of opening the cellar doors. In normal years, the temperature outside at this time of year is cool enough to make this quite sufficient.

After the first fermentation, which takes between ten days and two weeks, the wine is encouraged to go through its malolactic fermentation, which is almost essential for any white wine given Burgundy's cool climate and the high acid level of the grapes. Sometimes the start of this secondary fermentation is slow, and has to be helped along by heaters in the cellars, sometimes nature is allowed to take its course, and the malolactic process does not finish until the following spring.

The white wine is almost always chaptalized, that is sugar is added to raise the alcohol levels. Each year a fixed amount of chaptalization is permitted, and the sugar is added at the beginning of the first fermentation. New EEC rules now state that sweet concentrated grape must should be added, rather than sugar. A common scandal in Burgundy, particularly in cooler years when grapes are potentially low in alcohol, is an extravagant use of sugar, above the imposed limits.

After the two fermentations are complete, wines are racked (transferred from one container to another) and put into wood if they are finer wines, or into stainless steel or glass-lined cement tanks if lesser wines. Bottling will take place any time from the summer following the harvest up to about a year from the harvest.

The high-tech method replaces the traditional wooden equipment, such as the barrels or vats used for fermentation with modern stainless steel. Temperatures for fermentation will be strictly controlled, and they will generally be lower – 12-15° (53-59° F). Must will often be centrifuged to clean it before fermentation, and filtration will be used at various stages up to bottling. For lesser white burgundies, such as most of the Mâconnais wines, which are often made in the coopératives, this is just the right sort of technology: it produces clean, fresh, fruity wines intended for rapid quaffing.

But for the finer wines, what is called the "squeaky-clean approach" is not good enough. The younger generation of wineproducers, many of them university-trained in Dijon or even in California, are combining the best of the old with the best of the new. Wood is used for fermentation, but it is often new wood, or certainly small oak barrels. Allier, Limousin and Nevers are the woods preferred. A percentage of a wine will be fermented in new wood, some may be in second year wood, still more in stainless steel before a final blend is made.

The "new traditionalists" will mature their wine in new wood as well. Often the wines will remain on their lees for much of this period – say for 10 months. This is to give greater flavour to the wine. Little racking or filtration will take place – many producers do not even filter their wines before bottling – so that the wine is disturbed as little as possible. The less a wine is handled, the better the results, all other things being equal.

But while many traditional techniques are adopted by

younger wineproducers, they will also put into practice something learned from the squeaky-clean school: unstinted hygiene. Clean cellars are something found all over the New World, less often in the Old World. A good sign in any cellar, whatever its age or location, is a clean smell, raked sand on the floor and no musty barrels. Great wine can be made in dirty conditions, but it is harder, and that is a lesson the younger generation, now taking over in Burgundy, has learnt.

PRODUCERS

ROBERT AMPEAU & FILS   **→
6 Rue du Cromin, 21190 Meursault

Total v'yds owned: 10ha (247 acres)
Chardonnays produced: Puligny Montrachet Combettes, Meursault Perrières, Meursault Charmes, Meursault La Pièce sous le Bois, Meursault.

A strangely reticent man in a region where personalities are often larger than life, Robert Ampeau and his son Michel make a range of wines mainly from his Meursault holdings. Unusually too for the region, part of the vineyard is mechanically harvested. Both Charmes and Perrières are wines which can mature well, as can La Pièce sous le Bois, a strangely named Premier Cru which lies close to woods: the 79 of this (tasted in 1988) was still showing great signs of vitality, and was at its peak.

PIERRE BITOUZET   ***

Chardonnays produced: Corton Charlemagne, Savigny-lès-Beaune 1er Cru les Goudoulettes.

Pierre Bitouzet, régisseur (manager) of the Prince de Mérode estate, also has small amounts of his own vineyard, from which he produces around 250 cases a year of rich, tropical fruit tasting Corton-Charlemagne, which matures slowly; and also a round, full flavoured Savigny-lès-Beaune. The standards are high and reliable.

SIMON BIZE & FILS   →**
21420 Savigny-lès-Beaune

Total v'yds owned: 10ha (25 acres)
Chardonnay owned: 3.5ha (9 acres)
Chardonnays produced: Bourgogne Les Perrières, Savigny-lès-Beaune.

While the emphasis is more toward red wines in this region, Patrick Bize is making some light, fresh whites that are not overly expensive. His Bourgogne Perrières 88 tended to a slightly more austere style, while Savigny-lès-Beaune 88 managed a softer taste with more flowery character.

BONNEAU DU MARTRAY   ***→****
Pernand-Vergelesses, 21420 Savigny-lès-Beaune

Total v'yds owned: 11.1ha (27 acres)
Chardonnay owned: 9ha (22 acres)
Chardonnays produced: Corton-Charlemagne.

One of the great estates in Corton-Charlemagne, owned by Comte Jean le Bault de la Morinière, who lives in Paris. It regularly produces stunning wines from a mid-slope section of the Corton hill which faces south-west. Some idea of their comparative size can be seen from the fact that it manages to make over 50,000 bottles of Corton-Charlemagne each year. Recent vintages have returned to traditional ways, with fermentation in cask, even though the temperature is controlled. Of recent wines, the estate rates the 83 and 85 Corton-Charlemagne as its best: I would certainly agree, with the 83 in particular. The 86, too, is full of well-structured fruit that will certainly age in bottle well into the 21st century.

CAVE DES VIGNERONS DE BUXY   **
71390 Buxy

V'yds owned by members of coop: 484ha (1,200 acres)
Chardonnays produced: Montagny, Mâcon-Villages.

One of the most reliable of the Chalonnais and Mâconnais coopératives, making wines that appear widely, often under brand names of retailers. The installation is modern, with stainless steel in wide use, and the wines are clean, fresh and fruity. Occasionally wines have some wood ageing: such as an 85 Montagny les Loges, whose ripe, soft fruit was balanced with a deft touch of wood.

LOUIS CARILLON & FILS   **→***
Puligny-Montrachet, 21190 Meursault

Total v'yds owned: 12ha (30 acres)
Chardonnay owned: 7.8ha (19 acres)
Chardonnays produced: Bienvenues Bâtard-Montrachet; Puligny-Montrachet 1er Crus: Les Combettes, Les Champs Canet, Les Perrières, Les Referts, Les Champs Gains; Puligny-Montrachet;
Chassagne-Montrachet.

A sizeable estate in Burgundian terms with some prime possessions, especially in white wines. The wines are made in a pleasantly soft style, using 10 percent new wood for ageing, and are then aged in wood for up to a year. The style is generally open and generous, often with ripe tropical fruit flavours. The 86 was a better vintage than 85, while the 88s are wines that may have the ability to age longer than is normal with these wines. The range of Premier Cru Pulignys is especially interesting.

MAURICE CHAPUIS   ***
21420 Aloxe-Corton

Total v'yds owned: 10ha (25 acres)
Chardonnay owned: 1.40ha (3 acres)
Chardonnays produced: Bourgogne Blanc, Corton-Charlemagne.

It may not seem much land, but Maurice Chapuis, now in charge after his father Louis' retirement, makes good use of what he has. The well-balanced and structured Corton-Charlemagne is designed for longevity and its fruit opens out beautifully over a period of years, as a 78 (tasted in 1989) testified. The Bourgogne Blanc is also a fine wine, much better than the appellation would suggest.

CHARTRON & TRÉBUCHET ***→
13 Grand' Rue, Puligny Montrachet, 21190 Meursault

Chardonnays produced: Bâtard-Montrachet; Chassagne-Montrachet; Chassagne-Montrachet Morgeots; Chevalier Montrachet; Meursault; Meursault Charmes; Rully; St-Aubin; Puligny-Montrachet Clos de la Pucelle; Puligny-Montrachet Les Folatières.

A partnership of two *chefs de caves* who started together as négociants in 1983, and are now producing top-rank wines. Vintages of 86 (tasted in 1988) for example, showed a good, straight ripe style of Rully la Chaume; a poised St Aubin la Chatenière, pleasingly perfumed; a bigger, slow-developing Meursault, and a closed, firm Puligny-Montrachet les Folatières from their own domaine, citrusy, closed, full of wood, but with excellent fruit. Their other domaine wines include Chevalier Montrachet, and their *monopole* of Puligny-Montrachet Clos de la Pucelle, the 86 a soft, quite open wine, forward and with balanced acidity.

DOMAINE DU CHÂTEAU DE BEAUNE *→**
Château de Beaune, 21202 Beaune

Total v'yds owned: 100ha (25 acres)
Chardonnay owned: 14.8ha (37 acres)
Chardonnays produced: Beaune Clos St-Landry, Beaune du Château, Corton Charlemagne, Meursault Genevrières, Chevalier Montrachet, Montrachet.

This is the large domaine of the négociant firm Bouchard Père & Fils, the bulk of whose business is, of course, based on bought-in grapes and wine. Nothing wrong in that, but in this case the firm's best wines are certainly from its own vineyards which, as can be seen, are in some prime sites. Despite heavy investment in a modern cuverie, and some spectacular cellars under the old château in the town walls of Beaune, there are still disappointments even here. Wines can taste heavy and seem overchaptalized, even in years which should not warrant it: Beaune du Château, a non-vintage white is smooth and a little too sweet. Beaune Clos St-Landry 86 was closed, opening slowly in the mouth with a hint of opulence, Chevalier Montrachet 86 (the Bouchards are the biggest landowners here) was in a big style, with perhaps too much smoky flavour for the fruit, but could develop. Meursault Genevrières 86 had attractive perfumed fruit, and a pleasing elegance.

DOMAINE DU CHÂTEAU DE MEURSAULT ***
21190 Meursault

Total v'yds owned: 55ha (136 acres)
Chardonnay owned: 21.38ha (53 acres)
Chardonnays produced: Puligny-Montrachet Champs Canet; Meursault
1er cru; Meursault; Bourgogne Blanc Clos du Château;
Savigny-lès-Beaune.

Owned by the owners of the négociant firm of Patriarche, this is an estate based at the exquisitely maintained château in Meursault. In addition to owning some fine pieces of land, they have recently planted the land in front of the château, from which they produce a high-quality Bourgogne Blanc Clos du Château. The 89 of this, tasted from cask, was fresh and fruity with hints of malolactic and a pleasing creamy new wood taste. The 87 had 60 percent wood maturation, crisp and spicy; the 86 was soft and honeyed, already mature. More serious are the Meursaults, especially Château de Meursault: the 89, again tasted in cask, and partially fermented in wood, was rich and spicy. The 87 Château de Meursault was soft, creamy, even if still a little closed; the 86 concentrated with vanilla overtones, still with firm tannins.

RAOUL CLERGET →****
St-Aubin 21190 Meursault

Total v'yds owned: 17ha (42 acres)
Chardonnays produced: Chassagne-Montrachet; St-Aubin le Charmois;
St-Aubin Les Frionnes; Mâcon Villages; Rully; Puligny-Montrachet.

Both a domaine owner and a négociant, the firm of Raoul Clerget bears one of the oldest names in Burgundy, with family records back to 1270. This branch of the family is now controlled by Maurice Clerget. Their wines show a great influence of new wood, and are certainly on the big, ripe side. An 89 Premier Cru St-Aubin Les Frionnes is definitely in a heavy, old style, from 40-45 year-old-vines; the domaine Chassagne-Montrachet 89 is ripe and warm, with a good if strong wood presence; 86 Meursault (tasted in 1990) shows big mature fruit tastes, although it still needs time in bottle; Puligny-Montrachet 86 (tasted in 1990) has almost too much wood overlying the fruit which hints at baked apples and firm tannin.

J.-F. COCHE-DURY ****

Chardonnays produced: Bourgogne; Corton-Charlemagne; Meursault;
Meursault les Casses-Têtes; Meursault Chevalières; Meursault Perrières;
Meursault Rougeots.

One of the young generation of wine producers in Burgundy who are revitalizing traditional ways, Jean-Francois Coche-Dury is now seen as right at the top of his profession. Wines go through at least 50 percent barrel fermentation in new Allier wood, undergo few rackings, a long period in wood (as much as 22 months) and are bottled unfiltered. The results are often staggering: full of body, very concentrated flavours, which leap out of the glass. He makes tiny quantities of wine (223 cases of Meursault Perrières 86, for example). His 86s were better than his 85s, but that is splitting hairs. I have not tasted more recent vintages, but they should be well up to this standard.

DELAGRANGE-BACHELET **
Chassagne-Montrachet, 21190 Meursault

Total v'yds owned: 10ha (25 acres)
Chardonnay owned: 2.5ha (6 acres)
Chardonnays produced: Bâtard-Montrachet; Criots Bâtard Montrachet; Chassagne-Montrachet Morgeot.

This estate produces small quantities of intensely flavoured wines, with regular stirring of the lees during fermentation in barrel. The style is old, but is clean, and works well.

JOSEPH DROUHIN ***
7 Rue d'Enfer, 21200 Beaune

Total v'yds owned: 22.7ha (56 acres) and 35.3ha (87 acres) (in Chablis)
Chardonnay owned (in Burgundy): 7.4ha (18 acres)
Chardonnays produced (in Burgundy); Beaune Clos des Mouches; Corton-Charlemagne; Bâtard-Montrachet; Bourgogne la Forêt; Meursault Perrières; Montrachet Marquis de Laguiche; Chassagne-Montrachet; Chassagne-Montrachet Morgeot; Puligny-Montrachet; Puligny-Montrachet les Folatières.

A range of very fine wines from a négociant who has perhaps earned an even better reputation for his reds. There are some real stars here: top of the tree, undoubtedly, is the Meursault Marquis de Laguiche, the 85 intense, nutty and fruity with enormous rich tastes, seemingly lingering forever in the mouth. Beaune Clos des Mouches is another star: the 85 exhibits beautiful fruit flavours, great elegance and a charming light touch. Other wines, too, are worth searching out: the Puligny-Montrachet les Folatières 86 is a wine that needs to be aged for a good ten years. Joseph Drouhin also produces a range of Chablis from large holdings in that region.

DOMAINE DE LA FOLIE ** →
71150 Chagny

Total v'yds owned: 19.87ha (49 acres)
Chardonnay owned: 6.6ha (16 acres)
Chardonnays produced: Rully Clos de Bellecroix; Rully Clos Roch; Rully; Rully Clos St Jacques.

The Noël-Boutton family who run this estate specialize in the whites of Rully. The wines are good when drunk young, but are designed for some ageing, which they can certainly achieve.

JEAN-NOËL GAGNARD → ***
Chassagne-Montrachet, 21190 Meursault

Total v'yds owned: 2.32ha (6 acres)
Chardonnay owned: 0.66ha (2 acres)
Chardonnays produced: Chassagne-Montrachet 1er Cru; Chassagne-Montrachet Caillerets; Chassagne-Montrachet Morgeot; Bâtard-Montrachet.

A husband and wife team run this tiny domaine, which, although its main interest is in red wines, produces three or four very attractive whites that open out generously fairly early in their life. They tend to have tropical fruit characters, and are definitely on the rich side of burgundy.

DOMAINE GAGNARD-DELAGRANGE ** → ***
Chassagne-Montrachet, 21190 Meursault

Total v'yds owned: 4.8ha (12 acres)
Chardonnay owned: 2.69ha (7 acres)
Chardonnays produced: Montrachet; Bâtard-Montrachet; Chassagne-Montrachet Morgeot; Chassagne-Montrachet la Boudriotte; Chassagne-Montrachet.

This is a classic example of a fragmented estate: Jacques Gagnard (the brother of Jean-Noël) owns almost literally enough rows of vines in Le Montrachet to make a barrel a year. He believes that fermentation should start as soon as possible after picking and so does not follow the practice of allowing the must to settle in tank before it is put into wood for fermentation. There is a certain very traditional feel to some of his wines: an 86 Chassagne-Montrachet la Boudriotte, for example (tasted in 1988) was heavy and meaty, very big and literally beefy.

MAISON JEAN GERMAIN ***
11 Rue de Lattre-de-Tassigny, 21190 Meursault

Total v'yds owned: 1.58ha (4 acres)
Chardonnay owned: 1.58ha (4 acres)
Chardonnays produced: Meursault; Meursault La Barre; Meursault Meix Chavaux; Puligny-Montrachet Cuvée des Vignes; Puligny-Montrachet Les Grands Champs; St-Romain Clos sous le Château.

This is a small business (not to be confused with the producer of the same name in Chorey-lès-Beaune) with an unusual concentration on whites, making wines both from its own tiny domaine and from bought-in must. The wines are fermented in wood (of which a third to half is new) and then kept in wood for 15 months. The aim is to make a wine that will keep, and that is certainly true of a wine such as the 85 Puligny-Montrachet Les Grands Champs I tasted, which was quite lean, needing plenty of time in bottle. One of their more interesting wines is the St-Romain, which certainly shows what good, relatively inexpensive, quality can be produced from this village.

CHÂTEAU DE LA GREFFIÈRE **
La Roche-Vineuse, 71960 Pierreclos

Total v'yds owned: 12ha (30 acres)
Chardonnay produced: Mâcon Villages.

This 19th-century château, owned by Henri and Vincent Greuzard, has cellars dating from the 18th century. The size of the estate, large in Mâconnais terms, means that the Greuzards are a major influence in the area. Their wines are soft, broad, pleasantly perfumed and normally excellent value.

DOMAINE ANTONIN GUYON ** →
21420 Savigny-lès-Beaune

Total v'yds owned: 48ha (119 acres)
Chardonnay owned: 2.55ha (6 acres)
Chardonnays produced: Pernand-Vergelesses 1er Cru; Meursault-
Charmes; Corton-Charlemagne.

The size of this domaine puts it among the largest in Burgundy.
Whites are fermented at the relatively high temperature of 18°C
(64.4F) to give them considerable flavour and richness. One-
third new oak is used for maturation. The Corton-Charlemagne
is on the light side for this vineyard.

LOUIS JADOT ***
5 Rue Samuel Legay, 21200 Beaune

Total v'yds owned: 40ha (91 acres)
Chardonnays produced: Mâcon-Villages; Pouilly Fuissé; Savigny-lès-
Beaune; Chassagne-Montrachet; Chassagne-Montrachet Morgeot, Duc de
Magenta; Chevalier Montrachet Les Demoiselles; Corton-Charlemagne;
Meursault; Meursault-Blagny; Meursault Charmes; Meursault
Genevrières, Puligny-Montrachet Clos de la Garenne, Duc de Magenta;
Puligny-Montrachet les Combettes; Bourgogne Blanc.

Domaine wines are, of course, only a tiny part of this large
négociant business. In the general reflection of Burgundy, the
list is dominated by reds, but there are some serious whites as
well, with a generally high quality. The company ferments at
high temperatures to increase flavour extraction, and leaves the
wine in new oak for some time (depending on the wine). Their
basic white, Réserve des Jacobins, is a light, fruity, somewhat
uninteresting wine. But their lesser commune wines such as a
Rully Blanc la Fontaine have good, fresh acidity and a pleasing
roundness in a vintage like 85. There were good smoky tastes
with the Meursault Charmes 84, or the sumptuous Corton-
Charlemagne 83. Meursault 86 had decadently rich tropical
fruit. Meursault-Blagny matures well: the 83 (tasted in 1988),
showed excellent citrus flavours and was right at its peak. Jadot
markets the wines from the Duc de Magenta estate.

JAFFELIN *** →
2 Rue Paradis, 21200 Beaune

Total v'yds owned: 3.1ha (8 acres)
Chardonnay owned: none
Chardonnays produced: Bourgogne du Chapitre; Rully; St-Romain; St-
Aubin; Pernand-Vergelesses; Pouilly-Fuissé; Meursault; Chassagne-
Montrachet les Vergers; Corton-Charlemagne.

An exciting négociant firm, owned by Joseph Drouhin but run
separately by the energetic Bernard Repolt. Jaffelin is particularly interesting because of the way it has concentrated on
commune wines, bringing out the character of each village in a
range called Les Villages de Jaffelin. While they may not be the
greatest wines in Burgundy, they are certainly some of the best
of their kind. The Rully 88, 25 percent fermented in new wood,

has a slightly spicy, floral, quite full flavour; St-Romain 88 is attractively rustic, structured, heavy; the St-Aubin 88 concentrated, full of rich wood flavours, with 30 percent maturation in new wood; Pernand-Vergelesses 88 was still closed in 1990, full of wood, with a need for time in bottle. Like all Premiers and Grands Crus, these wines tend to have quite an amount of wood taste and are obviously designed for long ageing, but always have a good substructure of fruit.

FRANÇOIS JOBARD → ***

Chardonnays produced: Bourgogne Blanc; Meursault Blagny; Meursault Genevrières; Meursault Poruzot; Meursault Charmes.

François Jobard makes rich, early maturing wines that ooze flavour in a highly satisfying way. His basic Bourgogne Blanc is an attractive, wooded wine, with plenty of nutmeg spice; there is pleasing richness to the Charmes, while the Poruzot is lighter. His best wines are normally Genevrières, which show admirable balance between fruit and new wood.

MICHEL JUILLOT ** → ***
71640 Mercurey

Total v'yds owned: 25ha (62 acres)
Chardonnay owned: 1.8ha (4 acres)
Chardonnays produced: Mercurey Blanc; Montagny 1er Cru, Rully, Givry.

Some of the wines listed here are made by relations and family of Michel Juillot, but are included for convenience, because Michel himself is still the boss of the family. He is a serious producer, concentrating mainly on red wines, but produces small amounts of a harmonious white Mercurey Blanc: the 84 (tasted in 1989) was soft, balanced, still with some crisp fresh fruit; the 71 (also tasted in 1989) ripely mature, with asparagus tones – a delicious soft wine. M. Juillot tells me that this wine originally had to be sold for 7 francs because nobody wanted a white Mercurey. . . .

LABOURÉ-ROI ** → ***
21700 Nuits-St Georges

Chardonnays produced: Auxey-Duresses; Côte de Beaune Blanc la Grande Chatelaine; Meursault Clos des Bouches Chères; Chassagne-Montrachet Clos St Marc; Puligny-Montrachet 1er Cru Champs Canet.

This medium-sized négociant firm, firmly based in red wine country in Nuits-St Georges, also has domaine holdings in Meursault, Chassagne-Montrachet and Puligny-Montrachet, from which are now coming some vastly improved wines. The 85 Chassagne-Montrachet Clos St Marc had good nutty, smoky flavours, rich but firmly on the dry side of ripe; 85 Puligny-Montrachet Premier Cru Champs Canet (tasted in 1986) was powerful, quite forward, creamy and ripe, with a rich underlay of peppery wood. Lesser wines, such as an 83 Bourgogne Blanc showed well in a soft, slightly unfocused way. Labouré-Roi also distributes the wines of Domaine Chantal Lescure La Grande Châtelaine in the Côte de Beaune.

HENRI LAFARGE ** →
Le Bourg, Bray, 71250 Cluny

Total v'yds owned: 9.5ha (23 acres)
Chardonnay owned: 9.5ha (23 acres)
Chardonnays produced: Mâcon-Bray; Mâcon-Villages.

M. Lafarge produces light, attractive, floral Mâconnais wines that show what can be done in this region with a little care. His Mâcon Villages Bray 85 was a model of its kind, fruity and elegant, well-balanced, possibly able to age for three to four years from bottling.

DOMAINE MICHEL LAFARGE ** →
Volnay, 21190 Meursault

Total v'yds owned: 9.35ha (23 acres)
Chardonnay owned: 1ha (2 acres)
Chardonnay produced: Meursault.

Better known, of course, for its Volnays, Domaine Michel Lafarge makes small quantities of a poised Meursault from 1ha (2 acres) of vines in the village. Good use is made of new wood in this wine.

DOMAINE DES COMTES LAFON ****
Clos de la Barre, 21190 Meursault

Total v'yds owned: 13ha (32 acres)
Chardonnay owned: 6.7ha (17 acres)
Chardonnays produced: Meursault Clos de la Barre; Meursault Désirée; Meursault la Goutte d'Or; Meursault Charmes; Meursault Genevrières; Meursault Perrières; Montrachet.

One of the top two or three white estates in Burgundy making huge, long-lasting wines, full of concentration, showing to the sceptics why white burgundy is such a great wine. Despite their power, they are actually quite elegant wines, but their intensity comes from the estate's practice of leaving the wines on their lees for up to two years during barrel ageing, never racking them, and never filtering before bottling. If done with care, this shows that the less handling a wine has, the finer it will be. The estate, now under the control of Dominique Lafon, rarely releases a wine before two to three years after harvest. Every wine has some character that stands out: Clos de la Barre for its nutty flavours, la Goutte d'Or almost living up to its name with its golden fruit; Désirée a lighter, approachable style. The Charmes comes from vines which are nearly 70 years old, and is possibly the longest-lived of the Lafon wines. The finest, though, are Perrières and Genevrières, both complex, both elegant, and both so beautifully structured that their ability to age hardly notices in youth. Many of these wines are made in tiny quantities – 600 bottles on average for la Goutte d'Or, for example: but if you do find a bottle it really is worth the money.

HUBERT LAMY   **→
St-Aubin 21190 Meursault

Total v'yds owned: 13.5ha (33 acres)
Chardonnay owned: 4.43ha (11 acres)
Chardonnays produced: St-Aubin; St-Aubin 1er Cru; Puligny-
Montrachet; Chassagne-Montrachet; Criots-Bâtard-Montrachet.

Despite his holdings among the Montrachets, Hubert Lamy
believes in St-Aubin, and claims greatest pleasure from this
village's white wines. The fresh, floral quality both of the village
St-Aubin and the Premier Cru wines are immediately attractive.

MAISON LOUIS LATOUR   →***
18 Rue des Tonneliers, 21204 Beaune

Total v'yds owned: 47ha (117 acres)
Chardonnay owned: 9.5ha (23 acres)
Chardonnays produced: Bourgogne Blanc; Mâcon-Villages; Montagny;
Bâtard-Montrachet; Chassagne-Montrachet; Meursault; Puligny-
Montrachet; Montrachet; Meursault Ch de Blagny; Meursault
Genevrières; Corton-Charlemagne.

The house of Louis Latour produces around 3 million bottles a
year, of which only 10 percent come from its domaines. In terms
of white wine vineyards, the house owns a small amount in
Chevalier-Montrachet, and a comparatively huge (9ha/22
acres)) of the fabulous Corton-Charlemagne. This last is
certainly its finest wine, which can reach almost New World
proportions of toasty wood and ripe fruit and still retain, as with
an 83, tasted in 1990, a sense of balance and proportion. All the
whites are fermented in wood, and aged for at least nine months
in wood, while Grand Cru wines are treated to 100 percent new
wood. Apart from the Corton-Charlemagne, the best Latour
whites are often the Bâtard-Montrachets, which can reveal deep
honeyed fruit qualities. Latour has also pioneered the production of Chardonnay from the Ardèche, of which they now make
over one million bottles.

DOMAINE LEFLAIVE   ****
Puligny-Montrachet, 21190 Meursault

Total v'yds owned: 21ha (52 acres)
Chardonnay owned: 20ha (49 acres)
Chardonnays produced: Bâtard-Montrachet; Bienvenues Bâtard-
Montrachet; Puligny-Montrachet; Puligny-Montrachet Clavoillon; Puligny-
Montrachet Les Combettes; Puligny-Montrachet Les Pucelles; Chevalier
Montrachet; Meursault-Blagny.

Domaine Leflaive is at the summit of white Burgundy. Devoted
almost entirely to the art of making great white wine, this family-
run aristocratic estate succeeds admirably. For many people, to
drink a Leflaive wine is to taste the most perfect white wine there
can be. It all comes at a price, of course: Leflaive wines are some
of the most expensive white burgundies to be made. But even
with a domaine which is big by Burgundian standards,
quantities are still small: the number of bottles of wine from Les

Combettes, for example, of which Leflaive owns a mere 0.8ha (2 acres), can be counted in hundreds. The fermentation of the wines take place in a mix of Allier wood and small stainless steel tanks, and ageing is in wood, with about 25 percent new wood. I do not often have chances to taste these wines, but I treasure recent memories of the stylish and fragrant 85 Puligny-Montrachet; the 86 Bâtard-Montrachet, very creamy, honeyed, very rich; and the 86 Chevalier Montrachet, full of tropical fruits, with a delicious lightly toasty background, still somewhat firm, designed to last seemingly forever.

OLIVIER LEFLAIVE →***
Place du Monument, Puligny-Montrachet, 21190 Meursault

Total v'yds owned: none
Chardonnays produced: Bourgogne Les Sétilles; Auxey-Duresses; Rully 1er Cru; Mercurey; St-Aubin; Bâtard-Montrachet; Chassagne-Montrachet; Chassagne-Montrachet Les Baudines; Meursault; Meursault Charmes; Puligny-Montrachet Les Garennes; Corton-Charlemagne.

A négociant business, run by Olivier Leflaive, who also jointly runs the Domaine Leflaive. The wines are widely sourced, and in some ways I prefer the lesser wines in the range to the great names: an 88 Rully Premier Cru was richly woody and creamy; an 88 Mercurey soft, fresh and forward; the 86 Auxey-Duresses firm, quite toasty, but with good ripe fruit. At the top end of the range, both the 86 Meursault Charmes and 85 Corton-Charlemagne were disappointing, lacking weight.

DOMAINE LEQUIN-ROUSSOT ***
21590 Santenay

Total v'yds owned: 13.5ha (33 acres)
Chardonnay owned: 0.82ha (2 acres)
Chardonnays produced: Chassagne-Montrachet Morgeot; Chassagne-Montrachet En Cailleret; Chassagne-Montrachet Les Vergers; Bâtard-Montrachet.

The size of some of the holdings of the Lequin brothers would make a New World producer boggle: 0.11ha (0.3 acre) of Bâtard-Montrachet, 0.39ha (1 acre) of En Cailleret. And they have similar-sized holdings among their red wines. What they produce, albiet very often in tiny quantities, is of the best. The wines of Chassagne-Montrachet are, to my mind, their finest: an 85 En Cailleret was huge, rich, but beautifully shaped, obviously settling down for a long maturation in bottle. They use 20 percent new wood for maturing, and believe in long fermentation times.

MAISON LEROY →***
Auxey-Duresses, 21190 Meursault

Total v'yds owned: 24.36ha (60 acres)
Chardonnay owned: 3.43ha (8 acres)
Chardonnays produced: Bourgogne d'Auvenay; Auxey-Duresses; Meursault; Meursault Chaumes des Perrières; Meursault Les Narvaux; Meursault Genevrières; Puligny-Montrachet Les Folatières.

A négociant business owned by Mme Bize-Leroy, who is also joint owner of the Domaine de la Romanée-Conti. It is actually divided into three: the négociant firm, the Domaine Leroy (which mainly owns red wine vineyards), and the Domaine d'Auvenay, based in St-Romain, which owns small quantities of white wine vineyards. These white wines have, in a curious way, a strong affinity to the reds of Romanée-Conti: when young they are very firm, very closed up, very intense. Just like the reds, they seem to need many years in bottle before they are truly approachable.

MAISON PROSPER MAUFOUX   ** → ***
21590 Santenay

Total v'yds owned: none
Chardonnays produced: Château de Viré Mâcon Viré; St-Véran;
Montagny 1er Cru Le Vieux Château; Pouilly-Fuissé; Puligny-
Montrachet; Corton-Charlemagne; St-Aubin; Meursault Charmes;
Puligny-Montrachet les Folatières; Meursault; Chassagne-Montrachet;
Criots Bâtard Montrachet; Auxey-Duresses; Montrachet.

A family-run firm of négociants, based in the imposing château on the main square of Santenay. Among their wines, they have sole distribution for the Domaine St-Michel in Santenay, which produces some Puligny-Montrachet. They also distribute the Mâconnais wines of Château de Viré. The policy for the négociant wines is to buy must, and to keep the wines in wood for 10-16 months, but they are normally fermented in stainless steel. On the whole, the quality of the whites tends to be good, rather than exceptional, but I have certainly had fine bottles of Puligny-Montrachet from Prosper Maufoux, and had great pleasure from bottles of the firm's Mâconnais wines such as the St-Véran.

DOMAINE MICHELOT-BUISSON   ***
31 Rue de la Velle, 21190 Meursault

Total v'yds owned: 20ha (49 acres)
Chardonnays produced: Bourgogne Blanc; Meursault; Meursault Charmes;
Meursault Clos St-Félix; Meursault Genevrières; Meursault Limozin;
Meursault Les Narvaux; Meursault Perrières; Meursault Les Tillets.

No prizes for guessing that M. Michelot is a man of Meursault. Nor for appreciating that his wines reflect the essence of Meursault in a simple, uncomplicated, way. These are richly enjoyable wines, giving pleasure to those who like opulent buttery fruit and plenty of toasty oak. Some critics complain that the oak overpowers the fruit, but that is only true of leaner vintages, like 84. In both 85 and 86, the Michelot wines were glorious, often quite alcoholic: the Limozin, for instance, or the Clos St-Félix. His best wines are from his land in Genevrières and Charmes, with the Genevrières the more poised and long-lasting of the two.

MOILLARD   ** →
2 Rue F. Mignotte, 21700 Nuits-St-Georges

Total v'yds owned: 38ha (94 acres)
Chardonnay owned: 1.94ha (5 acres)
Chardonnays produced: Bourgogne Blanc; Bourgogne Hautes Côtes de
Nuits; St-Véran; Meursault Perrières; Chassagne-Montrachet la Romanée;
Corton-Charlemagne.

Also known as Moillard-Grivot, this large négociant firm
operates from large premises in Nuits-St-Georges. Most of the
wines are made in stainless steel before wood maturation, and
flash pasteurized before bottling, although some of the top
wines are not treated in this way. There has been a distinct and
welcome improvement in the whites, certainly since the early
1980s, and wines from the 85 vintage onward have been of
good, solid quality. Generally they are fat and rich and new oak
tastes abound. The Chassagne-Montrachet la Romanée and
their Corton-Charlemagne shone in both the 85 and 86
vintages, and were promising well in the 88.

DOMAINE JEAN MONNIER & FILS → ***
20 Rue du 11 Novembre, 21190 Meursault

Total v'yds owned: 17ha (42 acres)
Chardonnay owned: 6.5ha (16 acres)
Chardonnays produced: Meursault; Meursault Charmes; Meursault
Genevrières; Puligny-Montrachet; Bourgogne Blanc.

Wines here receive traditional treatment: fermentation and
ageing in wood much of it new. This applies to the lesser wines
as well as to the Grands Vins. They are stylish wines, which
mature well and which always seem to show well in tastings.

DOMAINE RENÉ MONNIER ** → ***
6 Rue du Dr Rolland, 21190 Meursault

Total v'yds owned: 16ha (40 acres)
Chardonnay owned: 6.8ha (17 acres)
Chardonnays produced: Bourgogne Blanc; Meursault Le Limozin;
Meursault Les Chevalières; Meursault Charmes; Puligny-Montrachet;
Puligny-Montrachet Les Folatières.

A sound, solid firm, founded in 1723 and still in the same family.
In their vineyards no weedkiller is used, which is believed to
guarantee quality in the long term. The cellars have one of the
best rounded vaults in the village. The wines are fermented and
matured in wood, 30 percent new, and bottled in the June
following the vintage.

BERNARD MOREY → ***
Chassagne-Montrachet, 21190 Meursault

Total v'yds owned: 8.8ha (22 acres)
Chardonnays produced: Chassagne-Montrachet Les Baudines; Chassagne-
Montrachet Les Caillerets; Chassagne-Montrachet Les Embrazeés;
Chassagne-Morgeot.

Bernard Morey produces intensely fruity, soft, rich wines that
tend not to age well, but which are highly enjoyable for all that. I

have particularly liked Les Embrazeés, a Premier Cru not often seen. Bigger wines such as Les Baudines or Morgeot, especially in vintages like 85, verge on too much of a good thing.

PIERRE MOREY →***

Chardonnays produced: Meursault; Meursault Charmes; Meursault Genevrières; Meursault Perrières; Meursault Tessons; Bâtard-Montrachet.

Pierre Morey is a believer in fermentation at a high temperature and minimal filtration. These practices give his wines a good intensity and concentration which can be stunning. His 86 wines were some of his best: my favourite was the creamy, oaky, ripe honey-favoured Bâtard-Montrachet. His village Meursault, too, can be an excellent wine.

JACQUES PRIEUR ** → ***
2 Rue des Santenots, 21190 Meursault

Total v'yds owned: 14ha (35 acres)
Chardonnay owned: 4.63ha (11 acres)
Chardonnays produced: Bourgogne Blanc; Meursault Clos de Mazeray; Meursault 1er Cru; Puligny-Montrachet Les Combettes; Chevalier Montrachet; Montrachet.

Since 1988, this domaine has been half owned by the merchant house of Antonin Rodet, but the Prieur family continues to be in charge. They describe their wines as ones which are designed for ageing, with greenness and firmness when young. The 85 Clos de Mazeray, from a vineyard which was once part of the Abbey of Citeaux, is a smooth, balanced wine, showing strong hints of the new oak used for maturation. An 85 Montrachet was surprisingly forward when tasted in 1988, very rich certainly but not suggesting the expected long ageing.

CAVE COOPÉRATIVE DE PRISSÉ ** →
71960 Pierreclos

Total v'yds of members: 356ha (880 acres)
Chardonnays produced: Mâcon-Prissé; Mâcon-Villages, St-Véran.

Of the number of coopératives which dominate much of the Mâconnais, this is certainly one of the best, and the wines regularly win prizes. I recently tasted an excellent Mâcon-Villages 88, soft, but full of fruit and refreshingly clean, while an 85 Mâcon-Villages was bursting with fruit. Apart from bottling its wines, the coopérative also supplies local négociants, such as Georges Duboeuf.

HENRI PRUDHON ** → ***
St-Aubin, 21190 Meursault

Total v'yds owned: 5.5ha (13 acres)
Chardonnay owned: 1.5ha (4 acres)
Chardonnays produced: St-Aubin, St-Aubin 1er Cru.

M. Prudhon's wines, made by his family for generations in St-Aubin, are an excellent example of the potential this appellation has for white wines. Partially aged in new oak, they are full of flavour, well balanced, and certainly with the ability to age.

DOMAINE RAGOT **
17 Rue de la Planchette, Poncey, 71640 Givry

Total v'yds owned: 6.8ha (17 acres)
Chardonnay owned: 2ha (5 acres)

While the vast majority of Givry wines are red, small amounts of white are made, of which this domaine's are excellent examples. I cannot taste any wood on the 86 Givry Blanc, but it is a good straightforward fresh tasting wine, rich and quite nutty, with a most attractive green/yellow colour.

DOMAINE RAMONET ***→
Chassagne-Montrachet, 21190 Meursault

Total v'yds owned: 13.6ha (34 acres)
Chardonnay owned: 6.7ha (16 acres)
Chardonnays produced: Bâtard-Montrachet; Bienvenues-Bâtard-Montrachet; Chassagne-Montrachet Les Ruchottes; Chassagne-Montrachet; Montrachet; Chassagne-Morgeot.

Also known as Ramonet-Prudhon, this domaine is run by André Ramonet, who has a high reputation in Burgundy. Certainly, the one and only time I was privileged to taste his Montrachet, it was sublime: the 85, still hardly ready to drink, yet with huge, intense flavours and rich concentrated honey, fruit and wood all perfectly in balance. Of his Chassagne-Montrachets, the Ruchottes seems to be better than the Morgeot, certainly in 85.

DOMAINE DE LA REINE PÉDAUQUE *→***
Aloxe-Corton, 21420 Savigny-lès-Beaune

Total v'yds owned: 25.5ha (63 acres)
Chardonnay owned: 2ha (5 acres)
Chardonnays produced: St-Aubin, Chassagne-Montrachet; Puligny-Montrachet; Meursault; Bâtard-Montrachet; Corton-Charlemagne.

Until very recently, the wines of this large négociant firm and landowner, based in Aloxe-Corton and in Corgoloin, might not have been in this book, because of their variable and often less-than-good quality. However, things are changing here, and recent wines are showing great improvements. Tasting the 89 wines in cask showed an impressive range: a smoky Chassagne-Montrachet; a potentially rich and soft St-Aubin; a huge, powerful Meursault that is obviously built to last; a soft, apples-and-custard Bâtard-Montrachet. From the domaine comes Corton-Charlemagne, which I have not tasted recently but it will presumably show the same improvements.

REMOISSENET ***
21200 Beaune

Total v'yds owned: 2.4ha (6 acres)
Chardonnays produced: Montagny; Bourgogne Blanc; Meursault; Puligny-Montrachet; Puligny-Montrachet Les Champs-Gains; Puligny-Montrachet

Les Folatières; Chassagne-Montrachet Morgeot; Puligny-Montrachet Clos de la Mouchère; Corton-Charlemagne; Le Montrachet du Domaine Thénard; Bienvenues-Bâtard-Montrachet; Meursault Charmes; Meursault Genevrières; Meursault Poruzots.

From the above impressive list, it is clear that the merchant house of Remoissenet is serious about white wine. In fact, there are those who argue that the white wines produced here are better than the reds. Certainly it makes wines of great elegance and ability to age. Even the basic Bourgogne Blanc, known as Marie Fanfare, is tastier than many similar wines from other houses. The finest wines are undoubtedly the Montrachet from the domaine of Baron Thénard, the Bienvenues Bâtard-Montrachet and the superlative Corton-Charlemagne (of which there are about 300 cases a year).

ROPITEAU FRÈRES   ** →
21190 Meursault

Total v'yds owned: 21.06ha (52 acres)
Chardonnay owned: 19.43ha (48 acres)
Chardonnays produced: Rully; Meursault; Meursault Perrières; Meursault Genevrières; Puligny-Montrachet Les Champs-Gains; Puligny-Montrachet.

This négociant house is certainly better known for its whites than its reds, and in particular for its range of Meursaults. The house is going for a flattering, rich style, which emphasizes wood tastes. The basic village wine, called Le Meursault de Ropiteau, is fermented in new wood, which certainly gave the 89, tasted from cask, a firm, spicy character which augured well; the 88 was soft, with an attractive nutty quality, with some good acidity. Meursault Perrières 88, was full of medium toast wood, again with this excellent spicy flavour, but also with excellent fruit. Puligny-Montrachet Les Champs-Gains 88 (tasted in 1990) had a creamy baked-apples taste, but was suffering at that stage from a little too much wood.

DOMAINE GUY ROULOT   ***
1 Rue Charles Giraud, 21190 Meursault

Total v'yds owned: 12.5ha (31 acres)
Chardonnays owned: 7.5ha (19 acres)
Chardonnays produced: Bourgogne Blanc; Meursault; Meursault Les Charmes; Meursault Les Luchets; Meursault Meix Chavaux; Meursault Les Perrières; Meursault Les Tessons; Meursault Tillets; Meursault Les Vireuils.

This is a proper Meursault estate, with wines from a wide cross-section of Premiers Crus, and village wines from individual vineyard sites, a practice which was pioneered by the late Guy Roulot. Two-thirds of production is of white wine, which is fermented in Allier wood, 20 to 30 percent new, and aged in wood for 10–12 months, on the lees. The village wines certainly display individual characters, which would be lost in blending: Les Vireuils is smoky, open fruited; Les Luchets is floral, elegantly perfumed; Meix Chavaux is more intense, concentrated; Les Tessons is a slow evolver, firm when young. Of the Premiers Crus, I prefer the Perrières with its nutty, toasty, yeasty character and excellent concentration.

DOMAINE ROUX PÈRE & FILS → ***
St-Aubin, 21190 Meursault

Total v'yds owned: 18ha (44 acres)
Chardonnays produced: St-Aubin; St-Aubin La Pucelle; St-Aubin 1er Cru La Chatenière; Chassagne-Montrachet; Puligny-Montrachet Les Enseignères; Meursault Les Poruzots.

In some ways, Marcel Roux put St-Aubin on the map as a quality white wine village and as an alternative to the pricier offerings from Meursault and the Montrachets. Through his négociant business he is also able to offer a small range of these top wines. I always enjoy the St-Aubin La Pucelle, the 85 was floral and fresh, with good almondy aromas, just hinting at the vanilla from the wood. The Premier Cru La Chatenière is from a steep slope which is a continuation of Le Montrachet vineyard, facing south-east. Of the top wines in the range, the best is the domaine Chassagne-Montrachet, the 86 honeyed and delicately toasty, with hints of apricots, never overtly woody.

DOMAINE ÉTIENNE SAUZET → ****
Puligny-Montrachet, 21190 Meursault

Total v'yds owned: 12.4ha (31 acres)
Chardonnay owned: 12.4ha (31 acres)
Chardonnays produced: Bâtard-Montrachet; Bienvenues Bâtard-Montrachet; Chassagne-Montrachet; Puligny-Montrachet. 1ers Crus: Les Combettes, Champ-Canet, Les Perrières, Les Referts; La Truffière.

One of the handful of Burgundy estates which make consistently excellent white wines. Great care is taken to allow the vineyards to express themselves, and it is possible to appreciate the differences between the light, soft, buttery Champ-Canet, the nutty, concentrated Les Perrières, the ripeness of La Truffière, or the elegance of Les Combettes. Wines are matured in 25 to 30 percent new Allier wood, and kept on their lees in wood for ten months before bottling. Their village Puligny is one of the most enjoyable around, the 85 soft, balanced, hinting discreetly at new wood.

JEAN SIGNORET **
Chardonnays produced: Mâcon-Clessé.

In a 1990 tasting of Mâconnais wines, M. Signoret's 85 Mâcon-Clessé stood out as a star: ripe, creamy, concentrated, deliciously fruity, just what the reputation of Mâcon was founded on and which it is in danger of losing. His 82, too, was an excellent wine, full of flavour and ripeness.

JEAN THEVENET ** → ***
Quintaine-Clessé

Total v'yds owned: 7ha (17 acres)
Chardonnay owned: 7ha (17 acres)
Chardonnay produced: Mâcon Clessé Quintaine.

M. Thevenet makes one of the top Mâconnais wines, full of fresh, fruity flavours. Low yields (half the permitted amount in the Mâconnais), no chemical weedkillers in the vineyard, stainless steel fermentation, all contribute to this. His 88, tasted from cask, showed excellent ripeness and concentration, with just a hint of wood. In 1983, because of weather conditions in the vineyards, he was able to make a curiosity: a botrytized wine Domaine de la Bon Gran, which although dry had definite hints of honeyed noble rot. However, the wines are designed for relatively rapid drinking: a 79 (tasted in 1989) was a disaster, vegetal, dried out and definitely too old.

DOMAINE MARCEL VINCENT   ***→
Ch Fuissé, Fuissé, 71690 Pierreclos

Chardonnays produced: Pouilly-Fuissé, Pouilly-Fuissé Vieilles Vignes.

Without doubt, M. Vincent's Pouilly-Fuissé is something special, showing what all the fuss is about with this appellation. The concentration of fruit even on his village Pouilly, with its rich oak and tropical fruits flavours is much nearer to Meursault than to the Mâconnais. As for his Vieilles Vignes, the smoky, toasty smell, and the intense fruit taste, as in the 85, is great white burgundy by any standards.

CAVE DE VIRÉ
Vercheron, Viré, 71260 Lugny

V'yds owned by members: 279ha (690 acres)
Chardonnays produced: Mâcon-Viré; Mâcon-Viré Vieilles Vignes.

Another of the handful of coopératives in the Mâconnais that shows the quality that careful selection and handling can produce. The wines are generally deliciously clean and fresh, light, with few pretensions. The firm makes a number of different blends: a basic wine, which often appears under retailers' names; a Grande Réserve, the 85 of which was light, nutty and absolutely fresh; a Cuvée Spéciale, the 85 elegant, with good wood flavours; and a Vieilles Vignes, the 85 rounded, soft, nicely toasty, quite full in the mouth.

MICHEL VOARICK   →***
21420 Aloxe-Corton

Total v'yds owned: 9ha (22 acres)
Chardonnay owned: 1.2ha (3 acres)
Chardonnay produced: Corton-Charlemagne.

Corton-Charlemagne is the only white that is produced at this domaine, but it is very good. Fermentation is in large wood, with maturation in small oak. The 86 was still very tight when tasted in 1989, but it suggested great intensity of flavour, great power, and was obviously a wine that needed long maturing in bottle.

Chablis

To taste Chardonnay, pure, unadorned and simple, it is best to drink Chablis. This is where the clean, fresh, appley acid tastes that are so elusive in areas like the Mâconnais of Burgundy, can be brought out with consummate ease.

Chablis is also the one area where Chardonnay reigns supreme. No other grape variety is permitted for appellation wines in the region at all. To look up to the slopes of the Grand Cru Chablis vineyards from the centre of the small town of Chablis, is to see Chardonnay.

Chablis is one of the most famous names in the wine world. Everyone has heard of it: it is synonymous with soft, smooth easy-to-drink white wine. But outside Europe only a minority of people who drink a wine called Chablis are actually consuming something that had its origins in France. The name "Chablis" has been stuck onto bottles of white wine made from the most curious collection of grapes in California and in Australias often slightly sweet, commercial wines, whose connection with the real thing is as remote as possible. Chablis: the name is easy to pronounce, easy to remember, and sells inexpensive white wine.

Production of true Chablis, while it has increased vastly since the early 1970s, is still comparatively small. In 1985, for example, some 11 million bottles of Chablis were produced, a below-average year. In 1981, a mere 6 million bottles were produced. Neither figure is impressive when put beside the production of a giant winery in California or a coopérative in the south of France. But, to put it further into perspective, the production of Chablis is equivalent to a quarter of the production of white wine in Burgundy and the Mâconnais.

Legally speaking Chablis is regarded as part of Burgundy. The wines are lumped together for statistical purposes. And there are definitely connections: many of the Burgundy négociants also produce a Chablis which they buy from growers or from the dominant coopérative La Chablisienne. Some négociants from Beaune own vineyards in Chablis. And, of course, the grape, the Chardonnay, is the same as white burgundy. But beyond that, the differences are equally strong. For a start, Chablis is halfway between Paris and Dijon: on a level with the southern vineyards of Champagne and north of the Loire. This is marginal wine country. Every year there is the risk of frost until May is almost over. Elaborate sprinkler systems have been devised to spray the vines with water at the first sign of frost – an immense investment, but one which has almost done away with the regular and total disasters which were a common occurence in the 1950s and 1960s. But even now, spring frost can wreak enormous havoc – the vintages of 1981 and 1985 were both affected.

The climate also influences the amount of wine produced. One year an enormous crop will be taken off the vines – probably with yields that are *too* high – the next almost nothing.

This seesawing effect upsets the Chablis producers every time the production drops, and they go about wringing their hands and doubling the price of their wine. With the next bumper year, prices remain high, demand falls and prices come down with a crash. A graph of the price of Chablis can look like a series of Alpine peaks and valleys.

And of course the climate influences the wine. The true taste of Chablis is steely green, minerally, crisp, appley fresh, almost - but never actually – tart. It should never be as rich as white burgundy, never as soft as Mâconnais wines, always have some raciness, some backbone and bite. This taste is harder and harder to find. Chablis producers often seem to want to emulate their confrères in Burgundy, making rich wines, creamy and soft, losing out on the acidity that should be the hallmark of this northern, cool-climate wine.

CHARDONNAY VINEYARDS

As in Burgundy, there is a series of categories into which Chablis falls, depending on where the vineyard is. From the lowest to the highest category, they are: Petit Chablis, Chablis, Chablis Premier Cru, and Chablis Grand Cru.

PETIT CHABLIS

Basic Chablis produced in the outlaying small vineyard areas. Much has been reclassified as Chablis (see below).

CHABLIS

By far the largest production area. It comes from the outer circle of vineyards surrounding the Premier and Grand Cru vineyards.

PREMIER CRU

Premier Cru vineyards are scattered about Chablis, with the site and aspect to the sun, so vital in this northern region, being as important as the soil. There is a happy wealth of confusion about the naming of Premier Cru wines, with a whole series of names being bandied about. But as it now stands, the Premier Cru vineyards are divided into 12 groups. Each group includes a number of vineyards which traditionally were separate Premiers Crus, and whose name may or may not appear on the label (here put in brackets after the principal name): Beauroy (Beauroy, Troesmes); Côte de Léchet; Fourchaume (Fourchaume, Vaupulent, Côte de Fontenay, Vaulorent, L'Homme Mort); Les Fourneaux (Les Fourneaux, Morein, Côte des Près-Girots); Mélinots (Mélinots, Roncières, Les Epinottes); Mont de Milieu; Montée de Tonnerre (Montée de Tonnerre, Chapelot, Pied d'Aloup); Montmains (Montmains, Forêts, Butteaux); Vaillons (Vaillons, Châtains, Séchet, Beugnon, Les Lys); Vaucoupin; Vaudevey; Vosgros (Vosgros, Vaugiraut).

GRAND CRU

Grand Cru vineyards run along the steep south-west facing slope on the bank of the Serein opposite to Chablis town. There are seven in all: Blanchot; Bougros; Les Clos; Grenouilles; Preuses; Valmur; Vaudésir.

The Chablis vineyards lie on both sides of the shallow valley of the Serein as it flows through the town of Chablis. The region was devastated during the phylloxera epidemic at the turn of the century, and many of the outlying areas were abandoned permanently; but the area under vine has grown enormously since the 1970s, fuelled by increased world demand. In the 1950s, there were a mere 500ha (1,230 acres) of vines producing Chablis, mainly the Grand Cru and some Premier Cru vineyards. Today, there are over 2,000ha (5,000 acres), and the total is growing. The latest move is to get rid of the appellation altogether and term all Petit Chablis vineyards Chablis.

So where is all the extra land, and should it be making Chablis? That is one of the two big controversies in Chablis at the moment (the other, the use of oak, I discuss in due course). The big question is whether the vines that grow on Portlandian clay can produce wines of a similar quality to those that grow on the traditional soil of Chablis Kimmeridgian clay. The expansionists say yes; their opponents say no. The expansionists have so far had their way, which is how the extra planting has come about.

The planting has chiefly affected the vineyards that produce straight Chablis. But some Premier Cru vineyards are also planted on the Portlandian soil, and for some it does raise question marks over the quality of Premier Cru wines. Straight Chablis vineyards have also been increased by the clever sleight of hand of changing Petit Chablis into Chablis. Producers of Petit Chablis felt that the word Petit meant their wine was inferior – which it was – so the word was dropped in the better Petit Chablis vineyards, leaving only derisory amounts of Petit Chablis production.

MAKING CHABLIS

Whether the expansion of the vineyards has affected the move towards a softer tasting Chablis is a moot point, promising infinite happy (and less happy) hours of discussion ahead. That discussion would also include the question of yields – ridiculously high in some years, even for the Premiers and Grands Crus. It would include the regular use of chaptalization of low alcohol, high acid musts (increasing the alcohol level by as much as 20 percent). And in the vineyard the discussion would include whether the clones of Chardonnay in use in Chablis are the right ones for quality, or are just rather good at producing high quantity yields and relatively low acids.

All this has certainly influenced the changing taste of Chablis. But I am inclined to think that what has happened in the cellars of the Chablis producers is of equal, if not greater, importance. New technology has arrived in the form of stainless steel tanks. Traditional Chablis production was to ferment in vats, and then to put the wine in small, old, 132 L barrels, called *feuillettes*, ready for bottling in the early summer after harvest. Now there is a split amongst the ranks of Chablis producers. There are those who wish to dispense with wood altogether and to make wines in stainless steel, aiming to emphasize fruit and freshness. Some of the best producers have adopted this approach.

Others, including to my mind the two best producers, have stayed with wood. But wood with a difference. Rather than old wood, they have started to use new wood, to get oaky, toasty tastes into their wines, greater richness.

But both sets of producers have adopted another practice which has probably had the greatest influence on the general trend of Chablis towards softness – whether the clean softness of stainless steel or the toasty softness of wood. And that change is the almost universal use of the malolactic fermentation to reduce the acidity. Until well into the 1950s, if not later, producers did not understand the function of the malolactic, and certainly could not control it. Now they can, and its effect of cutting acid levels is the one single act which, I believe, has changed the taste of Chablis.

PRODUCERS

JEAN-MARC BROCARD   →***
Préhy, 89800 Chablis

Total v'yds owned: 28ha (70 acres)
Chardonnays produced: Chablis, Chablis Domaine des Manants, Chablis Domaine Ste-Claire.

A grower in the southern part of Chablis, who also makes a Sauvignon de St-Bris. His wines often have a richness and opulence that suggests a more Burgundian than Chablisian taste. His Domaine Ste-Claire is particularly good – the 85 weighty, oaky, almost green/gold in colour, a beautiful, if big, wine. But Domaine des Manants 85 was also excellently nutty and rich. But is this Chablis or white burgundy?

LA CHABLISIENNE   *→***
8 Bd Pasteur, 89800 Chablis

Total v'yds controlled by members: 494ha (1,200 acres)
Chardonnays produced: Petit Chablis, Chablis, Chablis 1er Cru, Chablis Grand Cru. Wines under growers' names: Suzanne Tremblay, Domaine Jean Bourcey, Remy Lefort, Fèvre Frères, Alain Couperot, Jean-Claude Dauvissat, Michaut Frères and others.

Controlling about a third of the total production of Chablis, La Chablisienne is a vital part of the scene. It makes everything - from the simplest Petit Chablis through to Grand Cru. Much is pleasing enough – nutty, fresh – if somewhat neutral, and tending to appear under a number of guises, sometimes with retailers' own names on the label. But the coopérative also makes some grander wines: a 1er Cru Côte de Léchet 88, although without any wood tastes, was rich and creamy, perhaps lacking acidity. Their 1er Cru blend, Grande Cuvée, does have some wood maturation which gives a rich, soft, toasty taste. The Premier Fourchaume 86 was big and fat, again with some wood. The coopérative has adopted what could be seen as the questionable practice of putting the names of some of their better growers to individual *cuvées* of wine – without, it appears, any guarantee that the wine doesn't actually come from a common vat. But some of the wines produced like this are certainly good Chablis – Suzanne Tremblay and Fèvre Frères (not to be confused with William Fèvre) are names worth looking out for.

JEAN DAUVISSAT ***
3 Rue de Chichée, 89800 Chablis

Chardonnays produced: Grand Cru Les Preuses; 1er Cru Les Vaillons; 1er Cru Montmains La Forest.

Dauvissats abound in Chablis, and make life very confusing for us poor consumers. Mostly, they all make good wines, such as Jean Dauvissat's properly steely Premier Cru Chablis, such as Les Vaillons, the oaky, toasty Premier Cru La Forest; or the richer Grand Cru Les Preuses.

RENÉ & VINCENT DAUVISSAT ***→****
8 Rue Emile Zola, 89800 Chablis

Total v'yds owned: 9ha (22 acres)
Chardonnays produced: Grand Cru Les Clos; Grand Cru Les Preuses; 1er Cru La Forest; 1er Cru Vaillons; 1er Cru Séchet.

A small estate, run by more Dauvissats, with some prestigious holdings in Grand Cru and Premier Cru vineyards. Fermentation takes place partly in new wood, and maturation in used wood for eight to ten months. They are considerable wines, built to last: the balance between wood and fruit is always carefully considered. An 86 Les Preuses was particularly fine, not too heavy, with a crisp, tart, proper Chablis edge to it; the 86 Séchet (tasted in 1989) was lighter, more obviously spicy/oaky, needing time to settle down.

JOSEPH DROUHIN →***
7 Rue D'Enfer, 21201 Beaune

Total v'yds owned (in Chablis): 35.3ha (87 acres)
Chardonnays produced: Chablis; Grand Cru Les Clos; Grand Cru Les Preuses; Grand Cru Vaudésir; 1er Cru Vaillons; 1er Cru Côte de Léchet; 1er Cru Mont de Milieu.

The only Burgundy négociant to take Chablis sufficiently seriously to have extensive vineyards in the area. It makes fat, concentrated wines, generally with big wood tastes, that are, frankly, more Burgundy than Chablis, although certainly enjoyable. Even the basic Chablis 86 was rich and concentrated. This style, of course, means the wines age well, and Grand Cru Chablis of ten years is still improving in bottle.

JEAN DURUP ***
4 Grande Rue, Maligny, 89800 Chablis

Total v'yds owned: 150ha (370 acres)
Chardonnays produced: Petit Chablis; Chablis; 1er Cru Fourchaume; 1er Cru Vaudevey; 1er Cru Montée de Tonnerre; 1er Cru Montmains.

In the great controversy between those who advocate maturing Chablis in wood and those who prefer stainless steel, Jean Durup is definitely on the side of steel. He is also on the side of expanding the Chablis vineyards – and has made no mean contribution to this himself. His family has been making wine in the area since the 15th century. What he makes today is very direct, uncomplicated, tasting exactly how Chardonnay should. He uses estate names for even the basic Chablis: so, for instance, his Domaine de Valéry 85, a full wine, with yeasty characters, was very generous, perhaps lacking a little acidity. Ch de Maligny 86, Vigne de la Reine was light and fragrant, very fresh and creamy, slightly nutty. Fourchaume Premier Cru Domaine de l'Eglantière 85 was deliciously fresh and floral, even if it lacked the ultimate excitement a wine with its price tag should deliver.

WILLIAM FÈVRE   ****
Domaine de la Maladière, 14 Rue Jules Rathiés, 89800 Chablis

Total v'yds owned: 40ha (99 acres)
Chardonnays produced: Chablis; 1er Cru Fourchaume; 1er Cru Montmains; Grand Cru Les Clos; Grand Cru Bougros; Grand Cru Les Preuses; Grand Cru Valmur; Grand Cru Vaudésir; Grand Cru Grenouilles.

The great proponent of wood maturing in Chablis, William Fèvre, also happens to own more Grand Cru vineyards – 16ha – than any other grower. His techniques are firmly based on fermentation and maturing in wood: 100 percent for Grand Cru, 50 percent for Premier Cru and Chablis. He has also developed a new line of wines, called simply Chardonnay William Fèvre, using grapes from outside the Chablis appellations, which are also matured 50 percent in wood. Such is the expansionist policy here, that there is even a new vineyard in South America. The wines themselves are for me some of the best in Chablis: the use of wood gives them an edge of class and depth of flavour which is often lacking in wines without the benefit of wood. The 85 Premier Cru Vaulorent (Fourchaume) Domaine de la Maladière (tasted in 1987) certainly had plenty of wood, and it was apparent that it was set for a long life. The 86 of the same wine (tasted in 1988) was nutty, buttery, powerful and firmer than the 85. The 86 Vaudésir (tasted in 1988) was rich and oaky, but had excellent peachy fruit. Whether such wines are too powerful for their own good is the only question mark over a remarkable range.

DOMAINE ALAIN GEOFFROY   →***
4 Rue de l'Equerre, Beines, 89800 Chablis

Total v'yds owned: 25ha (62 acres)
Chardonnays produced: Chablis, 1er Cru Beauroy.

Unoaked but attractively elegant wines in the modern style, yet maintaining sufficient character. An 85 Beauroy Premier Cru had a good flinty bouquet – the smell that Chablis ought to have – and was cleanly balanced.

DOMAINE LAROCHE   ** → ***
L'Obédiencerie, 22 Rue Louis Bro, 89800 Chablis

Total v'yds owned: 76.33ha (189 acres)
Chardonnays produced: Petit Chablis; Chablis; 1er Cru Fourchaume; 1er Cru Les Vaillons; 1er Cru Vaudevey; 1er Cru Montmains; 1er Cru Beauroy; 1er Cru Côte de Léchet; Grand Cru Les Clos; Grand Cru Blanchot; Grand Cru Bougros.

An impressive estate, which also owns the négociant firm of Bacheroy-Josselin in Burgundy. A *sous marque* is Domaine La Jouchère. Fermentation of the Grands Crus is in wood, 40 percent new, while for the Premier Cru wines, there is 50 percent wood fermentation (20 percent of that new wood). For the Chablis and Petit Chablis, tank-fermentation is the order of the day. I find the basic wines rather lacking in character, but some of the Grands Crus – especially an excellent 86 Fourchaume (tasted in 1989) – show rich, toasty character, perhaps a shade too soft for its own good. There are separate bottlings of Vieilles Vignes wines, which can be outstanding.

LOUIS MICHEL
DOMAINE DE LA TOUR VAUBOURG   *** →
11 Boulevard de Ferrières, 89800 Chablis

Total v'yds owned: 20ha (49 acres)
Chardonnays produced: Chablis; 1er Cru Montmains; 1er Cru Vaillons; 1er Cru Fourchaume; 1er Cru Montée de Tonnerre; Grand Cru Vaudésir; Grand Cru Les Clos; Grand Cru Grenouilles.

Louis Michel is of the stainless steel school, which means his wines exhibit great fruit character without great complexity. In a way, this makes his straight Chablis one of his best wines: an 85 (tasted in 1987) beautifully balanced and with deep fruit flavours and good acidity, highly enjoyable. At a more serious level, Vaudésir is absolutely true to character – an 86 (tasted in 1988) is crisp and flinty, almost green to taste: perfect Chablis. I find his Montmains too soft, but Montée de Tonnerre is back to the real green Chablis character. Michel also makes wines under the Domaine de la Tour Vaubourg label.

J MOREAU & FILS   * → **
Route d'Auxerre, 89800 Chablis

Total v'yds owned: 59ha (146 acres)
Chardonnays produced: Chablis; 1er Cru Vaillons; Grand Cru.

The largest producer of Chablis, the firm of Moreau also has family holdings in Premier Cru and Grand Cru vineyards. The straight Chablis is dull, certainly clean and correct, but much too soft, rather like Mâconnais wines. More interesting things happen with the Premier Cru and Grand Cru wines, which, although showing no sign of wood, do have good depth of flavour and some crisply ripe acidity.

DOMAINE RAVENEAU   *** →
Rue de Chichée, 89800 Chablis

Total v'yds owned: 7.7ha (19 acres)
Chardonnays produced: 1er Cru Montmains; 1er Cru Montée de Tonnerre; Grand Cru Valmur; Grand Cru Les Clos; Grand Cru Blanchot.

A traditional estate, whose wines have appeared under the names of François Raveneau and Jean-Marie Raveneau. They are aged in wood for eight months and bottled without filtration. A Premier Cru Chapelot (Montée de Tonnerre) 87 (tasted in 1989) was full of ripe, serious fruit, almost Burgundy in style. Grand Cru Valmur 87 (tasted in 1989) was very closed, needing a long time to develop, while the 86 of this wine was richer and bigger but still needed time in bottle to open out, the same being true of 86 Chapelot (Montée de Tonnerre). Premier Cru Les Butteaux (Montmains) 86 (tasted in 1988) showed good spicy wood flavours on open, quite soft fruit.

A REGNARD & FILS   **
28 Boulevard du Dr Tacussel, 89800 Chablis

Total v'yds owned: 10ha (25 acres)
Chardonnays produced: Chablis, 1er Cru; Grand Cru

Mainly a négociant house, owned by the de Ladoucette family of Pouilly Fumé fame, making a full range of wines, from basic Chablis upwards, and including all the Grands Crus. A Chablis 85 (tasted in 1988) was a delicious, open, cleanly grassy wine that exhibited just what simple Chablis should be about. And that typicity is maintained right through the range. With this simplicity, the wines are not designed for ageing, and certainly the Premier Cru should be treated as if basic Chablis.

DOMAINE PHILIPPE TESTUT   →***

Chardonnays produced: Chablis; 1er Cru; Grand Cru Grenouilles.

This is the reincarnation of an old family domaine which was sold about the ears of Philippe Testut in one of those complicated family rows that are the bane of French viticulture. What was left was a small portion of Grand Cru Grenouilles, Premier Cru and straight Chablis vineyards, and here M. Testut makes absolutely sound, straight wines, some with barrel ageing, that always give pleasure.

DOMAINE ROBERT VOCORET   →***
Rue d'Avallon, 89800 Chablis

Total v'yds owned: 31ha (77 acres)
Chardonnays produced: Chablis; 1er Cru Montée de Tonnerre; 1er Cru Vaillons; 1er Cru Montmains; Grand Cru Les Clos; Grand Cru Valmur; Grand Cru Blanchot.

A serious old family estate, founded in the last century. Unusually, the wines are fermented in wood, and aged partly in wood, partly in tanks. The Grand Cru wines are, as a result of this treatment, floral and often quite broad. The 86 Blanchot was attractively flowery, although possibly too perfumed. On the whole, though, these are wines that can keep well.

Champagne

The Chardonnay forms one of the three pillars on which champagne is based. The other two are Pinot Noir and Pinot Meunier. Until the 1970s Chardonnay was very much the junior partner, with the two Pinots occupying much more than two thirds of the Champagne vineyard area. Even today, it only occupies 26 percent of the vineyards. That represents a fall from 28 percent in 1980, because new plantings since then have been of the two Pinots. But when we look at the Grand Cru and Premier Cru vineyards of Champagne – those from which the finest grapes come – Chardonnay takes a much more promi-nent place, occupying 45 percent of all the top vineyards of the region, with 36 percent and 19 percent planted to Pinot Noir and Pinot Meunier respectively. So it seems that Chardonnay occupies a privileged place in the best vineyards of Champagne.

Champagne is, of course, normally a blended wine, with varying proportions of the three grape varieties according to the contents of a grower's vineyard or to the recipe of a champagne house. The position of Chardonnay is to provide the lightness, freshness and bouquet of a champagne, while the Pinot Noir provides the weight, flesh and fruit and the Pinot Meunier is there for sweetness and ripeness.

The increase in the amount of Chardonnay planted in the Champagne region is a reflection of the changing taste in champagne. The preference for heavy, rich, weighty wines that would go well with food has been replaced by a desire for light, ethereal drinks that are better as aperitifs. Chardonnay has stepped forward to provide the poise and elegance that are what is now wanted.

While Chardonnay has gradually assumed a more important role in the blends of champagne, it has also been used to develop a style of wine that was once exceedingly rare: *blanc de blancs* champagne. Although, as Tom Stevenson records in his book *Champagne* (London 1986), all-white wines have been recorded in the region since the 13th century "when Aÿ achieved its earliest reputation", it was not until the 1920s that the term *blanc de blancs* was first used, by Eugène-Aimé Salon for his superb Salon-Le Mesnil champagne, and it is not until the 1960s that the demand for the style and character of *blanc de blancs* champagnes led producers to do more than make such a wine – generally a vintage wine – in years when the Chardonnay crop was particularly good.

At the time the producers didn't think much of such wines. According to Nicholas Faith (*The Story of Champagne*, London 1988), Maurice Pol Roger, of the house of Pol Roger once described *blanc de blancs* as being "de la flotte", that is just like water "implying that it has the same relationship to real Champagne as keg bitter does to real ale". Today, Pol Roger, under Christian de Billy, makes one of the lightest, freshest *blanc de blancs*. Fashions change, and so do the views of champagne houses.

Although certainly lighter in style, perhaps more acid, than the usual blended champagnes, a *blanc de blancs* also matures well. In fact, in its early years, a vintage *blanc de blancs* is a decidedly tart, green animal. Often such vintage wines will be released later than the equivalent blended vintage champagnes. With non-vintage *blanc de blancs*, of course, the better producers will be able to use a proportion of older wines to soften the slightly harsh character so that it is readily drinkable.

CHARDONNAY VINEYARDS

There are three categories of champagne vineyard, which are arranged within a sliding percentage scale. The lowest quality vineyards are rated at 80 percent, while the best are described as 100 percent – and vineyards fit anywhere in between according to where they are, the quality of what they regularly produce, and the grape varieties planted. Vineyards rated 100 percent are called Grand Cru, those between 90 percent and 99 percent inclusive are Premier Cru. Until 1990, this system was meant to indicate the payment a grower could expect for his grapes. Top prices were paid for 100 percent vineyards, and the right percentage was paid for vineyards down the scale (so that an 80 percent vineyard received 80 percent of the price obtainable from a 100 percent vineyard). All very logical, and it worked. Now, a new, more open system based upon a minimum price, above which a free market can operate, means that prices will vary more widely – and probably force up the price of champagne.

However, the scale of vineyard quality remains. Chardonnay occupies 52 percent of the Grand Cru (that is 100 percent vineyards). These can come from 17 villages in the Champagne region. The most important of these from the point of view of Chardonnay are in the Côte des Blancs, a strip of hills, facing north-east, running south from Epernay. However, Chardonnay is also grown to a smaller extent in the mainly Pinot Noir villages of the other top vineyard area, the Montagne de Reims, as well as in the Marne Valley to the west of the region and in the separate vineyard area of the Aube, to the south.

The Grand Cru villages in which Chardonnay predominates (percentage of the grape appear in brackets) are: Avize (100 percent); Chouilly (97.99 percent); Cramant (100 percent); Le Mesnil-sur-Oger (100 percent); and Oiry (98.8 percent).

Premier Cru villages in which Chardonnay predominates (again the percentages in brackets) are: Bergères-les-Vertus (93.17 percent); Billy-le-Grand (66.1 percent); Bisseuil (55 percent); Coligny (90 percent); Cuis (88.05 percent); Etréchy (95 percent); Grauves (77.72 percent); Trépail (87.19 percent); Vaudemanges (73.53 percent); Vertus (81.93 percent); Villeneuve-Renneville (98.95 percent); Villers-Marmery (95.18 percent); Voipreux (91 percent).

MAKING CHAMPAGNE

The champagne process of a second fermentation in the bottle rather than in large tanks which gives the characteristic bubbles has been widely described elsewhere. It is worth noting one characteristic that sets champagne producers of Chardonnay wines apart from most still wine Chardonnay producers: the very last thing a champagne producer wants is the taste of oak on his wines. So that even if, as is the case with some of the smaller champagne growers and a few of the top houses like Krug, Alfred Gratien and Bollinger, wooden barrels are used for fermentation, they are old barrels giving no wood taste and are only there to give a slight hint of gentle oxidation to the wine. Other producers use stainless steel or glass-lined tanks for fermentation.

The blending of still wines before they go into bottle for the second fermentation is another familiar subject of many books and articles. But again one point with respect to Chardonnay is worth making. Blending with three grape varieties is infinitely more difficult than blending with just the one – Chardonnay. And I have been told more than once by blenders in champagne houses, that putting together their *blanc de blancs* while, of course, a serious business (after all a lot of money rides on it) is child's play compared with the strain of making up the blend for the normal champagne.

In good Chardonnay years (which may not be the same as good "normal" champagne vintage years), a house may decide to make a vintage *blanc de blancs*, using grapes just from that year. This style of wine will need even longer ageing in the bottle than the more usual non-vintage *blanc de blancs*.

THE WINES

Many producers make *blanc de blancs* champagnes. The top champagne houses will use wines from all over the region to make up their blend. A grower will only have the use of grapes from his own vineyards: which means it is much less likely that a grower in the predominantly Pinot Noir Montagne de Reims will make a *blanc de blancs*, while a grower in the Côte des Blancs who bottles and sells his own wine is almost obliged to make a *blanc de blancs*.

(Note: a *crémant* is a wine which is bottled at slightly lower pressure than an ordinary champagne, and is particularly successful with Chardonnay.)

THE STILL WINE OF CHAMPAGNE

While most Chardonnay goes into making champagne, either as a blend or as a *blanc de blancs*, there is still some production of a still white wine in the Champagne region, called Coteaux Champenois. On the odd occasions when I have tasted this wine, I have found it to be rather thin, and it is easy to see why the wine of this region is better sparkling than still. The wines come from the Côte des Blancs.

CHAMPAGNE HOUSES WHICH PRODUCE A BLANC DE BLANCS ARE:

Ayala ** (Vintage Blanc de Blancs Brut, made up of blends from the growths of Cramant, Le Mesnil-sur-Oger and Vertus, a light, frothy, creamy wine)

Billecart-Salmon *** (Vintage Blanc de Blancs Brut, excellent acidity and medium weight)

G. Billiard (non-vintage Blanc de Blancs, but in fact normally the product of one year)

F. Bonnet & Fils *** (Vintage Blanc de Blancs, typical of the house style which is dominated by Chardonnay, from vineyards in the Côte des Blancs)

Bricout & Koch (non-vintage Blanc de Blancs Brut)

Albert le Brun (non-vintage Blanc de Blancs Brut)

Canard-Duchêne **→ (Vintage Blanc de Blancs Brut, lively, light, fresh wines)

De Castellane ** (non-vintage Blanc de Blancs Brut, ripe, somewhat sweeter in taste than the normal *blanc de blancs*)

De Cazanove (Cuvée Spéciale)

A. Charbaut →*** (non-vintage Blanc de Blancs Brut and very lively, refreshing Vintage Certificate, Cuvée de Réserve)

A. Chauvet ** (Cachet Vert, a very fruity wine, quite full)

Delamotte Père & Fils (non-vintage Blanc de Blancs)

Deutz **→*** (Vintage Blanc de Blancs Brut, a lemony-crisp wine when young, warm and biscuity when mature, sold in a clear glass bottle)

Duval-Leroy ** (non-vintage Crémant Blanc de Blancs Brut, well balanced, soft, creamy mousse)

H. Germain (non-vintage Grande Cuvée Vénus and vintage Blanc de Blancs Brut)

Georges Goulet ** (non-vintage Goulet "G" Blanc de Blancs Brut, vigorous, slightly too heavy wine, but full of fruit)

Charles Heidsieck ***→ (Vintage Blanc de Blancs Brut, non-vintage Blanc de Blancs Brut, quite full in style in past years, now lighter and fresher)

Henriot **→ (Crémant vintage, non-vintage, both very light and fresh in style when young, the vintage maturing well over ten years)

Jacquesson →*** (Brut Zéro vintage and non vintage, the Brut Zéro a wine without dosage, and needing many years in bottle)

Krug **** (Clos du Mesnil, the ultimate in Blanc de Blancs, surprisingly weighty, but also ethereal in its bouquet and flavour)

Larmandier *→** (non-vintage Cramant Blanc de Blancs Brut, which is sold after three years' bottle age, and non-vintage Brut Perlé)

R. & L. Legras (Grand Vintage, Vintage Présidence, Vintage Cuvée St Vincent, Coteaux Champenois Blanc)

Abel Lepitre **→ (Vintage Réserve Blanc de Blancs and non-vintage Cuvée No. 134, the vintage a delicious flowery wine whose bouquet leaps from the glass)

Marie Stuart *→** (non-vintage Blanc de Blancs Brut, very light style)

Montaudon (Blanc de Blancs Brut)

Mumm ** (non-vintage Crémant de Cramant Blanc de Blancs Brut, a dry style for a Mumm champagne, very tight mousse, and good acidity)

Oudinot →** (non-vintage Blanc de Blancs, very fruity wine, perhaps too much so)

Bruno Paillard *** (non-vintage Crémant Blanc de Blancs, soft mousse, with fragrant, mouthwatering fruit, impeccable)

Joseph Perrier **→ (non-vintage Cuvée Royale Blanc de Blancs Brut, smooth, light, fragrant, heady bouquet)

Philipponnat ** (Vintage Cuvée Première Blanc de Blancs, a wine that normally needs time in bottle)

Pol Roger →**** (Vintage Cuvée de Blancs de Chardonnay, honey and summer flavours, a classic Blanc de Blancs)

Rapeneau (non-vintage Blanc de Blancs)

Louis Roederer ***→ (Vintage Blanc de Blancs Brut, a fresh, creamy, very dry wine, top quality)

Ruinart **** (Vintage Dom Ruinart Blanc de Blancs, intense, elegant, stylish, lemony and racy)

Sacotte (Vintage Blanc de Blancs)

Salon **** (Vintage Cuvée "S", the firm's only wine, a vintage which is made only in exceptional years, of which there have been just 23 since the house was founded in 1914. Well worth seeking out a bottle of this superlative wine)

A. Secondé Prevoteau (non-vintage Princesses de France Blanc de Blancs Brut, from a single vineyard at Aguzon)

Taittinger **→*** (Vintage Comtes de Champagne, green, dry, quite weighty in style)

J de Telmont **→ (non-vintage Crémant Blanc de Blancs, a wine which matures well)

De Venoge *** (non-vintage Crémant Blanc de Blancs Brut, perfumed, honey flavours, deliciously soft)

Vollereaux (non-vintage Blanc de Blancs Brut)

CHAMPAGNE GROWERS

Major growers in predominantly Chardonnay Grand Cru villages who bottle a *blanc de blancs* include (non-vintage unless otherwise indicated, but often the wines from one year):

In Avize: Michel Gonet; Jacques Selosse (*** non-vintage Blanc de Blancs and Vintage Cuvée Special Club, both of top quality from a small traditional firm)

In Chouilly: Vazart-Cocquart (look for non-vintage Blanc de Blancs Brut Réserve); Lucien Vazart; Voirin.

In Cramant: Bonnaire-Boquemont (** good quality vintage Blanc de Blancs); Pierre Gimonnet & Fils (**→ light, fresh Vintage Spécial Club); Lilbert-Fils; Pertois-Lebrun; Sugot-Feneuil Fils.

In Le Mesnil-sur-Oger: Charlemagne-Peters; François Gonet; André Jacquart; Launois Père & Fils (*** excellent bottle-aged non-vintage Cuvée Réserve and top-quality Vintage Spécial Club); Pierre Peters.

Other French Chardonnays

From its home base in Burgundy and its traditional vineyard areas of Chablis and Champagne, the Chardonnay has begun to spread to other viticultural areas of France. It has been planted to produce quality white wines in a world market which is clamouring for these products but is not willing to pay the prices of white burgundy or Chablis. In other cases, the Chardonnay has infiltrated already established areas, either replacing local grapes or being grown alongside them. In yet others, it has long been a highly respected part of the local scene.

ALSACE

Chardonnay can only be grown in Alsace to make Crémant d'Alsace, the local sparkling bottle-fermented wine. It is used here in a blend with any of Pinot Blanc, Pinot Auxerrois, Pinot Noir, Pinot Gris and Riesling. Most Crémant d'Alsace is, in fact, made from Pinot Blanc and Pinot Auxerrois.

ARDÈCHE

A major Burgundy producer, Louis Latour, has moved out of his region to grow Chardonnay less expensively. He now produces 1 million bottles of Chardonnay de l'Ardèche (∗∗→) from vineyards in this region, lying in hills to the west of Valence.

CORSICA

Chardonnay is definitely an infiltrator among the traditional grape varieties and wines on France's Mediterranean island. Turning up among the local white varieties such as Vermentino and Pagadebit, it is rather like a city slicker gate-crashing a village fête. At the moment, any Chardonnay planted is on the eastern side of the island around Bastia. It cannot be an *appellation controlée* wine and is only allowed in the island's splendid *vin de pays*, the Vin de Pays de l'Ile de Beauté. In the Mediterranean climate of the island, Chardonnay can ripen as early as the end of August, which does not augur well for the development of the grapes. However, a local coopérative, the Union des Vignerons Associés du Levant makes straight 100 percent varietal Chardonnay which is stainless steel-fermented, treated in the most modern way and sold for rapid drinking. It is a pleasant enough wine, very clean and fruity, but not likely to set the world on fire.

HAUT-POITOU

The newly created (with the 1989 vintage) appellation area of Haut-Poitou lies south of the Loire and west of Poitiers and Châtellerault, centred on the small town of Neuville. Production is dominated by the local coopérative, which has set high standards and created an international market for the wines of this area which had sunk into insignificance since the heady days of the early Middle Ages when they were the most widely consumed wines in England.

Of the two major white grape varieties grown in this area Sauvignon Blanc is the best known, but Chardonnay comes second in importance, with 30 percent of the white wine vineyard. The wine is fermented in stainless steel, with temperature control and, once bottled (in the late winter following the harvest), is designed for early drinking. Chardonnay de Haut-Poitou (∗∗) is a fresh, soft wine, gently buttery, certainly tasting of the variety. There is also a sparkling wine, Diane de Poitiers, made from 100 percent Chardonnay.

JURA

The Jura is an unspoilt upland region lying east of Burgundy on the borders with Switzerland. Chardonnay arrived from Burgundy during the Middle Ages when the Jura was part of the great Duchy of Burgundy. Locally the grape became known as the Melon or the Gamay Blanc. Today it is grown along with the local white grape, Savagnin, in a number of the Jura appellations. In L'Etoile, it is the principal grape in the white wine of the area, occasionally, but not necessarily, blended with a little Savagnin. In Château-Chalon it is used on occasion in what must be its most unusual manifestation, as part of the blend for the sherry-like Vin Jaune. The white Vin d'Arbois is normally made from Chardonnay, with a little Savagnin, to produce a clean, pure wine, which is normally soft and rounded. In the regional, catch-all appellation of Côtes de Jura Chardonnay again forms an important element, either producing a 100 percent wine or, more usually, blended with Savagnin. Some Chardonnay sparkling wine is also made.

LOIRE

The most significant new plantings of Chardonnay outside its traditional areas are in the Loire Valley, specifically in Touraine. Here the general appellation of Touraine covers new plantings of Chardonnay which are sold as Chardonnay de Touraine, alongside the better known Sauvignon de Touraine. The smaller and very localized appellations of Cheverny and Valençay also have plantings of Chardonnay. Further west, in Anjou, some producers are now blending it with Chenin Blanc in their basic Anjou Blanc, presumably to cut down on the piercing acidity inherent in the Chenin, while right at the mouth of the river, the tiny Fiefs Vendéens VDQS area also permits production of a rather tart Chardonnay. The river-long sparkling appellation of Crémant de Loire also includes Chardonnay in the permitted blend.

PROVENCE

France is full of almost forgotten vineyards. One of the more unusual survivors is that of Bellet, in the suburbs of Nice in the hills behind the Côte d'Azur. Here about 50ha of vineyard produce what is, on the whole, a not particularly exciting white wine, made mainly from the traditional Rolle. Since 1955 Chardonnay has also been permitted for blending with this local grape to give it a lift and some freshness.

LANGUEDOC-ROUSSILLON

The Chardonnay is not allowed for any of the *appellation contrôlée* (AC) wines of the Midi. However, some producers are using it to produce Vin de Pays d'Oc, which is the huge region-wide, catch-all *vin de pays* for any wines produced in Languedoc and Roussillon. Of those I have tasted, one stood out to show the potential of Chardonnay even this far south in France – a wood-fermented and matured Chardonnay Vin de Pays d'Oc from Hugh Ryman, the Australian-trained son of the owner of Château la Jaubertie in Bergerac: the 89 of this was big, rich, creamy, full of tropical fruit, piles of luscious toasty tastes, not particularly French in style, but certainly a star (∗∗∗).

RHÔNE

One of the new VDQS appellations in the southern Rhône – Côtes du Lubéron – has plantings of Chardonnay, and the white from the model estate of Château Val-Joanis stands out in this region for its crisp, elegant, fruity flavours (∗∗→). Further north, almost in Burgundy, the white wines from the tiny area of the Côteaux du Lyonnais are made from Chardonnay. And away to the east, in the valleys of the Alps, the still wines of Die, called Châtillon-en-Diois, provide yet another out-of-the-way and rewarding oasis of Chardonnay.

SAINT-POURÇAIN

At Saint-Pourçain-sur-Sioule, near the source of the Loire and due west of the Mâconnais region of Burgundy, there is yet another long-established home for Chardonnay. However, only recently has it claimed a prominent place over the local white grape, the Sacy. Many producers (not that there are many here) make a top white wine which is either a blend of Chardonnay and Sauvignon Blanc or just 100 percent Chardonnay, while reserving the Tressalier for their less expensive white wines. Some producers also make a bottle-fermented sparkling wine, a blend of Sacy and Chardonnay.

SAVOIE

Two appellations in the Savoie are allowed to use Chardonnay in their white wines: Vin de Bugey and Vin de Savoie. The vineyards of Savoie itself are in the spectacular Alpine scenery of eastern France, around Chambéry, while Bugey's vineyards are further to the west, halfway towards Lyon.

Vin de Savoie is the area-wide appellation, with certain villages being permitted to add their names, as special *crus* (or growths) to the general AC. The *cru* where Chardonnay is to be found is Jongieux, to the west of the Lac du Bourget.

In the vineyards of Bugey, wines coming under the appellation of Roussette de Bugey are made with some Chardonnay in the blend, as are some of the whites from the *cru* villages of Vin de Bugey VDQS. Quantities in all cases are tiny.

California

If California is the most fashion-conscious wineproducing region in the world, then Chardonnay must be the trend-setter of wine; its style changing almost as often as a designer's collection. From lusciously ripe, over the top wines, through lean almost ascetic wines, to the current fad for "food wines" (what wine isn't?), the California producers have rung the changes in the style of Chardonnay they think the market will buy and enjoy. While fashions are famously unpredictable, the planting of Chardonnay has gone remorselessly on. Far exceeding Cabernet Sauvignon, with its relatively stable demand, and the vastly more ephemeral Sauvignon Blanc, Chardonnay is commanding the highest prices from grape-growers and wineproducers alike: it is currently the most sought-after grape and has become the ultimate pinnacle in white wine production throughout California.

Vineyards to suit Chardonnay have been the inspiration behind the development of the Carneros region of southern Napa and Sonoma. There, Chardonnay has paired up with Pinot Noir to create that elusive "holy grail" of winemakers, so difficult to make and so perfect when done well. While many producers in warmer regions rely on the pairing of Cabernet Sauvignon and Chardonnay as their premium varieties, in Carneros and similar cooler parts of the state, the Burgundy-style twinning of Chardonnay and Pinot Noir has become the new status symbol of an up-and-coming winery.

THE CHARDONNAY ARRIVES

Chardonnay is a relative newcomer on the California wine scene. Whether it was brought in with the original consignments of vines that were delivered to Count Agoston Haraszthy in the 1860s, the Hungarian who established the Buena Vista vineyards in Sonoma, is unknown but it is a reasonable assumption since the consignment also included Pinot Noir. But what became of that Chardonnay – if Chardonnay there was – is unrecorded.

That very little Chardonnay was produced is evident from the furore and acclaim that surrounded the sale in 1961 of a large consignment of Chardonnay in cask from the Hanzell winery in the Sonoma Valley. The owner, James Zellerbach, had spent over a decade quietly making wines in the Burgundy style he had learnt to appreciate while a diplomat in Europe: when he died his wife sold the wine remaining in the winery. The taste of these wines, when finally made public, showed that California could certainly hope to emulate the taste of great burgundy.

Role models are important in developing industries, none more so than winemaking. So it is hardly surprising that the wine-drinking Californian of the 1960s and 70s should have been brought up on a diet of "Burgundy" and "Chablis". What was never explained was that the one grape that was definitely not in those blends was Chardonnay, simply because it was still too rare and expensive. They used Chenin Blanc, French Colombard and anything that was cheap and cheerful. But white burgundy, with its soft, creamy tastes, was none the less the role model for these wines even if they were usually sweetened to satisfy the taste of people equally used to Coke. At the more serious end of the wine business, the combination of the inspiration of those wines from the Hanzell winery, and the new innovative use of French oak, which was pioneered by the likes of Joe Heitz and Robert Mondavi, paved the way for the great Chardonnay cult of the late 1970s and 1980s.

MAKING CHARDONNAY

The changes in the styles of Chardonnay – from enormously overblown and overoaked to too-lean to somewhere in the middle - have been echoed in the techniques used in the winery. Grapes are no longer picked superripe as they were in the 1970s but just before full ripeness to preserve natural acidity. The use of wood, too, has changed. Over toasty-wines, often matured in highly spicy American oak, have given way to more elegant examples, matured in French oak – from the all five of the French forests which supply the wine trade with casks – with medium to low toast being preferred to a very burnt smoky character, as the Robert Mondavi winery discovered in its famous toasting experiments.

Technology, apart from the use of wood, is high tech. Cool fermentation in stainless steel may be out of fashion with top Chardonnays, which are now fermented in wood, but the pressing of grapes is by way of the soft pneumatic presses, and yeasts are specifically developed for the fermentation process. "Cellars" are more usually air-conditioned rooms which are spotlessly hygienic. Bottling, too, will be carried out under the most sterile conditions. Seeing the contrast between all this high tech and the rows of oak barrels is something I always enjoy.

The use of techniques like lees contact for wine maturing in barrels is a relatively recently "rediscovered" phenomenon but one which has been enthusiastically taken up by winemakers for their top Reserve wines. Malolactic fermentation, to lessen the acids in a wine, is only practised in certain circumstances and rarely up to 100 percent, for most of California's vineyards are too hot for acidity to be a problem. But those winemakers who want to create the full luscious taste while still using slightly underripe fruit will make use of it: others will be found to be *adding* citric acid to give their potentially too soft wines a bite.

CHARDONNAY VINEYARDS

The most interesting development of the past decade has been the move in Chardonnay plantings away from the hotter vineyard areas, such as the northern Napa Valley, to cooler climate vineyards. California was the first wine region of the world to categorize its vineyard areas according to their sunshine hours. Back in the 1880s, an assistant professor at Berkeley University had divided California into the five viticultural areas by their climates – a categorization that still hold true today. But it is surprising that it took producers so long to realize that Chardonnay, eminently suited to cool-climate Burgundy, would naturally take to cooler zones in California. Perhaps it was a symptom of the general lack of interest in vineyard sites as opposed to winery technology that was a phenomenon of much New World wine production until the early 1980s.

Now, though, the move to cooler vineyards is firmly underway. There are plantings in Anderson Valley in Mendocino County, which are as far north and as near to the sea as any serious vineyard plantings can go. There are plantings in the Russian River Valley in Sonoma, only separated from the ocean by the coastal ranges which funnel wind and fog through valleys on to the vineyards in summer. Further south, Monterey, exposed to the ameliorating effects of the Pacific Ocean, has become a home for Chardonnay vineyards.

Most important of all, has been the development of the Carneros region in southern Napa and Sonoma. Recognized early in the 19th century by pioneers like General Vallejo (the last Spanish governor of California) and Agoston Haraszthy as a good source of grapes, it was virtually "rediscovered" in the 1980s and its rolling sloping hills are covered with the magical combination of Chardonnay and Pinot Noir to form a mini-Burgundy. It has few wineries itself with most grapes going to established wineries in Napa or Sonoma.

Given that vineyards closer to the fogs of San Francisco Bay are cooler, it follows that Chardonnay produced from southern Sonoma (such as Sonoma Valley) and the southern part of the Napa Valley, as far north as the Stag's Leap region, will be better balanced than that made further north. In the Napa Valley, for instance, the small hills that cut the valley at Yountville are seen as a convenient division between great Chardonnay territory and great Cabernet Sauvignon territory. The only exceptions are the increasing number of vineyards being planted on the hillsides themselves as opposed to on the valley floor.

PRODUCERS

ACACIA WINERY   ***
2750 Las Amigas Road, Napa

Total v'yds owned: 20.2ha (50 acres)
Chardonnay owned: 20.2ha (50 acres)
Chardonnays produced: Napa Valley Carneros; Napa Valley Carneros "Marina Vineyard".

One of the southernmost Napa vineyards, Acacia was started in 1979 to prove that Carneros was the right place for Chardonnay. It succeeded in that to a considerable degree, with its crisp, sometimes austere offerings that, for many, owed more to France than California. Now part of Chalone (qv), standards have been maintained, with such barrel-fermented, wood-aged offerings as the 88, restrained, crisp, leaning toward a future creaminess. There are two Chardonnays: the blended wine from a number of Carneros vineyards, and the single vineyard Marina Vineyard, generally somewhat richer both in toasty oak and fruit. Both repay time in bottle, especially Marina Vineyard.

ALDERBROOK VINEYARDS   **→

2306 *Magnolia Drive, Healdsburg, Sonoma*

Total v'yds owned: 22ha (54 acres)

From its first vintage in 1982, this small winery in northern Sonoma, which purchases grapes from Dry Creek Valley and Russian River Valley, has made a name for its Chardonnay. In a big, rich, tropical-fruit, oaky style they have even been known, as in the 85, to be slightly sweet, but normally remain just the very rich side of dry.

ALEXANDER VALLEY VINEYARD   *→**

8644 *Highway 128, Healdsburg, Sonoma*

Total v'yds owned: 101ha (250 acres)

Better known for its reds, this vineyard, which produced its first wines in 1975 has developed a definite style of Chardonnay, tending to leanness certainly until the mid-1980s, with more recent vintages, such as the 87, tasting richer, with an attractive if unusual rhubarb and cream taste, which turns it into a pleasant garden wine rather than one for too serious appreciation.

AU BON CLIMAT   ***

2800 *San Marcos, Box 113, Los Olivos*

Total vineyards owned: none
Chardonnay produced: Benedict Vineyard.

This Santa Barbara winery has concentrated on the great Burgundy varieties of Pinot Noir and Chardonnay, They produce wines in small quantities, using bought-in grapes from Santa Barbara. Their Chardonnay is toasty and oaky with additional flavours of tropical fruits – definitely in a ripe, relatively forward style, aged in quite strongly toasted wood. The wines mature within three years. Since the 87 vintages, there has also been a single vineyard Benedict Vineyard which stands in for the previous blended Reserve Chardonnay.

BERINGER   **→

2000 *Main Street, St Helena, Napa*

Total v'yds owned: 890ha (2,200 acres)
Chardonnay owned: 283ha (700 acres)
Chardonnays produced: Proprietor Grown; Private Reserve.

One of the historic St Helena wineries founded in 1881 by German brothers Jacob and Frederick, and still using the Germanic-style Rhine House in St Helena. Production, of course, is now in modern cellars. Vineyards have been developed in Napa Valley and there are impressive plantings in Knights Valley, just north of Calistoga in Sonoma County. There are two styles of Chardonnay: the heavily oaked Private Reserve which has varied in quality over recent years (86 very good, with rich, open fruit and spicy wood tastes, the 87 disappointing), and the less obvious (and less expensive) Proprietor Grown Chardonnay, which has good rich fruit flavours, and a better balance between wood and fruit.

BOUCHAINE →**
1075 Buchli Station Road, Napa

Total v'yds owned: 13ha (31 acres)
Chardonnay owned: 10ha (25 acres)
Chardonnays produced: Carneros; Carneros Estate Reserve.

Vineyards in the Napa Valley and Carneros supply the fruit for vintages of Chardonnay from 86 onward. Previously Napa fruit was used which led to a certain heaviness not apparent now. The first Chardonnay vintage was 1980. From 86 on, there is also a Chardonnay Reserve, using exclusively Carneros fruit. The wines are barrel-fermented, and this is generally obvious in the rich, toasty tastes and considerable intensity in good vintages like 85 and 86. Some critics believe this winery has still not realized its potential: perhaps with Carneros vineyards now mature, things will improve faster.

BUENA VISTA **→
18000 Old Winery Road, Sonoma

Total v'yds owned: 444ha (1,100 acres)
Chardonnays produced: Carneros; Private Reserve.

The first Sonoma winery, founded by the Hungarian Agoston Haraszthy in the 1870s. Currently owned by the German Racke company, production has been transferred from the historic cellars (now a museum and tasting room) to a modern winery. The fruit for Chardonnays comes from the firm's Carneros vineyards, and in recent years they seem to have improved immensely. Wood tastes are there but are secondary to good, ripe, tropical fruit, as in the soft, buttery 86 Carneros. Earlier vintages, such as the 84, showed good balance but lacked the current intensity of fruit. Private Reserve Chardonnay is more woody and creamy, and improves with bottle age.

CAKEBREAD CELLARS **→
8300 Highway 29, Rutherfords, Napa

Total vineyards owned: 30ha (75 acres)
Chardonnay owned: none
Chardonnays produced: Napa Chardonnay; Chardonnay Reserve.

Cakebread had a reputation for big, rich toasty Chardonnays. And, despite an obvious decrease in rich, buttery flavours and an increase in acidity in recent vintages, their wines remain on the weighty side. Most of their fruit is bought from land near Oak Knoll Avenue, north of Napa and the rest comes from the Yountville area. Of recent vintages, 85 was a better, riper-tasting wine than the rather lean 86, while 87 had great freshness and clean, citric flavours, which balanced well with a hint of wood.

CALERA WINE   ** → ***
11300 *Cienega Road, Hollister, San Benito*

Total vineyards owned: 10ha (25 acres)

Up in the cool climate of the hills way behind Monterey Bay, Josh Jensen has made quite a name for Calera with Pinot Noir. So it is quite logical that this winery, whose first vintage was in 1975, should have Chardonnay as its second string. The 86 Chardonnay, very toasty and dry, was followed by a single vineyard 87 from young vines in Mount Harlan Vineyard, very rich, almost crudely so, maturing quickly, but worth seeking out by those who don't want subtlety in their Chardonnays. The straight 87, on the other hand, took quick maturity to extremes, and, when tasted (in 1990), was hard and definitely too old.

CARNEROS CREEK   **
1285 *Dealy Lane, Carneros, Napa*

For a vineyard in the prime Chardonnay country of Carneros, Carneros Creek has had mixed reviews. It has done much better with its Pinot Noirs and its Merlot. Best of recent vintages was the 85 Chardonnay, while 87 Los Carneros was much less toasty than the wines have been in the past.

CHALONE VINEYARDS   ****
Stonewell Canyon Road, Highway 146, Soledad, Monterey

Total v'yds owned: 69ha (170 acres)

High up in a remote corner of the Gavilan Mountains, near the Pinnacles National Monument, east of Soledad, Chalone Vineyards produces what some regard as one of California's best Chardonnays. The climate, cool and dry, lends itself to the pairing of Chardonnay and Pinot Noir, which is exactly what Chalone has specialized in since the 1960s. From its base here, it has expanded to purchase other wineries, most notably Carmenet in Sonoma (now famous for its Cabernets), which suggests its formula has been hugely successful. It makes big, rich, barrel-fermented wines: less overt, over-the-top New World style, more a superior burgundy from a very good vintage putting oak and buttery qualities before tropical fruits. The 85 and 86 were huge (the 86 the better of the two) and very much in this mould, but I found myself preferring the lighter, slightly more elegant 87. The wines last well, with bottle-ageing potential of anything up to 10 years.

CHATEAU ST JEAN   *** →
8555 *Sonoma Highway, Kenwood, Sonoma*

Total v'yds owned: 49ha (120 acres)
Chardonnay owned: 14ha (35 acres)
Chardonnays produced: St Jean Estate; Robert Young Chardonnay; McCrea Vineyards Chardonnay; Belle Terre Chardonnay; Jimtown Ranch Chardonnay; Sonoma County Chardonnay; also Brut-Blanc de Blancs méthode champenoise.

Chardonnay has been one of the claims to fame at this winery at the foot of Sugarloaf Ridge; the others being Late Harvest Johannisberg Riesling and (since 1980) three *méthode champenoise* cuvées. The buildings of the winery, modelled in part on a medieval castle, house a high-tech operation, which was established in 1973. Now owned by the Japanese Suntory firm, it is producing top flight Chardonnays, nearly all from single vineyards. They are flavoursome wines, normally bursting with fruit: the Robert Young Vineyard in the Alexander Valley is the best known wine – and generally the finest: spicy, citrusy and oaky flavours all well in balance. Other Alexander Valley wines include the Belle Terre Vineyards and the Jimtown Ranch, which I find has the best ageing potential in the range. There is also a lighter McCrea Vineyards from Sonoma Valley and a blended Sonoma County which, like the rest, is well up in quality.

THE CHRISTIAN BROTHERS   **→
2555 Main Street, St Helena, Napa

Total v'yds owned: 480ha (1,190 acres)

The address above is the original Greystone building where the Christian Brothers made their wine from the founding days in 1882. Today, it is a showplace rather than a winery, and winemaking operations are south of St Helena in a brand new winery. There are other changes at the Christian Brothers: they have new owners (the British firm Grand Metropolitan) and they have changed their philosophy from producing middle-of-the-road blended wines to a move upmarket in premium varietals. With their vineyards making them one of the largest landowners in the Napa Valley, they are well placed to exploit differences in climate for their varietal wines. One of the varieties they are concentrating on is Chardonnay, now all matured in French oak. The barrel-fermented 85 Private Reserve, made from Oak Knoll and St Helena fruit, was matured in Nevers and Vosges wood, and is full of flavour, quite lively and easily drinkable, but a distinct and welcome improvement on their wines up until the early 1980s. They also make an unusual blend of California Chardonnay and white burgundy, called Montage, which is something of a curiosity.

CLOS DU BOIS   ***→
5 Fitch Street, Healdsburg, Sonoma

Total vineyards owned: 218ha (540 acres)
Chardonnay owned: 109ha (270 acres)
Chardonnays produced: Barrel Fermented Chardonnay; Winemaker's Reserve Chardonnay; Flintwood Chardonnay; Calcaire Chardonnay.

When founder-owner Frank Woods sold Clos du Bois in 1988 to the British/Canadian company Allied Lyons-Hiram Walker, he bequeathed a substantial vineyard holding in Alexander Valley, a reputation for high quality Chardonnays – and no winery. Still working from his rented winery in Healdsburg, winemaker John Hawley continues to produce a big range of Chardonnays for the new owners. The main production is the Barrel Fermented Chardonnay, made in a broad style with increasing amounts of malolactic fermentation, and designed for relatively early drinking. There are also two single vineyard wines: Flintwood, from Dry Creek, a suitably onomatopoeic name since the wine, like the 87, can be quite austere; Calcaire, made from chalky soils in the Alexander Valley, full, rounded, very tropical fruit in character. The top wine is Winemaker's Reserve (previously called Proprietor's Reserve), a big, oaky, toasty wine that needs time in bottle.

CLOS DU VAL   ∗∗ → ∗∗∗
5330 *Silverado Trail, Napa*

Total v'yds owned: 107ha (265 acres)	
Chardonnay owned: 45ha (110 acres)	
Chardonnays produced: Carneros Estate Chardonnay; Joli Val Chardonnay.	

The sister company of Taltarni in Victoria, Australia, Clos du Val has long had a reputation for its Cabernet Sauvignon and Bordeaux blends, made by its French winemaker Bernard Portet. While the main vineyards were in the Stag's Leap district of the Napa Valley, (much better suited to reds) Chardonnay fared less well. Now with fruit from the Carneros vineyards maturing and coming on stream, there is an impressive performance on the Chardonnay front. The wines are fermented partly in tank and then finished in light to medium toasted French Nevers oak, in which they are also matured for six to eight months. The 85 Chardonnay, made with fruit from Yountville, central Napa Valley, is austere, light, understated with only hints of wood flavours. The 87 Carneros Chardonnay is much creamier, richer, more attractive, with good acidity and wood flavours, obviously a wine that will mature in bottle.

CONGRESS SPRINGS VINEYARD   ∗∗∗ →
23600 *Congress Springs Road, Saratoga, Santa Clara*
From its first vintage in 1976, Congress Springs has been well known for its barrel-fermented Chardonnays. which come from vineyards in two areas: the Santa Cruz Mountains and Santa Clara County, including the single vineyard San Ysidro Vineyard. The wines are almost uniformly rich and toasty, but vary in intensity and keeping qualities. The basic Santa Clara Chardonnay is the softest and most easy-drinking of the three, while the Santa Cruz Mountains from the estate's own vineyards is smoky, quite toasty, sometimes quite tart (especially in 87) but generally on the firm side (as in 86). The third wine, San Ysidro Vineyard, is the best – elegant and well balanced – the 87 slightly honeyed but with good citric flavours and well in the forefront of California Chardonnays.

CUVAISON   ∗∗∗ → ∗∗∗∗
4550 *Silverado Trail, Calistoga, Napa*
Since its takeover in 1979 by a Swiss banking family, Cuvaison has made its reputation on Chardonnay. Despite the northern Napa address, the fruit for its wines comes from 162ha (400 acres) of vineyards owned in the Napa County part of Carneros.

I have tasted the wines a number of times over the years, and it is really with its 85 and 86 wines that Cuvaison has come into the top league of California Chardonnays. Careful blending, a mix of barrel fermentation and tank fermentation, followed by maturation in new French oak, and the gradual maturing of the Carneros vineyard all play their part. The 82 was a light wine which had a tendency to gooseberry flavours. The 84 was again light but was beginning to show some creamy, toasty character, while the 85 (tasted in 1987) showed lychee flavours, although its closed-up character suggested a good run at bottle ageing. The 86 (tasted in 1989) made from 100 percent Carneros fruit, had excellent balance, with soft, creamy tastes, but with a good firm edge to it that indicated, again, the ability to age in bottle.

DE LOACH VINEYARDS   ***
1791 Olivet Road, Santa Rosa, Sonoma

If you want to taste the classic, all-California blockbusting Chardonnay, De Loach Vineyards, north-west of downtown Santa Rosa, would be the place to visit. Tropical fruits, oak, toast, butter, it's all there, and I like it. There are two styles, the slightly less opulent Russian River Valley, which has honey and spices, but certainly ripe, sweet fruits. The special bottling OFS (which stands for Our Finest Selection) is a wine that sometimes needs taming, and is possibly better in cooler years like 1987.

DEHLINGER WINERY   →***
6300 Guerneville Road, Sebastopol, Sonoma

Serious wines, produced in a serious way by owner Tom Dehlinger in his wood-frame winery. While earlier wines (the first release was in 1976) were better among the reds, since the mid-1980s, it has been Chardonnay that has stolen the limelight. They are big wines, bursting with rich Russian River Valley fruit, with a good tinge of acid right through them. Both the 85 and 86 were highly praised, an accolade with which I won't disagree. The 87 was leaner, as befits the vintage, and all the wines need some ageing.

EDNA VALLEY VINEYARDS   ***
2585 Biddle Ranch Road, San Luis Obispo, Central Coast

Total v'yds owned: 223ha (550 acres)
Chardonnay owned: 113ha (280 acres)
Chardonnays produced: Edna Valley Estate Bottled; Estate Reserve.

If any doubt the possibility of producing great Chardonnay almost as far south as greater Los Angeles, then they should look at the microclimate of Edna Valley. A fog-bound shallow valley, it is open to the cooling breezes from the ocean less than 8km (5 miles) away. Established in 1980, with Chalone vineyards (q.v.) responsible for the winemaking, the label rapidly made a name for itself, both with Chardonnay and with Pinot Noir. They have a refreshing quality which is not always evident in some of the bigger blockbusters, and there is always a taste of intense fruit, coupled with some acidity. However, richness is always present, derived from barrel fermentation, maturation in French oak, and ripe fruit. The 86 was a great wine, the 87 lighter and crisper, the 88 (tasted in 1990) very rich and initially spoilt by tartness on the aftertaste, which hopefully will disappear with bottle age.

FAR NIENTE ** → ***
Off Oakville Grade, Oakville, Napa

Total v'yds owned: 49ha (120 acres)

From its renovated stone cellar in Oakville, Far Niente has wowed a generation of Chardonnay (and come to that Cabernet) drinkers with its restrained ''food wines'' and especially its heavy bottle and deliberately archaic label. If I seem a little cynical, it is because I've had some bad experiences with bottles of Far Niente Chardonnay. Two bottles of 86 in a tasting had bad bottle stink, and earlier vintages seemed too lean for their own good. However, 87 is much better, still lean, with acid rather than tropical fruit flavours, but well married to spicy oak.

FERRARI-CARANO ****
8761 Dry Creek Road, Healdsburg, Sonoma

Total v'yds owned: 146ha (360 acres)
Chardonnay owned: 73ha (180 acres)
Chardonnays produced: Alexander Valley Chardonnay; Reserve Chardonnay.

At the far end of Dry Creek Road, near the Lake Sonoma dam, Ferrari-Carano winery is one of the new stars on the California wine scene. From a standing start in 1981, with no track record, it has achieved immense things over only five vintages (in 1989) of Chardonnay. The owners, Don Carano, a Nevada attorney, and his wife Rhonda, have been busy buying land in Dry Creek Valley, in Alexander Valley and more recently in Carneros. At present, fruit for the Chardonnays comes from Alexander Valley but in time Carneros fruit will also be used. From this now extensive property, they are making Chardonnays with 85 percent barrel fermentation, with the remainder fermenting in small tanks. They are then aged for twelve months in French oak. The 86 was elegant, smoky, spicy; the 87 was even better, still restrained, harmonious and elegant, with balanced hints of wood and good concentration and intensity.

FETZER **
1150 Bel Arbres Road, Redwood Valley, Mendocino

Total v'yds owned: 283ha (700 acres)
Chardonnays produced: Sundial, Mendocino; Barrel Select; Special Reserve.

A family company, run by ten brothers and sisters, Fetzer has grown dramatically since its founding in 1968. The firm now owns two large wineries in southern Mendocino, and draws on grapes from Mendocino and Lake County as well as using grapes from Oregon and Washington in its inexpensive Bel

Arbors range. A new departure is the changeover of their vineyards to strictly organic production, although it is too early to say if this makes any difference to the taste of the wines. Among their Chardonnays are some fairly mediocre offerings, but the Barrel Select, using a blend of Mendocino and Lake County fruit, and the single vineyard Sundial Vineyard, 100 percent Mendocino, are both more serious offerings.

FLORA SPRINGS   *** →
1978 West Zinfandel Lane, St Helena, Napa

Total v'yds owned: 162ha (400 acres)
Chardonnay owned: 36ha (89 acres)
Chardonnays produced: Estate Chardonnay; Barrel Fermented Chardonnay.

A splendid old stone building, nestling into the hills on the west side of Napa Valley, houses a winery which in its modern guise dates from 1978. Under the ownership of the Komes family, it has built up substantial vineyard holdings in St Helena, in Oakville and in the Chiles Valley east of Napa. While the reds are now going apace, early successes were with Chardonnay, from which the company makes two wines. The Estate Chardonnay is the lighter of the two, spending some time during fermentation in stainless steel before being transferred to wood. It is then given up to seven months' ageing in wood. The 87 was delightfully perfumed, clean, softly rich, quite light and not too creamy. The 88 was equally delicate, and with a stronger citrus undertow. The Barrel Fermented Chardonnay is much richer, spending all its fermentation in wood. The 87 is a smooth, rich wine, that has some pineapple character; the 88 is bigger, and, when tasted in 89, seemed to have an unbalanced citrus taste which should soften down, given some bottle age.

FOLIE À DEUX   ** → ***
3070 St Helena Highway, St Helena, Napa

Total v'yds owned: 5ha (13 acres)

Owners Dr Larry and Evie Dizmang set out their small winery north of St Helena in 1981. The name, they say, comes from the well-known saying in the wine trade that to make a small fortune in the wine industry, you need to start with a large one. Their total annual production of 10,000 cases certainly puts them in the boutique or small winery category. They make a well-balanced Chardonnay, which moves easily between wood flavours and crisp, open fruit. The 87 was, given the vintage, a better wine than 88, and never lost sight of honeyed fruit flavours and eating-apple freshness.

FORMAN WINERY   *** → ****
1501 Big Rock Road, St Helena, Napa

Total v'yds owned: 24ha (60 acres)
Chardonnay owned: 7ha (17 acres)
Chardonnay produced: Forman Chardonnay.

Ric Forman, formerly winemaker at Sterling Winery and at Charles F Shaw, has gone solo with a small operation based on vineyards on the slopes of Howell Mountain and at Rutherford, both in Napa Valley. He made his first Chardonnay in the 84 vintage, and has continued to receive rave reviews ever since. The 86, barrel fermented, is intense, very toasty, but manages to keep just the right balance of fruit and crisp acidity; the 87 is beautifully smoky and will obviously develop in bottle; while the 88 has excellent tropical ripeness but, again, maintains the crispness and deftness of touch.

FREEMARK ABBEY   ** → ***
3022 St Helena Highway North, St Helena, Napa

Total v'yds owned: 105ha (260 acres)
Chardonnay owned: 36ha (90 acres)
Chardonnay produced: Carpy Ranch.

Dating from 1967, Freemark Abbey has built and maintained its reputation for small quantities of classic varietal wines. The Chardonnay, from fruit grown in the St Helena district is, as the warm climate of this part of the Napa Valley would suggest, a big wine even in cool years. It is oaky and rich, sometimes veering towards blowsy, but not quite reaching it. Recent vintages have concentrated more on fruit than wood, which is no bad thing. The 85 (tasted in 1990) had matured well, with hints – not at all unpleasant – of artichokes and crisp green vegetables.

GRGICH HILLS   ***
1829 St Helena Highway, Rutherford, Napa

Total v'yds owned: 36ha (90 acres)

For those of you who, like me, thought Grgich Hills were a range of imaginary hills somewhere in Napa, the truth is that Mike Grgich is the winemaker and the grower is Austin Hills. Grgich, who was a winemaker at Robert Mondavi and Chateau Montelena, set up in 1977. Grapes for their Chardonnay come from east of Rutherford and east of Napa City, and are due to come from a new vineyard in Carneros. Chardonnays are the wines which have made Grgich Hills' name, and the team continues to produce outstandingly good examples. The wines tend to be lean and quite austere when young, despite the added richness and complexity of barrel fermentation. The 85 has turned into a splendid example from a top vintage, while the 86 was in the leaner style. The 87 was tart when tasted in 1990, and definitely needed more time in bottle.

HANDLEY CELLARS   → ***
3151 Highway 128, Philo, Mendocino

Total v'yds owned: 8ha (20 acres)

There is not much further north or much cooler in California wine country than Handley Cellars in Anderson Valley on the road to Navarro, only a few miles from the coast. And yet Milla

Handley, who started here with the 1982 vintage, makes a surprisingly rich and creamy Chardonnay, using family-owned vineyards in Dry Creek Valley in Sonoma. The 87, one of Milla's best wines, is buttery, creamy and with 25-30 percent barrel fermentation in new wood. The 87 Anderson Valley Chardonnay, by contrast, from grapes grown around the winery, reveals the cooler climate with its citrus characters – green and lemony with a crisp, clean, fresh aftertaste.

HANZELL VINEYARDS   ** →
18596 Lomita Avenue, Sonoma

Total v'yds owned: 13ha (33 acres)
Chardonnay owned: 7ha (17 acres)
Chardonnay produced: Hanzell Chardonnay.

Big flavours are the hallmarks of the Chardonnays from this winery situated on the western slopes of the Mayacamas Mountains just north of Sonoma town. The winery is credited with introducing the California wine industry to the use of French oak back in the 1950s and 1960s, and they certainly still make generous use of it today. The style is big and bold, with an edge towards a vegetal quality which needs time to soften and mature in the bottle: so that the 82, for example (tasted in 1990) had ripe petrol/wood tones, and a softer version of a vegetal character on ripe, mature fruit.

HESS COLLECTION   ***
4411 Redwood Road, Napa City, Napa

Total v'yds owned: 113ha (280 acres)

Wines from this small winery, which now occupies the La Salle cellars, formerly owned by The Christian Brothers (qv), started with the 83 vintage and immediately attracted attention, showing the quality of the hillside vineyards on Mount Veeder. If Cabernet Sauvignon was the top star, Chardonnay was never far behind, the 86 with its buttery, oaky flavours, using fruit from the same Mount Veeder vineyards that also provide the Cabernet Sauvignon.

WILLIAM HILL WINERY   ** →
1775 Lincoln Avenue, Napa City, Napa

Total v'yds owned: 374ha (925 acres)
Chardonnays produced: Silver Label Chardonnay; Reserve Chardonnay.

From hillside vineyards on both sides of the Napa Valley and from Carneros, Bill Hill is producing two Chardonnays. The Silver Label is a lighter, softer style, almost ready for drinking when released. The oaky Reserve is the more serious wine, the 86 tasting nutty, buttery and oaky, with excellent but not too heavy fruit. The 87 Reserve is toast and toffee, with ripe pears: the 88 is big, ripe and creamy. These more recent wines from this winery seem to be a very satisfactory compromise between the much earlier over-oaked wines, and the in-between wines which leant too far towards austerity.

JEKEL VINEYARD   ** →
40155 Walnut Avenue, West Greenfield, Salinas, Monterey

Total v'yds owned: 131ha (325 acres)
Chardonnay owned: 46ha (114 acres)
Chardonnays produced: Estate Bottled; Private Reserve; Gravelstone
Vineyard and Sceptre.

Cool-climate Monterey, with its coastal winds and fresh
temperatures, is home to Bill Jekel's winery. Vineyards are
around the winery at Greenfield with newer plantings along the
Salinas River. The low growing season here gives the Arroyo
Seco Chardonnays considerable flavour, always with a firm
edge. The 85 is rich and buttery, the 84 very wooded and with
less obvious fruit and the 87 tart and fresh. An unusual,
honeyed botrytized Chardonnay Private Reserve was made in
1983, taking advantage of the appearance of noble rot.

JORDAN VINEYARD   → ***
1474 Alexander Valley Road, Healdsburg, Sonoma

Total v'yds owned: 94ha (232 acres)
Chardonnay owned: 32ha (79 acres)

From the splendidly outrageous "French" chateau atop a hill
above Alexander Valley, Tom Jordan has been making one of the
best publicized California Cabernet Sauvignons since 1976. The
first Chardonnay to be produced, from the 81 vintage, was
always a second string. But wines such as the 82, with its
intense malolactic fermentation softness and richness, and its
ageing in French oak for five months, or the lighter 86, a fast
maturer with soft, understated fruit, have certainly made a
mark.

KENDALL-JACKSON VINEYARD   ** → ***
640 Matthews Road, Lakeport, Lake County

Total v'yds owned: 40ha (100 acres)
Chardonnays produced: Vintner's Reserve; Proprietor's Reserve; Anderson
Valley De Patie Vineyard.

The rapid growth of this Lake County winery, from nothing in
1981 to 400,000 cases by 1988 owes much to the fact that it can
produce extremely drinkable wines. The Chardonnays are
mainly made from a blend of fruit grown in both Lake County
and Mendocino (and therefore labelled simply as California
wines). The Vintner's Reserve, named after winemaker Jed
Steele, is soft, tropical fruit in style and immediately attractive.
The barrel-fermented Proprietor's Reserve (named after owner
Jess Jackson) is oaky and buttery, with the 87 honeyed, not bone
dry, creamy and smooth. A single vineyard Anderson Valley De
Patie Vineyard wine has also been made in tiny quantities. The
87 is very complex, benefiting from the extra dimensions of
cool-climate fruit, and made to age well in bottle.

LA CREMA VINERA   ** →
4940 Ross Road, Sebastopol, Sonoma

Total v'yds owned: none
Chardonnays produced: Regular Chardonnay; Reserve Chardonnay.

After changes of ownership, La Crema now seems firmly set on a path of Burgundy-style wines, with Chardonnay the mainstay among the whites. Jason Korman, the owner since 1985, has dropped the single vineyard wines that were made in previous years and now concentrates on two Chardonnays, a regular and a reserve bottling, both barrel-fermented. The regular style, a blend of fruit from Mendocino and Sonoma, is light and soft in style, the 88 with baked apples and smoky wood. The Reserve, which includes Monterey fruit, has been big and alcoholic, very old style, but enjoyable none the less, although the 88 is more complex and spicy, and would benefit from bottle ageing.

MATANZAS CREEK →****
6097 Bennett Valley Road, Santa Rosa, Sonoma

Total v'yds owned: 23ha (58 acres)
Chardonnay produced: Matanzas Creek Winery.

Since its founding in 1978, Matanzas Creek has produced a stream of Chardonnay that has maintained a consistently high standard, even while the style has changed from overt oak to more complex, Burgundy-style wines. Grapes from these wines come from a variety of Sonoma sources: Carneros, Russian River Valley, Sonoma Valley, Sonoma Mountains and from around the winery in Santa Rosa. They are barrel-fermented, with long lees contact, and mainly French oak barrels. The wines reflect the vintages accurately: the 87 quite austere, firm in structure, with appley overtones, needing time to develop; the 88 more tropical in flavour, but still with a streak of acidity.

MAYACAMAS VINEYARDS →***
1155 Lokoya Road, Napa

Total v'yds owned: 20ha (50 acres)
Chardonnay owned: 11ha (28 acres)
Chardonnay produced: Mayacamas Vineyard Chardonnay.

From vineyards high up on the eastern slopes of the Mayacamas Mountains, and in their pre-Prohibition winery, Bob and Nonie Travers have built up a serious reputation for long-lived Cabernet Sauvignon. But, logically considering the cool nature of these vineyards, they also manage to produce a slow-maturing Chardonnay, which has been known to last ten years or more – a long time by California standards. In the past, the wines also tended to be heavy with wood (perhaps that is why they aged), but now the fruit is being given a chance to come through, as witnessed by the well-balanced 86.

ROBERT MONDAVI WINERY **→****
7801 St Helena Highway, Oakville, Napa

Total v'yds owned: 439ha (1085 acres)
Chardonnay owned: 135ha (334 acres)
Chardonnays produced: Robert Mondavi Chardonnay; Chardonnay Reserve.

Considering the size of the production at this winery (at around 500,000 cases, and another 1.5 million cases at the Wood-bridge Winery in Lodi, Mondavi is up with the big boys of California), it is a reflection of the care and commitment here that virtually every wine produced is of a consistently high standard. Vineyards along the Rutherford Bench and further south in Yountville will be supplemented with grapes from Carneros, as well as fruit from contract growers. Mondavi's reputation goes across the board, both reds and whites, but certainly one of his great successes is with the Reserve Chardonnays. This is just what we expect from California Chardonnays: the barrel-fermentation intensity, the light but definite oak toast, the buttery flavours, ripe fruit. The 86 was a very fine wine, followed closely by the 85, while the 88 was stylish and elegant as befits the cooler vintage. The regular Chardonnays are inevitably less exciting, rather straight and just too clean: although 87 was a classic wine, the 88 a shade too tart.

CHATEAU MONTELENA ***
1429 Tubbs Lane, Calistoga, Napa

Chardonnays produced: *Napa Valley Chardonnay*; *Alexander Valley Chardonnay*.

Right at the north end of the Napa Valley, hard up against Mount St Helena, is the stone winery and pretty Chinese gardens of the Montelena Winery. A 1969 revival of a pre-Prohibition winery has now produced a succession of top-class wines, sourcing fruit from both the Napa Valley and the Alexander Valley just across the pass in Sonoma County. The styles of the two Chardonnays thus produced are inevitably quite different: the smooth tropical fruits and wood tastes of the 88 Napa Valley Chardonnay contrasting with the cooler, citrus and grapefruit freshness of the 87 Alexander Valley. The Napa wines age better in bottle.

MONTICELLO CELLARS ** → ***
4242 Big Ranch Road, Napa

Total v'yds owned: 101ha (250 acres)
Chardonnay owned: 42ha (105 acres)
Chardonnays produced: *Jefferson Ranch Chardonnay*; *Corley Reserve*.

It would not take long to discover that Monticello's owner Joe Corley is a fervent admirer of Thomas Jefferson. The name gives it away, and even more so does the house at the winery, a copy of Jefferson's Monticello mansion in Virginia. Even the wines sport the distinguished statesman's name. If this strikes outsiders as slightly obsessional, the wines show a different sort of obsession: with quality. From the mid-1980s (the first wine was made in 1981 from vines planted in 1972), there has been a fine run of good vintages of Chardonnay, from the vineyards around the winery in southern Napa, which have put Monticello well up the ranks of California Chardonnay pro-ducers. They are quintessential California, but above the obvious fruit and wood characters there is also a sense of balance and subtlety. So the 86 Jefferson Ranch, partly barrel-fermented, is full of its quota of ripe fruit, with a touch of apricots, but finishes with crisp acidity; the less immediately appealing 86 Corley Vineyard, more serious, barrel-fermented, but also warmer and richer, had the ability to age in bottle.

MOUNT EDEN VINEYARDS   *** →
22020 Mount Eden Road, Saratoga, Santa Clara

Total v'yds owned: none
Chardonnay produced: MacGregor Vineyard Edna Valley.

Top-class wines are coming from this small winery, located in the Santa Cruz mountains, just outside Saratoga. Chardonnay is certainly the star here, with a range of two wines produced. Until the 1987 vintage, the regular wine was known as MEV, from the MacGregor vineyard in Edna Valley: an elegant wine, full of toast and fruit, and obviously able to age well. Now known as MacGregor Vineyard Edna Valley, the 88 was a slight disappointment, but still came in with crisp, fresh flavours. The top wine is the Estate Chardonnay, the 87 bursting with fruit, topped generously with oak and stirred together with just the right amount of acidity. The 88 Estate promises even better.

NAVARRO VINEYARDS   ** →
5601 Highway 128, Philo, Mendocino

Total v'yds owned: 20ha (50 acres)
Chardonnays produced: Mendocino Chardonnay; Premiere Reserve.

In the idyllic, rural conditions of the northern end of the Anderson Valley, Ted Bennett and Deborah Cahn make wines from rolling, sloping vineyards that are well into cool climate country. While their intention has been to make good Gewurz-traminer (which they do), their greatest wine success has been with Chardonnay. It is cool, clean wine with plenty of citrus flavours, like the 87 Mendocino Chardonnay (made with the addition of 15 percent nearby Potter Valley fruit), definitely lemony with only a touch of wood; or the 87 barrel-fermented Premiere Reserve, tasting softer due to malolactic fermentation, and with a shot of toasty oak, but still full of crisp citrus fruit. They also make a basic Chardonnay, which contains 15 percent Colombard.

NEWTON VINEYARD   ***
2555 Madrona Avenue, St Helena, Napa

Total v'yds owned: 42ha (105 acres)
Chardonnay owned: none
Chardonnay produced: Newton Vineyard Chardonnay.

Owned by Englishman Peter Newton (who founded and then sold the Sterling winery further north in the Napa Valley), this is one of the most spectacular vineyards in Napa. The winery is topped by a Chinese pagoda and a formal garden, the vineyards terraced in the manner of the Douro in Portugal, the slopes overlooking the valley sometimes almost vertiginous. The emphasis here is on red wine, but there is also some Chardonnay which in its understated way, is a match for the reds. The 87 (tasted in 90) is creamy, with smooth subtle wood tastes, spicy, with some pleasant not overdone acidity. The 88 (also tasted in 1990) is bigger, initially firm and chewy, needing bottle age to come round.

JOSEPH PHELPS   ** →
200 Taplin Road, St Helena, Napa

Total v'yds owned: 137ha (340 acres)
Chardonnay owned: 47ha (116 acres)
Chardonnays produced: Napa Valley Chardonnay; Carneros Sangiocomo.

Much better known for its range of single vineyard Cabernet Sauvignons, the Joseph Phelps vineyards in Napa and Carneros are now beginning to produce some much better than average Chardonnays that are developing character. The two wines produced are the Carneros Sangiacomo, and the Napa Valley, the barrel-fermented Sangiocomo the better one, the 88 with its nutty, earthy, gently crisp and quite firm fruit, the 87 Napa quite austere, slightly one-dimensional, although with some pleasant oak flavours.

RUTHERFORD HILL   **
200 Rutherford Hill Road, Rutherford, Napa

Total v'yds owned: 182ha (450 acres)
Chardonnay owned: 113ha (280 acres)
Chardonnays produced: Jaegar Vineyards Chardonnay; Cellar Reserve Chardonnay; Rutherford Knoll Special Cuvee.

Under the same ownership as Freemark Abbey (qv), Rutherford Hill (formerly Souverain) is housed in a picturesque modern version of a traditional wooden barn, high up above the eastern side of the Napa Valley. While these are by no means the greatest Napa Chardonnays, they are highly enjoyable, not too expensive wines, which, while still relying on a certain amount of oak, seem to have brought forward good fruit tastes as well. Three Chardonnays are made: the top wine is the Cellar Reserve, while there are two single site wines Jaeger Vineyard and Rutherford Knoll Special Cuvee, of which the 87 is a pleasantly smoky wine.

SAINTSBURY   *** →
1500 Los Carneros Avenue, Carneros, Napa

Total v'yds owned: 6ha (14 acres)
Chardonnays produced: Regular Chardonnay, Reserve Chardonnay.

Considering the amount of vineyard now in Carneros, and its importance to Napa's Chardonnay viticulture, there are surprisingly few wineries actually based there. Saintsbury is one - and indeed was one of the pioneers of the area, starting with a first vintage in 1981. Pinot Noir and Chardonnay are all that are made here. In fact, there are two Chardonnays: a regular and a reserve. The Reserve, from selected vineyards, which has 100 percent barrel fermentation, 100 percent malolactic, and lees contact, plus nine months in Nevers oak, is, as all this would suggest, a powerful wine. The 87 is rich and creamy, very tasty for the vintage; the 88 is big, not quite too much, but certainly a huge mouthful of wine. The regular Chardonnay is prettier, lighter and fresher in style, with only seven months in wood, the 88 full of approachable fruit flavours, very easy to drink.

SANFORD   ** → ****
7250 Santa Rosa Road, Buellton, Santa Barbara

Total v'yds owned: 6ha (15 acres)
Chardonnay owned: 3ha (8 acres)
Chardonnays produced: Sanford Chardonnay; Barrel Select Chardonnay.

Two Chardonnays come from Richard Sanford's winery, a regular and a Barrel Select. The regular, in a lighter style, has been made from a blend of fruit across the Central Coast, but now is based on fruit from Sanford's Santa Ynez vineyards as well as from growers mainly in that area. It varies in quality, from an excellent 87 to a less than satisfactory 88 with too much tartness.

However, the Barrel Select, based on Santa Barbara fruit, is a fine wine, rich and voluptuous, with layers of honey and tropical fruits: the 88 especially had these characters, while the tighter 87 added a smoky complexity.

SHAFER VINEYARDS   ** →
6154 Silverado Trail, Napa

Total v'yds owned: 60ha (150 acres)
Chardonnay owned: 26ha (66 acres)
Chardonnay produced: Shafer Vineyard Chardonnay.

Vineyards in the Stag's Leap district of Napa and now Carneros too supply the fruit for the Chardonnays from this medium-sized winery, owned by John Shafer. The wines have a small amount of wood character, but the overall impression is of lightness and freshness, the 87 crisp and clean, the 88 with a nice zip of citrus and eating apples, balanced by a very light touch of wood.

SILVERADO VINEYARDS   ***
6121 Silverado Trail, Napa

Total v'yds owned: 137ha (338 acres)

Since its beginnings in 1976 this Stag's Leap district winery, owned by the Disney family, has pushed firmly into the forefront of Napa wineries, with the Chardonnays playing a major part. Vineyards in Stag's Leap, in Yountville, in Coombsville near Napa City and new plantings in Carneros all contribute to the wines. Both 86 and 87 Chardonnays showed well: the 87 was lean, as befits the vintage, but had good toffee and ripe apple flavours; the 88, soft and spicy, had smooth well-balanced wood, and a delightful creamy finish.

SIMI WINERY
*** →

16275 Healdsburg Avenue, Healdsburg, Sonoma

Total v'yds owned: 121ha (300 acres)
Chardonnay owned: 52ha (130 acres)
Chardonnays produced: Simi Chardonnay, Reserve Chardonnay.

The translation of winemaker Zelma Long to presidency of this Moët Hennessey-owned company has had little effect on the high quality of much that is produced in this historic winery, founded by the Simi brothers in 1881. Chardonnay has been high on the list of the successes, and is the largest production here. Fruit comes from their own vineyards in Alexander Valley, from elsewhere in Sonoma and from Mendocino County. Of the two wines, the regular Chardonnay, partially barrel-fermented and then aged in wood for five months, is fresher in style, with over 50 percent Mendocino fruit in the 86, with its citrus character and zippy finish. The Reserve Chardonnay, a blend of fruit from Sonoma Carneros, from Alexander Valley and Sonoma Valley, is 100 percent barrel-fermented and has six months' wood ageing on the lees. The 85, buttery, creamy, very rich and full-blown is typical of this style.

SONOMA-CUTRER
*** → ****

4401 Slusser Road, Windsor, Santa Rosa, Sonoma

Total v'yds owned: 242ha (600 acres)
Chardonnay owned: 182ha (450 acres)
Chardonnays produced: Les Pierres Vineyard; Cutrer Vineyard; Russian River Ranches.

Chardonnay is the beginning and the end at winemaker William Bonetti's Russian River Valley winery, just north of Santa Rosa. There are three made and, in their different ways, they all say almost everything that has to be said about California Chardonnay. There is the marginally less impressive Russian River Ranches Chardonnay, the 88 light and elegant with crisp fruit flavours, the 87 surprisingly rich for the vintage with spicy flavours in abundance; the Chardonnay Cutrer, the 86 rich and buttery with toasty oak much to the fore; and, right at the top, the single vineyard Les Pierres Chardonnay from a vineyard in the southern Sonoma Valley, austere when young, needing time to mature. The 86, full of power and firmness, was still giving plenty of acidity in 1990; the 87 (also tasted in 1990) was smoother and creamier, and will mature faster. Both are top-notch wines.

STAG'S LEAP WINE CELLARS
** →

5766 Silverado Trail, Napa

Total v'yds owned: 18ha (44 acres)

While red wines have established the success and fame at Stag's Leap Wine Cellars, owner Warren Winiarski has also made a steady production of Chardonnay, which, while not in the same league as his Cabernet Sauvignon, is very enjoyable wine in its own right. Using Napa fruit and a proportion of barrel fermentation, the Reserve Chardonnays have shown considerable style with the restrained, smooth, orange and honey flavours of the 87 and the smoky, citrusy 88.

STONY HILL VINEYARDS ***→
PO Box 308, St Helena, Napa

Total v'yds owned: 16ha (40 acres)
Chardonnay owned: 10ha (24 acres)
Chardonnay produced: Stony Hill Estate Chardonnay, SHV.

Stony Hill, founded back in the 1950s, was one of the earliest of the boutique wineries which came to wider prominence in the 1960s and 1970s. From the start owner Eleanor McCrea has concentrated on white wines in her mountainside vineyards under Spring Mountain, and Chardonnay has been the lead variety. Until the 87 vintage there was just the one Chardonnay, sometimes called SHV (Stony Hill Vineyard; the secondary label made of bought-in grapes from a vineyard on Howell Mountain): the 88 still closed in, rich and heavy, the superb 85 just beginning to show its full-blown stature. The 87 vintage produced a new wine to pair this from their own vineyards, which I have not yet tasted.

SWANSON VINEYARDS →***
1275 Manley Lane, Rutherford, Napa

Total v'yds owned: 65ha (161 acres)
Chardonnay owned: 19.5ha (23 acres)
Chardonnays produced: Blended Chardonnay; Reserve Chardonnay.

Swanson's is a new venture, which released its first Chardonnay in 1990, based on grapes from Carneros, and from the central Napa, including the winery's own vineyards in Oakville, immediately next door to the Opus One vineyard. No expense has been spared in this operation and winemaker Marco Cappelli has made two Chardonnays from the 88 vintage, which will form the pattern for future years. There is a blended wine using 70 percent Napa and 30 percent Carneros fruit, crisp and melony in character, soft, fresh and ready for early drinking. And there is the more serious 100 percent barrel-fermented Reserve Chardonnay 88, fuller and fatter, more peachy and buttery, which will need time in bottle.

TREFETHEN ***
1160 Oak Knoll Avenue, Napa

Total v'yds owned: 244ha (603 acres)
Chardonnay owned: 71ha (175 acres)
Chardonnay production: 250,000 bottles

From a considerable vineyard holding on the Napa Valley floor at the cool southern end of the valley, the Trefethen family makes a considerable quantity of highly regarded Chardonnay. The style is lighter than most with what the winery describes as "judicious" wood ageing complementing the fruit rather than overwhelming it. "Poised" would sum up a wine such as the 86

Chardonnay, or the crisper 87. The wines have a reputation for maturing well and are sometimes released as Library Selection wines. Certainly a 79 I tasted back in 1985 gave considerable pleasure with its light gold colour and smooth taste.

VICHON   **→
1595 Oakville Grade, Oakville, Napa

Total v'yds owned: none

Now owned by Robert Mondavi (qv), Vichon was started as a partnership in 1981 and sold in 1985. The wines are made from Napa grapes grown by contract growers. Chardonnay is the star wine here, with a nicely balanced 85, a firmer 86 and a complex 88 which gives hints of citrus and oak underlying quite sweet ripe fruit.

VILLA ZAPU   **→***
3090 Mount Veeder Road, Napa

A new winery, making its debut with an 85 Chardonnay, using grapes grown in four different Napa vineyards. The style is in the big, bold California tradition, and the label, an extravagant surrealistic creation, reinforces this. The 87 was less successful, but 88, mainly barrel-fermented, and with 30 percent malolactic fermentation, with its ripe wood and fruit tastes, and smoky, spicy flavours works extremely well.

WENTE BROTHERS   **→
5565 Tesla Road, Livermore, Alameda

Total v'yds owned: 931ha (2,300 acres)
Chardonnay owned: 344ha (850 acres)
Chardonnays produced: Arroyo Seco Chardonnay; Livermore Valley
Ranches and Selected Vineyards Lots.

Vineyard holdings in the Livermore Valley and in Monterey provide the bulk of the grapes for this family winery, originally established in the 19th century. The style of the Chardonnay Reserve, using Livermore fruit, is open, ripe, and pleasantly fat: the 86 showed especially well. Chardonnay from the Arroyo Seco vineyards in Monterey has been somewhat more commercial: the 84 was fragrant and perfumed with comfortable softness, but the 88 much better with good, oaky, toasty flavours, and a smooth, creamy taste.

MARK WEST VINEYARDS   **→
7000 Trenton-Healdsburg Road, Forestville, Sonoma

Total v'yds owned: 25ha (62 acres)
Chardonnays produced: Sonoma County Blend; Estate Chardonnay;
Artists Selection Chardonnay.

With vineyards about as far west in the Russian River Valley as possible before meeting the coastal range of mountains, Mark West Vineyards are firmly in cool-climate country. Perhaps best known for Gewurztraminers, they also make a Burgundian duo of Chardonnay and Pinot Noir. There is quite a range of them, from a regular Sonoma County blend, through an Estate Chardonnay, a Reserve Chardonnay to an Artists Selection Chardonnay, which has individually designed labels. I haven't tasted their wines for a few years, but the 80 showed decent maturity in 1986, while the 83 (also tasted in 1986) had a smooth, almost unctuous taste, a ripe petrolly mature finish and only a tiny touch of acidity.

CHATEAU WOLTNER   **→***
154 Main St, St. Helena

Total v'yds owned: 22ha (55 acres)
Chardonnay owned: 22ha (55 acres)
Chardonnays produced: Blended Chardonnay; St Thomas Chardonnay; St Titus Chardonnay.

Starting with the 1985 vintage, the previous owners of Ch La Mission Haut-Brion in the Bordeaux Graves region of France, have set up shop on the slopes of the Howell Mountain with fine views over the Napa Valley. They started with an enormous 85 Chardonnay, which was generously over-oaked, and included a blend and two single vineyard wines, St Thomas and St Titus. I preferred the 86 wines, which allowed the fruit to show through, and both the single vineyard wines showed considerable breeding. A name to watch.

ZD WINES   ***→
8383 Silverado Trail, Napa

Total v'yds owned: 1.5ha (3.5 acres)
Chardonnay owned: none
Chardonnay produced: California Appelation Chardonnay.

From an almost makeshift winery on the east side of the Napa Valley, Norman de Leuze makes his ripely attractive Chardonnays, using purchased grapes from all over the valley, now including Carneros. The Chardonnays are barrel-fermented in a mix of American and French oak. The name ZD indicates, he says, Zero Defects, and there is little wrong with wines of the quality of the 85 Chardonnay (tasted in 1989), spicily mature, with restrained elegant, but always ripely tropical fruit; or the mature 82 (tasted in 1989) biscuity like an old champagne, smooth and creamy, with excellent mature fruit flavours; or a barrel sample of 88 (tasted in 1989) with excellent crisp greengage fruit, obviously demanding time in cask and bottle.

NORTHWESTERN STATES OF THE USA

Oregon

Oregon hit the wine world's headlines back in 1979 when a Pinot Noir, entered by David Lett of Eyrie Vineyards, beat all comers bar one in a worldwide tasting of Pinot Noirs. It did for Oregon's wine industry what a similar competition in 1976 had done for California's – it gave the state international recognition, and bolstered a new-found confidence in its ability to produce world-class wines.

That success was for a Pinot Noir. And that elusive grape variety has continued to produce top-rate wines in Oregon, produced by an ever-increasing number of small wineries. It would seem logical, therefore, to assume that Chardonnay would do equally well. But it has not been that simple. The reasons for this are not hard to find, and the solutions are already being worked out. The ''problem'' is climate or, more exactly the wine producers' reaction to it. Although Oregon is further south of Washington State, it is the coolest viticultural region of the three northwestern states which produce wine. The vineyards are close to the cool Pacific Ocean, from which fogs and rain pour regularly across the low coastal range of hills that separate the main vineyard area of the Willamette Valley from the ocean.

The growing season is long and comparatively cool, giving time for grapes to ripen but also leaving the Chardonnay with high natural acidity. The problem has been that producers in Oregon have been slow to recognize this high acidity – more familiar perhaps to Chardonnay producers in Chablis than in, say, Meursault.

In true American fashion, copying the principal style of California Chardonnay, Oregon producers have turned to toasty new oak barrels so enthusiastically that they have overwhelmed the fruit. Even when they do succeed in getting the balance right, the high natural acids mean the wines must be given time to mature. Keeping Chardonnay in cellars for maturation is not something that comes easily to a wineconsuming public more used to the instant offerings from further south in California.

Happily, this is a matter that can be easily resolved. If Oregon can produce world-beating Pinot Noir, it certainly can produce similar quality Chardonnay.

THE CHARDONNAY ARRIVES

Although wineproducing grapes were grown in Oregon back in 1854, in the Rogue River Valley (which is so far south it is almost in California), not until the 1950s and 60s were any proper plantings of Vitis vinifera made, although the Concord grape, a Vitis labrusca, was already producing grapes for jam. The first commercial winery in Oregon was at Hillcrest in 1961, and Eyrie

Vineyards followed in 1966. Chardonnay was planted at the same time as Pinot Noir.

CHARDONNAY VINEYARDS

Chardonnay is the number two variety in the state after Pinot Noir, and well ahead of other successful varieties like Rhine Riesling or Gewurztraminer. The main centres of Oregon grapegrowing are in the Willamette Valley which runs due south of Portland from the state boundary with Washington State to the north. All the main wineries are also situated here. Other vineyards are in the Umpqua Valley and Rogue River Valley, and a few are further east. To all intents and purposes, the wines in the directory section that follows are all grown from Willamette Valley fruit, although a number of Oregon wineries also use fruit from Washington State which, with a much larger vineyard area, has a fruit surplus which is also exported to California.

MAKING CHARDONNAY

Wine production in Oregon is still very much a cottage industry. Wineries are just as likely to be in tin sheds as in smart buildings with tasting rooms. Most, with a few exceptions, are ten years old or less. On such a small-scale basis, the producers have chosen only such equipment as they really need. So modern presses and crushers may stand alongside equipment that has been re-used from some other agricultural purpose, such as dairy farming. Essentially, high tech is used where it is useful, and not just for the sake of being modern. And the return to techniques like barrel fermentation for Chardonnay happened before the high-tech phase which swept through California ever hit Oregon. New French wood is used – perhaps too enthusiastically – for fermentation and maturing.

PRODUCERS

ADAMS VINEYARD   **
1922 NW Pettygrove St, Portland

A tiny winery, on the edge of the built-up area of Portland, but it has made a name for its Chardonnays which have elegance and balance, coupled with a judicious use of oak. There are two styles produced – a regular and a reserve, and the Reserve, especially in years like 86 need plenty of time in bottle to come round. In some ways, perhaps, the use of wood in these reserve wines is overgenerous, and a wine like the 85 regular Chardonnay gives full rein to the generous fruit flavours that are there.

ADELSHEIM   ** → ***
22150 NE Quarter Mile Lane, Newberg

Total v'yds owned: 10ha (25 acres)
Chardonnay owned: 2ha (6 acres)
Chardonnays produced: Oregon Chardonnay; Adelsheim Vineyard Reserve Chardonnay.

Owner David Adelsheim is one of Oregon's most respected authorities on viticultural techniques. The Chardonnays tend to have considerable oak, with high initial acid levels, so that they are slow to develop. The 85 was certainly an example of this tendency, still very closed when tasted in 1988, but certainly with potential. I preferred the riper 86, but it probably will not last as long.

AMITY VINEYARDS   **→
18150 Amity Vineyard Road, Amity

Total v'yds owned: 40ha (100 acres)	
Chardonnay owned: 0.80ha (2 acres)	
Chardonnay produced: Willamette Valley Chardonnay.	

In a large barn-like building, owner Myron Redford has made a considerable reputation for his Pinot Noirs. His Chardonnay may be less impressive, but this stainless-steel fermented, taut, sometimes high acid wine is very typical of Oregon Chardonnay. As with so many of these wines, it needs time in bottle to soften its sharp edges – the 85 was typical of this, crisp and taut when tasted in 1988, in the lean style of a northern cool-climate wine.

THE EYRIE VINEYARDS   ***
PO Box 204, McMinnville, Dundee

Total v'yds owned: 19ha (46 acres)	
Chardonnay owned: 2ha (4.5 acres)	
Chardonnays produced: Willamette Valley; Yamhill County.	

The owner, retiring David Lett, has been in the business of making small quantities of top quality wines for over 20 years. He has concentrated on the duo of Pinot Noir and Chardonnay to great effect. Both his 86 Chardonnay, with its very rich, buttered toast tastes, and very full palate – and the 85, leaner and crisper, more cool climate with excellent fruit quality, were excellent wines. I was somewhat disappointed by the 87 which seemed to take leanness to extremes, and was rather too light, not something to be expected in a vintage from a hot year, but perhaps it just needs time in bottle.

KNUDSEN-ERATH   **
17000 NE Knudsen Lane, Dundee

Total v'yds owned: 18ha (45 acres)	
Chardonnay owned: 7ha (18 acres)	
Chardonnay produced: Knudsen-Erath Chardonnay.	

The beautiful vineyard of Knudsen-Erath (the name comes from the two families which own it) is on a steep hillside just outside the small town of Dundee in Willamette Valley. Here Dick Erath makes Pinot Noirs that have earned him a reputation as one of Oregon's best, and Chardonnay which is good but not quite that good. Tastings have suggested that the lean character of the Chardonnays does soften with time to give a good, steely style of wine. There are two wines produced: a regular and a Vintage Select, both of which are barrel-matured.

PONZI VINEYARDS   ***→
Route 1, Box 842, Beaverton

Total v'yds owned: *5ha (12 acres)*
Chardonnay owned: *1ha (3 acres)*
Chardonnays produced: *Willamette Valley (Regular and Reserve).*

This is probably Oregon's top Chardonnay producer at the moment – things move fast in this state. The winery, a homely wood and stone building, more roof than walls, is on the edge of Portland, at the beginning of the Willamette Valley vineyard area. Dick Ponzi manages to get the balance just right between the crisp nature of Oregon Chardonnays and the use of wood, resulting in wines that are surprisingly ripe and rich, the fruit buttressed by the wood. There are two bottlings – the regular and the reserve and, as is often the case, the regular is the better balanced wine in youth, the 86 with a good showing of fruit and an underlay of oak; the Reserve 86, meanwhile, is moving toward a luscious, ripe style, more fruit than buttery oak.

SHAFER VINEYARD   ***
Star Route, Box 269, Forest Grove

Away to the west of Portland, isolated from the main vineyard area of Willamette Valley, Shafer Vineyards is run by Harvey Shafer who left the construction industry to become a wineproducer – and managed to make a success of his wines from day one in the 1980 vintage. Ten years on, he is consistently coming up with some of the best Chardonnays in Oregon. As with so many wineries, two Chardonnays are produced: a regular wine which includes bought-in grapes and an Estate wine, which comes from the home vineyard. Both wines typically exhibit a lean character when young, but the wood and fruit balance is always there: an 85 Chardonnay was appley rather than buttery, light and floral in character, immediately attractive after three to four years.

TUALATIN VINEYARDS   ***
Route 1, Box 339, Forest Grove

Bill Fuller, owner of Tualatin, was one of the pioneers when, back in 1973, he set up shop in an old barn that had been a strawberry-packing shed. Things are somewhat smarter now, but the family atmosphere hasn't changed. Interestingly, in a state whose proudest vinous claim to fame is its Pinot Noirs, Tualatin's reputation rests as much on its Chardonnays. The company manages to coax very ripe flavours out of the grapes, and to come up with, as in the 85, piles of taste, enough to sustain any amount of oak, although always with an edge of appley acidity to it. The 86, as befits the vintage, was somewhat leaner.

YAMHILL VALLEY VINEYARDS   **
Oldville Road, McMinnville, Dundee

Another of the group of wineries that exists around the township of McMinnville in Dundee's Red Hills. Yamhill is a new winery - the building wasn't constructed until 1985, when the vineyards first became mature enough, but Chardonnays are already setting a track record of quality. From the 85 vintage, Yamhill made a softly ripe wine that is open and quite luscious, while from 86, it managed to coax ripeness from fruit in a cool year to make a wine that has pleasing baked-apple flavours, underlined with rather than dominated by new wood tastes.

Washington State

After California, Washington State has more vines than any other state in the United States. But the development has been within 20 years, from the point in the late 1960s when a Gewurztraminer from the Yakima Valley attracted the attention of the California wine industry's *éminence grise*, André Tchelist-cheff, who had been called in to advise the State Government on the suitability of growing grapes for wine. At that time, a firm called American Wine Growers had been experimenting with wine grapes in vineyards near Seattle. And it was they who, under the name Chateau Ste Michelle, launched the first commercial Washington State wines in the early 1970s. From the start Chardonnay was there, and it has rapidly established itself as one of the leading varieties in the State, with more area-units than Cabernet Sauvignon which along with Merlot and Sauvignon Blanc are the principal varieties planted in the State.

The development of viticulture has obviously been a fairly whirlwind affair, which nearly ran into disaster because the vineyard plantings disliked the irrigation techniques employed on other crops in the dry eastern parts of the State. At great cost, vineyards had to be uprooted and replanted on the same sites so that new irrigation schemes could be designed. Since the mid-1980s, things have moved really fast – the crop of 17,272 tonnes (17,000 tons) in 1985 had increased to 46,738 tonnes (46,000 tons) by 1988. Between 1981 and 89, the area under Chardonnay increased from 302 to 646ha (746 to 1,596 acres).

The style of Washington Chardonnays is still evolving. Many of the wines are still correct rather than exciting, and it is difficult to identify a true Washington style. But it does seem to be mid-way between the ripe, rich tastes of a Napa Chardonnay in California and the cool, crisp, high acid taste of an Oregon Chardonnay. Although the State is to the north of Oregon, the vineyards are situated in warmer areas than in Oregon, to the east of the Cascade Ranges and away from the influence of the ocean.

CHARDONNAY VINEYARDS

The main growing area in Washington is in the Columbia River Valley, which runs in a huge arc south from the Cascades down to the Oregon state boundary and then north again to Spokane.

While Columbia River forms one large AVA (Approved Viticultural Area), two smaller areas within it are where the bulk of vineyards are now found.

Of these areas, the Walla Walla Valley, shared jointly by Washington and Oregon, is regarded as red wine country. The larger Yakima Valley, on the eastern slopes of the Cascade Ranges is where the bulk of the Chardonnay and other white varietals are planted. This is an east–west river valley, between a low range of hills called the Rattlesnake Hills to the north and a similar range, the Horse Heaven Hills, to the south. Even within this relatively contained area vineyards are still widely scattered and there are few, if any, regions with continuous vineyards.

The climate is one of extremes. Hot days in the summer are followed by cold nights, with temperatures dropping by as much as 30° C (86° F). It is very dry, desert country – with only 250mm (about 10 inches) of rain a year – and scrub forms the natural vegetation. Vineyards obviously have to be irrigated – by diverting the Columbia River and its tributaries into a complex system of canals and drainage channels.

However, this continental climate with its hot summers also has very cold winters, which can start with serious frosts in October right at the end of the ripening season. These are anxious days for the grower: there is always a fine line to be trod between leaving the grapes to gain extra ripeness and picking them before the onset of the frosts, to give the vines a chance to go dormant, thus protecting them from the cold.

MAKING CHARDONNAY

Washington is dominated by a handful of large producers, two of which, Chateau Ste Michelle and Columbia Crest, are owned by the same company.

Their wineries, which happen to produce some good Chardonnays, are huge by any standards, certainly as large as the big boys of the Napa Valley, and are fully equipped with state-of-the-art equipment. At the other extreme, there is still a pioneering spirit about some of the smaller wineries, where the winemaker is the owner, and his wife (or her husband) runs the tasting room. However, even here, compared with Oregon, Washington seems to have moved faster toward the smart wineries and organized tasting rooms.

The winemaking follows techniques familiar in California. There is a general tendency to barrel-ferment Chardonnays in French oak, to give them a certain amount of lees contact during maturation and to age them for anything up to eight or nine months in French wood. Malolactic fermentation is encouraged for a part of a blend, but normally the ripeness of the grapes is sufficient to allow a portion to keep its tart malic acid.

Many wineries are designing wines that can be drunk soon after release, while also making a reserve, or a single vineyard wine, that repays bottle ageing. However, again compared with Oregon, the softer style of Washington Chardonnays means most can be drunk sooner rather than later. It is still too early in the production of Chardonnay in Washington to say whether the better wines also age well.

PRODUCERS

ARBOR CREST ** →
4506 Buckeye, Spokane

Total v'yds owned: 32ha (80 acres)
Chardonnay owned: 8ha (20 acres)
Chardonnay produced: Chardonnay; Cameo Reserve Chardonnay.

Despite the fact that the winery is a long way from any vineyards, Arbor Crest has set itself high standards, under the winemaking direction of Scott Harris. Fruit for the Chardonnays is a blend from a number of different sources in the Columbia Valley. The 87 Chardonnay, light in character, soft in flavour, has perhaps a shade too much oak. The 88, with richer fruit, allowed the smoky character of the wood to enhance rather than dominate. Neither wine seems to be designed for long ageing.

BARNARD GRIFFIN ** →
1707 W 8th Place, Kennewick

On the edge of the Yakima Valley vineyard area, this firm produces a barrel-fermented Chardonnay, the 88, aged on its lees in new French wood, giving a rich, sweet wine, buttery and spicy, soft, perhaps lacking acidity for ageing, but attractive for youthful drinking.

CHINOOK WINES → ***
PO Box 387, Prosser

The small Chinook winery is owned by winemaker Kay Simon, who previously worked at Chateau Ste Michelle (qv), and her husband Clay Mackey. In their small farmhouse winery, they make a Chardonnay in a ripe, toasty style, the 86 with balancing delicacy, the 88 much more creamy, but still with good acidity. The 87 was the biggest wine of the three, much more toasty and ripe, broad and rich.

COLUMBIA WINERY ***
1445 120th Avenue NE, Bellevue

Total v'yds owned: none
Chardonnay owned: none
Chardonnays produced: Otis Vineyard; Woodburne Collection; Wycoff Vineyard, Signature Series.

In such a comparatively close-knit wine scene as Washington's, it is somewhat confusing to find two major wineries with Columbia on their wine labels. This one, Columbia Winery, was formerly called Associated Vintners when it was set up right at the beginning of the development of Washington's vineyards in 1962. Now, under the winemaking direction of David Lake, a Canadian Master of Wine, it is producing some excellent Chardonnays (as well as its main claim to fame, the Cabernet Sauvignons). Columbia Valley Chardonnay 88 (tasted in 1990) is soft, buttery, light, fresh, not too overt, while the 85 of the same wine (also tasted in 1990) with its mature, petrolly flavours, shows that four years is about the right ageing time for this wine. Single vineyards wines under David Lake's signature include the Brookside Chardonnay, the 87 of which (tasted in 1990) showed signs of lasting well, with its baked-apple fruit and creamy, restrained taste; while the 86 Wyckoff Chardonnay was somewhat less satisfactory, having a slight vegetal character, and showing signs of drying out.

COVEY RUN ** → ***
Box 2287, Zillah
On the slopes of the Rattlesnake Hills, facing south over the Yakima River, this winery has a superb view right across the Yakima Valley. It started out life as Quail Run, but the name was changed to avoid confusion with California's Quail Ridge winery. In the attractive wooden winery, they make Chardonnay from Yakima Valley grapes. The 88, which spent nine months in Limousin oak, still shows more fruit character than wood; while the 87, tending to taste bigger all round, had more wood than fruit when tasted in 1989. All that probably means is that the wines need time in bottle to balance out.

THE HOGUE CELLARS ** →
Box 2898, Prosser
Founded with the 1982 vintage, the Hogue Cellars immediately made an impact with wines that were eminently drinkable and not too complex. Their Chardonnay fits perfectly into this scenario: the 87 (tasted in 1989) was already absolutely mature, nice open flavours, some wood and soft acidity with a peachy ripe aftertaste. The 88 (tasted in 1990) with 85 percent malolactic fermentation, showed similar readily drinkable qualities – medium weight, and good forward buttery fruit.

KIONA VINEYARDS ***
Box 2169, Benton City

Total v'yds owned: none
Chardonnay owned: 2ha (4.5 acres)
Chardonnay produced: Kiona Chardonnay; Yakima Valley.

At the eastern end of the Yakima Valley vineyard area, Kiona's vineyards stand isolated at the end of a dirt track that seems to lead into the desert. It gives the visitor a vivid reminder of the essential need for irrigation on this dry side of the Cascade Mountains. Kiona started out in 1980, and its wines have won good critical acclaim. Their Chardonnay, a barrel-fermented wine, using Yakima Valley fruit, is in a light style with piercingly fresh tastes, the 88 light, delicate, with just the right flavour of wood; the 87, even better, apricots and other stone fruits just supported by the toasty vanilla taste of the wood.

CHATEAU STE MICHELLE → ***
1 Stimson Lane, Woodinville
This is by far the largest Washington winery, with its head-quarters and small cellars on the western side of the Cascade Mountains, but drawing its grapes from the main vineyard areas of the Columbia Valley, where the main winery is located.

Besides the Chateau Ste Michelle name, they also market wines under the name of Columbia Crest. The main winery, at River Ridge south of the Yakima Valley vineyards, is a startling French chateau, set in landscaped gardens, and splendidly out of place in the context of dusty Washington State. There are a number of Chardonnays produced. Under the Chateau Ste Michelle label there is a regular Chardonnay, the 87 elegant, wooded, the 88 much riper, with bananas and tropical fruit and much less obvious wood; a superior Cold Creek Chardonnay, the 87 light, elegant and complex; and another superior bottling, River Ridge Vineyard, the 87 citrusy, light, with only a hint of oak. Under the Columbia Crest name, there is a Vintage Select, the 87 a rather heavy wine; and a regular Chardonnay, the 88 fresh and designed to be drunk young.

SALISHAN VINEYARDS   ** →
Route 2, Box 8, LaCenter

| Total v'yds owned: 5ha (12 acres) |
| Chardonnay owned: 1ha (2.5 acres) |

Away from the main Washington vineyard area of Columbia River, Salishan is located in southwestern Washington State, near Oregon's Willamette Valley. The cooler growing conditions here produce a very light, quite acid Chardonnay style, which is crisp rather than rounded. The 87 Chardonnay showed this very well, light and fresh, with only a hint of wood at the end, leaving a very clean, fresh acid feel. The wines tend to need longer in bottle than most Washington wines – again, more in the style of Oregon.

SNOQUALMIE   → ***
1000 Winery Road, Snoqualmie

Situated in the mountainous country on the route between Seattle and the eastern Washington vineyards, Snoqualmie is in an appropriately Alpine-looking winery, not far from the waterfalls of the same name. Joel Klein, the owner, used to work at Chateau Ste Michelle before setting up on his own. The grapes for all his wines come from the Columbia Valley, an hour's drive to the east. His Reserve is the more impressive of the two Chardonnays he makes, a barrel-fermented wine that, with the 87 (tasted in 1989), combines good spicy tastes with a crisp baked-apple flavour, not too heavy in style, and with a balanced cutting edge of acidity. The regular Chardonnay 87 was lighter, more citrusy, a much less woody, toasty wine, one which needs to be drunk young.

STATON HILLS   **
2290 Gangl Road, Wapato

At the western end of the Yakima Valley, Staton Hills is one of the best places in the valley for its tasting facilities. The Chardonnay, with barrel-fermentation and maturation in Allier and Tronçais oak, is in a broad style, the 87 rather one-dimensional, full of spicy fruit, the 88 more interesting, with its soft wood and tropical fruit tones well integrated.

STEWART VINEYARDS → ***
Box 3578, *Sunnyside*

The attractive red barn that houses this winery is some way from the vineyards on Wahluke Slope, which is fast making its name as one of the best vineyard sites in the Columbia Valley. The Chardonnay, a Columbia Valley wine, is aged in French oak. The 87 was a fine big wine, full of tropical flavours, while the 88, more lightly oaked, was more in a delicate style. Both worked.

PAUL THOMAS ***
136th Pl NE, *Bellevue*

Along with his rather fine line in fruit wines such as rhubarb and raspberry, Paul Thomas has started making some acclaimed Chardonnay in his winery in an industrial estate on the outskirts of Seattle. He makes two styles of Chardonnay: a reserve and a regular. The 88 regular was a successful, complex wine, combining the nutmeg and ginger of wood with a smooth, creamy fruit taste, while the 87 of the same wine was lighter with less complexity. The Private Reserve 87 was leaner, more citrusy, less immediately appealing, best after four to five years in bottle.

Other American Chardonnays

NEW YORK STATE

Two areas of *Vitis vinifera*, as distinct from the native *Vitis labrusca*, are producing some interesting Chardonnays in New York State. First, in the Finger Lakes, a group of well-established wineries has been joined by some exciting newcomers who are making Chardonnay (and other wines) in a very boldly American style. Chief among these wineries are Wagner Vineyards, Finger Lakes Wine Cellars, Glenora Wine Cellars, Vinifera Wine Cellars, Woodbury Vineyards and Herman Wiemer. Second, a new wineproducing area in the state is Long Island, where a small group of wineries has been growing up, enjoying a more gentle maritime climate than the vineyards of the Finger Lakes. The biggest of these is Banfi, owned by the Villa Banfi company, which released its first Chardonnay in 1986, another is Hargrave Vineyard in North Fork. Both have received good reviews.

CANADA

Across the international boundary one or two of the Canadian wineries are producing more than just inexpensive wines from American vines. The two best Chardonnay producers are Chateau des Charmes and Inniskillin, both at Niagara.

OTHER STATES

In Texas, Chardonnays have come from Pheasant Ridge at Lubbock and Fall Creek near Austin, both with good toasty oak flavours. In Virginia, some rather lean, tart Chardonnays have been made by Barboursville Vineyards and Meredyth Vineyards.

Australia

Perhaps even more than Cabernet Sauvignon, it has been Chardonnay that created Australia's international reputation in the 1980s. The full-blown, rich, fat, buttery styles, reeking of new wood, and absolutely clean to taste have given not only the Burgundians, but also the Californians a run for their money. Australia seems to have the considerable ability to produce its great wines in decent quantities and at decent prices.

That said, if any grape variety has suffered under the pressure of demand, it has been Chardonnay. It has proved such a runaway international success that demand rapidly out-stripped supply during the late 1980s, forcing up prices. But since this was Australia, and not hidebound Europe, growers simply adopted the obvious solution: they planted more. By the time of the 1990 harvest, the balance of supply and demand was getting back onto an even keel. There was even talk of a fall in Chardonnay prices – almost unheard of in the wine world.

THE CHARDONNAY ARRIVES

The grape is a relative newcomer to the big time in Australia. For some years, it was confused with Pinot Blanc, and it is still possible to see wines incorrectly labelled Pinot Chardonnay. Although true Chardonnay was planted in small quantities, its rise to fame and fortune started in the Hunter Valley in 1971 when Murray Tyrrell, of Tyrrell's, released the first commercial Chardonnay, his Vat 47. Significantly, he gave it small oak matur-ation: significant because the use of small barrels to mature anything in Australia was unusual then, certainly for whites.

From these small beginnings, the grape moved fast, travelling south from the Hunter Valley, into South Australia (reached in the mid-1970s) and Victoria, as well as into Western Australia and Tasmania. Now, not only is it used for still wines, but the burgeoning sparkling wine industry is demanding the classic champagne blend of Chardonnay and Pinot Noir, encouraged by champagne producers who have begun to invest in Australian wines.

MAKING CHARDONNAY

Oak and Chardonnay have gone hand in hand in Australia, and it has been the taste of oak combined with the ripe fruit that has propelled Chardonnay forward as the premium white variety. The use of small wood, usually French, has imparted the spicy, buttery tastes that, added to the ripe, sometimes tropical fruit flavours, give Australian Chardonnay its most familiar charac-teristics. That there has been a recent tendency to play down this super-richness could be due to the fact that more grapes are coming from cooler vineyards, or, more probably, a general feeling on the part of producers that the public does not want wines that are too rich. I think they are wrong: Burgundy can do the subtle wines perfectly well. What we want from Australia, please, are the blockbusters!

At the beginning of the Chardonnay craze, the fruit was fermented in the Australian high-tech way, using stainless steel, controlled temperatures – generally quite low, around 12-15° C (53-59° F) or less – and using specially chosen dried yeasts for fermentation. Only after fermentation had finished were barrels used. The whole thing was regarded very scientifically. Gradually, however, a modicum of French tradition has crept into this shiny modern scene. Now we find that many producers are fermenting their best Chardonnay in barrels rather than tanks to enhance the wood flavours. They are also leaving the wine on its lees for prolonged periods to give greater intensity and richness.

Few producers are letting their wine go through malolactic fermentation. A loss of acidity is just what they do not want in Australia, given the high sugar levels and low acidity of the fruit. In fact, there is a common tendency to add acidity, in the form of citric acid, to stop the wines being just too fat. This shot of citric is what gives some Australian Chardonnays their somewhat bitter, sharp aftertaste.

The oak barrels that producers are using are generally French: Allier, Tronçais and Limousin seem to be the preferred woods, with Nevers increasing in popularity. Barrels are imported made up, despite the extra expense, because producers find that Australian coopers cannot make up the barrels quite so well as their French counterparts. Some producers, looking perhaps to lessen expenses, perhaps to increase spicy tastes, use German or American oak which is certainly less costly than French wood: this is normally made up in Australia.

CHARDONNAY VINEYARDS

The Australians have yet to decide finally where Chardonnay works best. But certain ground rules have already been established – and the trend has been to look for cooler-climate vineyards, either in the far south, or high up. Chardonnay, being treated as a premium grape, is not widely planted in the irrigated vineyard areas and tends to be found in the up-and-coming quality areas.

New South Wales

The original source of Chardonnay in the country is the Hunter Valley. Despite its position north of Sydney, both the Lower Hunter and, especially, the cooler Upper Hunter are home to a number of top quality Chardonnay producers. The vineyards are helped by the cloud cover over the valley which lowers the temperature during the growing season. The style is generally rich, well oaked, although some Upper Hunter wines have greater delicacy.

Victoria

Chardonnay is grown in most of the many small, isolated wine regions of Victoria. Certain areas are proving better than others: the Yarra Valley, one of the coolest districts is coming up with some show stoppers. Other areas which also lend the benefits of a cool climate to Chardonnay growing are Geelong, the Pyrenees, and some of the high vineyards of Bendigo and Ballarat. The wine region of north-east Victoria, renowned for its fortified wines, is not good Chardonnay country, unless, as with new vineyards on the slopes of the Australian Alps, it is planted at higher altitudes.

South Australia
Chardonnay is planted in every vinegrowing area of the state, from Clare to Coonawarra. But it is the cooler areas, such as Coonawarra and McLaren Vales, which are proving to be best for Chardonnay. Top wines come out of Coonawarra, far to the south of Adelaide. The Adelaide Hills, to the east of the city of Adelaide, also provide the chance for vineyard planting at higher altitudes. Just over the ridge the high Eden Valley has good Chardonnay, but the valley floor of the Barossa Valley tends to be too warm. Some vineyards in Clare are producing good quality grapes, despite the greater heat here.

Western Australia
The Margaret River and Mount Barker, in the south of the state, are the best areas, and many of the small wineries in these two areas are coming up with some of the country's best wines. Swan River, to the north of Perth, is generally too hot, and producers here buy their fruit from the southern areas.

Tasmania
There are small plantings of Chardonnay on the north coast at Piper's Brook, some of which is going into bottle-fermented sparkling wines.

PRODUCERS

ALLANDALE   **
Lovedale Road, Pokolbin, New South Wales

Total v'yds owned: 6ha (15 acres)

Re-founded on a late 19th-century farm in 1977, Allandale is a small estate which relies mainly on bought-in grapes. Reds and whites are made, but Chardonnay is the most popular wine. It tends to full, buttery tastes which can lack acidity and sometimes have too much oak, but which give a rich mouthful.

BALGOWNIE   ** → ***
Hermitage Road, Maiden Gully, Victoria

Total v'yds owned: 14ha (35 acres)
Chardonnay owned: 4.2ha (10 acres)
Chardonnay production: 19,000 bottles

Currently owned by Mildara (qv), Balgownie was founded in 1969 by Stuart Anderson, a pharmacist, who now acts as consultant to the winery. The vineyard, in the Bendigo district of

Victoria, is mainly planted with Chardonnay and Cabernet Sauvignon. Late spring frosts can be a hazard for Chardonnay, but the area enjoys a long ripening season which enhances the intensity of the fruit. Two Chardonnays are produced here. Premier Cuvée, is a blend of which only a small percentage is from Balgownie's fruit: the 87 is rich, sometimes too much so. The superior 88 Estate Chardonnay, made entirely from Balgownie fruit, is much subtler, with creamy, yeasty tastes and a light touch of wood – Limousin has been used here.

BANNOCKBURN VINEYARDS   **→
Midland Highway, Bannockburn, Victoria

Total v'yds owned: 18ha (44 acres)
Chardonnay owned: 4.5ha (11 acres)
Chardonnay production: 20,000 bottles

The success stories from this winery are wines using the Burgundy grapes Pinot Noir and Chardonnay. So it comes as no surprise to learn that winemaker Gary Farr spent some time at Domaine Dujac, and makes wines, as he says, "using traditional French methods". Founded in 1974, Bannockburn is in Geelong, in a cool growing area south-west of Melbourne. Earlier vintages of Chardonnay tended to be too oaky, but this has now been toned down, and the 88 Chardonnay (tasted in 1990) produced a fine, deliciously mature wine, which showed great elegance. The 86 Chardonnay, benefiting from an excellent vintage, had a more flowery, almost honeyed character.

JIM BARRY   *
Main North Road, Clare, South Australia

Total v'yds owned: 105ha (259 acres)
Chardonnay production: 300,000 bottles

Originally known as the St Clare Cellars, Jim Barry Wines is the home ground for one of the most respected names in Clare Valley. Jim Barry has been making wine in the area since 1947, and set up his own winery in 1968. It is one of the largest concerns in the valley, making 300,000 bottles a year, with Jim's son Mark as winemaker. The Chardonnay, which has prolonged skin contact during fermentation, is a distinctly unexciting wine: the 87 (tasted in 1990) I found characterless, almost antiseptic in its clinical taste.

BERESFORD WINES   *→
PO Box 93, McLaren Vale, South Australia

Total v'yds owned: none
Chardonnay production: 36,000 bottles

This newly established winery (founded in 1986) owns no land, but buys in grapes from the McLaren Vales, Padthaway and Coonawarra regions. The barrel-fermented Chardonnay stays on lees for nine months. This gives a pleasingly rich taste, but one designed for early drinking. The 87 (tasted in 1989) was in a spicy style, almost gingery, with well-integrated acidity, but was beginning to dry out when tasted in 1990. The 88 (also tasted in 1990) was forward, easy-drinking, fresh and clean, and with more fruit and less wood.

BERRI-RENMANO *
Berri, South Australia

Total v'yds owned: 8ha (20 acres)

Do not be fooled by the tiny size of the vineyard holding. This is one of the giants of the Australian industry, with 15 percent of total national production. It is a cooperative, relying on grapes from members, mainly in the Riverlands area of the Murray River, which is the source for much of the bag-in-box wines which are so popular with the Australian consumer. However, Berri-Renmano also produces some superior Chardonnays. In the Berri Estates range is a Barossa Valley Chardonnay: open, fruity, with some nuttiness and toasty ripeness – a wine for easy drinking. In the top Renmano Chairman's Selection range is a big, almost blowsy wine, definitely from very ripe fruit, deep in colour with plenty of oak – good, gutsy stuff.

BOWEN ESTATE * → **
PO Box 4B, Coonawarra, South Australia

Total v'yds owned: 24ha (59 acres)

A small, family-owned estate, founded in 1972, with vineyards at the southern end of the famous "terra rosa" (red soil) of Coonawarra. The vineyards are mainly planted with red wine varieties, but small amounts of a restrained, quite classically elegant Chardonnay are produced, which are, unusually, fermented and matured in German oak puncheons (casks).

BROKENWOOD ** →
McDonalds Road, Pokolbin, New South Wales

Total v'yds owned: 16ha (39 acres)

Celebrating its 20th birthday in 1990, this was one of the pioneers of the great influx of boutique wineries in the Hunter Valley. Founded as a part-time venture, it soon became a successful business, and has established a high reputation. Without doubt, the best wines are based on the Hunter's "natural" grapes, Shiraz and Semillon. The Chardonnay, which sometimes seems too spicy from the wood or, alternatively, too full of top-heavy tropical fruits, is well to the rich side of the spectrum, although the 88 (tasted in 1989) had well-integrated acidity.

BROWN BROTHERS → ***
Glenrowan-Myrtleford Road, Milawa, Victoria

Total v'yds owned: 160ha (395 acres)

An archetypal family firm, run by father John Brown and his four sons, who have expanded a small 100-year-old winery into one of the largest in Victoria. The winery is in Milawa, south of Rutherglen in north-eastern Victoria where there is also a vineyard, but fruit for their Chardonnays comes more from cooler vineyard areas, such as the King Valley to the west, and from the newly planted 800 m (2,624 ft) high Whitlands Vineyards in the foothills of the Australian Alps, which claims to be the highest vineyard in Australia. They make a range of Chardonnays: their basic wine is a blend of grapes from around Victoria, crisp, delicate, only slightly tinged with wood. The Family Selection range produces two Chardonnays: the riper style of the Victoria blend, with a touch of mangos, and the lighter, delicately perfumed King Valley wine. Whitlands wines are, as would be expected, lighter still, restrained, with a good shot of wood from barrel fermentation, quite green when young, but with good ageing potential.

CAPEL VALE   ***
Lot 5, Stirling Estate, Capel North West Road, Capel, Western Australia

Total v'yds owned: 32ha (79 acres)
Chardonnay owned: 14ha (35 acres)
Chardonnay production: 140,000 bottles

Capel Vale has Chardonnay vineyards in three Western Australia viticultural areas: Capel Vale home vineyard on the coast of Geographe Bay, some 250 km (155 miles) south of Perth; a little further south in the Margaret River area; and much further south in the Mount Barker area. While some grapes are bought-in for other wines, Chardonnay is made entirely from the Pratten family vineyards. Fermented partly in oak and partly in tank, the Chardonnay is richly endowed with tropical fruit flavours and considerable intensity, placing it firmly near the top in Western Australia's Chardonnay hierarchy.

CHITTERING ESTATE   ** →
Chittering Valley Road, Lower Chittering, Western Australia

Total v'yds owned: 25ha (62 acres)

It is early days for this showpiece estate north of Perth. Joint-owner Steven Schapera trained at the University of California, Davis, the leading California wine school, and has put together a state-of-the-art winery. The first release was in 1987, and Schapera is quoted as saying he hopes his Chardonnay will outshine all its competitors in Western Australia. I have not had a chance to taste the wine, but all reports are very promising.

COLDSTREAM HILLS   *** →
Lot 6, Maddens Lane, Coldstream, Yarra Valley, Victoria

Total v'yds owned: 15ha (37 acres)
Chardonnay owned: 6ha (15 acres)
Chardonnay production: 50,000 bottles

James Halliday is normally described as Australia's leading wine writer. But this lawyer turned wine enthusiast, who then turned to wineproducing, could now be called one of the country's leading winemakers. From his Coldstream Hills vineyard in the cool-climate Yarra Valley near Melbourne, he is producing Pinot Noir and Chardonnay which are both highly acclaimed. He makes two Chardonnays from Yarra fruit. The single vineyard 86 Lilydale Chardonnay was a well integrated wine, with just the right amount of acidity from the Yarra's cool growing climate. Even better was the barrel-fermented 88 Four Vineyards Chardonnay, the first vintage to come from Halliday's new winery, ripe with elegant citrus fruit, the hint of honey from the malolactic fermentation, and a very sophisticated balance between fruit and wood. New with the 89 vintage was a Chardonnay under the Halliday label using Padthaway fruit from South Australia.

DELATITE ** →
Stoney's Road, Mansfield, Victoria

Total v'yds owned: 24ha (59 acres)
Chardonnay owned: 2ha (5 acres)
Chardonnay production: 8,400 bottles

Delatite, an isolated cool-climate vineyard on the southern slopes of the Great Dividing Range, is perhaps better known for its Germanic grapes, Rhine Riesling and Gewurztraminer, than for its Chardonnay. They make two Chardonnays, both new to the range, one under the estate label, Delatite, and the other, from bought-in grapes, under the name of the family which owns the estate, Ritchie. The 87 Delatite estate wine (tasted in 1990) was quite delicate, with quite crisp acidity, already mature, but still attractively clean, and little hint of wood.

EVANS & TATE ** →
Swan Street, Henley Brook, Swan Valley, Western Australia

Total v'yds owned: 24ha (59 acres)

This firm, established in 1971, owns vineyards in two distinct viticultural areas. From the Swan Valley, it produces a highly regarded Shiraz; while from vineyards in the cooler Margaret River area, it produces, among other wines, two Chardonnays. The first Chardonnay, released in 1986, came some 12 years after the move into Margaret River and immediately attracted critical acclaim. The Margaret River Redwood Vineyard Chardonnay is the top wine, while the newly introduced Two Vineyards Chardonnay comes in at a lower price.

FOREST HILL ** → ***
PO Box 49, Mount Barker, Western Australia

Total v'yds owned: 22ha (54 acres)
Chardonnay owned: 3ha (7 acres)
Chardonnay production: 48,000 bottles

This was the pioneer vineyard of the cool-climate Mount Barker viticultural area, established on the Pearse family farm by the government's viticultural institute in 1965. Now run by the Pearses, for a period of seven years, the estate's wines were formerly known as Conti Forest Hill, after the then winemaker Paul Conti. The main production is of Cabernet Sauvignon, but there are plantings of Chardonnay which produce a cool, elegant, subtle wine, which matures well (the 86, tasted in 1990, was just reaching its peak), and exhibits good wood and acid balance.

ANDREW GARRETT ** →
Kangarilla Road, McLaren Vales, South Australia

Total v'yds owned: 200ha (500 acres)

For the McLaren Vales, home of boutique wineries, this is large-scale production, with a total of 720,000 bottles a year. The grapes come from three locations: one in the McLaren Vales, the second in Padthaway (both of which supply Chardonnay); the third source is in the Clare Valley. More Chardonnay is sourced in McLaren Vale. On occasions Garrett's Chardonnays can be light and quite zippy. At other times, such as in the good vintage of 86, they can be quite heavy with wood, after 11 months on lees in the barrel, and maturation in a mix of Limousin, Nevers and American oak, giving altogether too much spiciness for the fruit.

GROSSET WINES → ***
PO Box 64, Auburn, Clare Valley, South Australia

Total v'yds owned: 5ha (12 acres)
Chardonnay owned: None
Chardonnay production: 24,000 bottles

A small winery at the southern end of Clare which has quickly established a high reputation, especially for its Chardonnays which sells out fast. The winery was founded by Jeffrey Grosset in 1981, and the first Chardonnay vintage, using bought-in fruit, was 1983. He aims for a restrained style with his Chardonnay, reducing the use of pressings and the amount of extract, and allowing only a small amount of malolactic fermentation (about 5 percent). A small amount is also fermented in wood, but Grosset worries about the lack of control this introduces. The wine is certainly restrained in style, gentle. The 87 (tasted in 1990) already had a mature taste, more of a wine to go well with food than some richer Australian Chardonnays.

THOMAS HARDY * → ***
Chateau Reynella, Reynell Road, Reynella, South Australia

Total v'yds owned: 824ha (2,036 acres)

This is one of the giants of the Australian wine industry. It owns a number of companies and sells under a number of names: Chateau Reynella, Houghton, Stanley Leasingham and, of course, Hardys itself. Their Chardonnays come from vineyards in Padthaway and from around their historic headquarters at Chateau Reynella just south of Adelaide. They make a range of Chardonnays; the least expensive being in the attractively labelled Bird Series: clean, easy-to-drink wines, without wood characters, very fresh and zippy. Up one notch to the Nottage Hill Chardonnay, the 89 full of flavoursome fruit, ripe, tropical, very forward. The top of the range is the newly introduced Eileen Hardy Chardonnay (named after the original Thomas Hardy's mother, whose portrait is displayed on its appalling label), the 87 a hugely rich wine, bursting with fruit and wood, and very much in the grand style of Australian Chardonnays.

HEEMSKERK ∗∗
Pipers Brook, Tasmania

Total v'yds owned: 30ha (74 acres)

On the northern coast of Tasmania, this vineyard grows Pinot Noir and Cabernet Sauvignon as well as Chardonnay. More vineyards are now planted (50ha [125 acres] in the West Tamar area), and much of the production is destined for a joint-venture sparkling wine with Louis Roederer Champagne, whose first releases were in 1990.

HENSCHKE ∗∗→∗∗∗
Moculta Road, Keyneton, South Australia

Total v'yds owned: 81ha (200 acres)
Chardonnay production: 12,000 bottles

From vineyards situated high up in the Mount Lofty ranges to the south-east of the Barossa Valley come a range of stunning award-winning wines, the best certainly the reds, but with some good classy Chardonnay as well. New vineyards at 600m high in the Adelaide Hills produced their first Chardonnay in 1989. The Henschke family contrast a very traditional method of red wine production with state-of-the-art white wine technology. The 87 Eden Valley Chardonnay was light in style, with pleasing buttery wood overtones, but quite restrained in character. They also own vines in the Barossa Valley.

HILL-SMITH see YALUMBA

HOUGHTON ∗∗→
Dale Road, Middle Swan, Western Australia

Total v'yds owned: 144ha (356 acres)
Chardonnay owned: 16.7ha (41 acres)

This Western Australian outpost of the Hardy empire has a long and distinguished history (established 1836) and is now the home of a large range of wines, dominated by the immensely successful Houghton Supreme (known locally as white burgundy) which is one of Australia's best-selling white wines – and also happens to taste very good. It has a dash of Chardonnay in its predominantly Chenin Blanc blend. But Houghton's also make some good varietal Chardonnays: from the Moondah Brook vineyard, north of the Swan Valley, is an estate Chardonnay which matures well, in a biscuity style. In the Gold Reserve range, there is a wood-matured Chardonnay, which exhibits good tropical wood flavours.

HUNGERFORD HILL
*→ **

Broke Road, Pokolbin, New South Wales

Total v'yds owned: 110ha (272 acres)

A marketing-oriented company, with a wine village and restaurants at its winery in the Lower Hunter Valley, Hungerford Hill was founded in 1967. There are vineyards in the Lower Hunter and also in Coonawarra, South Australia. They make three Chardonnays: the Hungerford Hill Collection Chardonnay, which is designed for early maturation and tends to lack acidity; the Pokolbin Chardonnay, from grapes grown in the Hunter Valley vineyards; and a Show Reserve Chardonnay, richer, more buttery, but still rather middle of the road.

HUNTINGTON ESTATE
→ ***

Cassilis Road, Mudgee, New South Wales

Total v'yds owned: 40ha (99 acres)
Chardonnay owned: 4ha (10 acres)
Chardonnay production: 12,000 bottles

Reds are by far the most important element in the production mix of this Mudgee estate. Founded in 1968, it has a reputation for making good use of the high-quality fruit that Mudgee produces. However, they also make two Chardonnays, one in an absolutely clean fresh style, with no oak ageing, designed for early drinking; the other with some wood maturation, which repays bottle ageing. Both exhibit great fruit quality.

TIM KNAPPSTEIN
→ ***

2 Pioneer Avenue, Clare, South Australia

Total v'yds owned: 46ha (114 acres)
Chardonnay owned: 12ha (30 acres)
Chardonnay production: 60,000 bottles

Two separate areas provide grapes for this Clare-based winery: the Clare Valley itself and the Adelaide Hills. Most of the Chardonnay comes from the cool growing conditions of the Adelaide Hills. The Wolf Blass company (qv) has a majority shareholding in the winery, but the vineyards are still owned by the Knappstein family, and they still make the wine. While Rhine Riesling is the most important seller among the whites, there is also a good quantity of Chardonnay, produced using modern high-tech fermentation, as well as barrel fermentation. The 88 Chardonnay, produced from Clare fruit, and the fifth vintage the wine has produced, has delightful sweet appley overtones, is crisply ripe, and has only slight hints of wood (the mix is 70 percent French and 30 percent American). Tasted in 1990, it needed a little time to reach its peak.

KRONDORF
**

Krondorf Road, Tanunda, South Australia

Total v'yds owned: 24ha (59 acres)

Part of the giant Mildara (qv) group, Krondorf operates
independently from its Lyndoch winery in the Barossa Valley. It
was founded originally in the 1860s by German settlers. Fruit is
bought in from all over South Australia, but only two ranges of
wine are produced: a basic range and a Show Reserve or Limited
Release range. The Chardonnay in this range is a blend of
McLaren Vale, Eden Valley and Barossa Valley fruit, and is
partly barrel-fermented, with some high toast barrels giving
quite a pronounced taste. The 89 Limited Release, tasted 90,
was a quite forward style, full and quite fat, with definite tastes
of wood, and with some honeyed richness.

LAKE'S FOLLY ** →
Broke Road, Pokolbin, New South Wales

Total v'yds owned: 14ha (35 acres)
Chardonnay owned: 4ha (10 acres)
Chardonnay production: 20,000 bottles

Dr Max Lake was instrumental in bringing boutique wineries to
the Hunter Valley where he planted his first vineyard in 1963.
While his first wines were reds, he planted Chardonnay in 1969,
releasing his first vintage of this wine in 1974. The first vintages
rapidly accrued a fine reputation to the winery, and they still
command great respect. But recent tastings have disappointed
me: the 87 (tasted in 1990) had all the right characters, big fruit,
plenty of wood tastes, a shot of citric to balance the richness –
but lacked the extra dimension of style and individuality that
earlier vintages offered. Maybe that is the fate of pioneers –
everybody else is doing the same thing now.

LEEUWIN ESTATE *** → ****
Gnaroway Road, Margaret River, Western Australia

Total v'yds owned: 89ha (21 acres)
Chardonnay owned: 17ha (42 acres)
Chardonnay production: 36,000 bottles

One of the showpiece wineries of Western Australia, Leeuwin
Estate has built up a formidable reputation both for its reds and
its whites. The high-tech winery is complemented by a
restaurant and an open-air concert arena, as well as the usual
tasting room. Early advice for the success of the winery came
from the Californian Robert Mondavi, and there are similarities
in the very confident style not only of the winery, but also of the
wines. The Chardonnay is matured in new French wood, and
has rich buttery characters, the 84 (tasted in 1990) still full of
forward toasty tastes, maturing well and slowly for an
Australian Chardonnay with considerable complexity of fruit,
wood and acidity. The 86 was fresher, lighter, while the 85 is full,
weighty, but still excellently balanced, with top-class style.

PETER LEHMANN **
Para Road, Tanunda, South Australia

Vineyards owned: none

The first release of a Chardonnay from this winemaker (who buys in grapes principally from Barossa Valley growers) was in 1988. Already tasting mature in 1990, with only a hint of wood, it also had petrolly tastes, which gave it an almost Semillon character.

LINDEMANS ** →
McDonalds Road, Pokolbin, New South Wales

Total v'yds owned: 1,010ha (2,500 acres)

Sold to the Penfolds group (qv) two years ago, Lindemans was already one of the three largest producers in the country in the days when it was owned by American tobacco firm Philip Morris. From its original vineyard region in the Hunter Valley, it has expanded to extensive properties in Coonawarra, Padthaway (both in South Australia) and at Mildura in Victoria. Much of the production is of inexpensive (and on average ordinary) cask wines and what they like to call "beverage wines" (in Australian terms, a wine that is drunk fast, in large quantities and without much thought). There are, however, some finer varietal wines, of which the very best are single vineyard reds, but which also include the soft, unoaky Premium Selection Chardonnay, the South East Australian Chardonnay (made using blends of fruit from South Australia and Victoria) and, further up the range, the Padthaway Chardonnay, which does have some wood character, and which has much of the right character of cool-climate fruit.

GEOFF MERRILL ***
Mount Hurtle Winery, Reynella, South Australia

Total v'yds owned: 20ha (49 acres)
Chardonnay production: 72,000 bottles

Geoff Merrill, former winemaker for nearby Chateau Reynella, now runs an acclaimed winery at Mount Hurtle in the Adelaide Hills. He makes two ranges of wine: the lesser Mount Hurtle range, and the top Geoff Merrill label, which includes a Chardonnay. Until new plantings made in 1990 come on stream, most of the fruit is bought in, either from McLaren Vale or the Barossa Valley. Typically, the 86 Chardonnay had 81 percent McLaren Vale fruit and 19 percent Barossa. The style – as in the 85 – is full of strongly toasty wood, overrestrained, elegant fruit and highly – but attractively – perfumed flavours. This is top-quality winemaking.

MILDARA * → **
Wentworth Road, Merbein, Mildura, Victoria

Total v'yds owned: 254ha (627 acres)

Mildara, which also owns Krondorf in South Australia and the Morton Estate in New Zealand, is one of the larger Australian producers. The main plant is in the Riverlands region of Victoria, from where its bulk wines come. But in 1955 purchases of land in Coonawarra meant the producer could make premium varietals. In Chardonnay, these include Jamiesons Run, orginally a blended wine, now with a high proportion of Chardonnay, barrel fermentation, six months in wood, giving – as in the 89 – an austere, quite firm, almost tannic style of wine, green when young and repaying some bottle ageing. Church Hill, from Murray River vineyards, is in a fresh, light, crisp style, with no hint of wood.

MONTROSE →***
Henry Lawson Drive, Mudgee, New South Wales

Total v'yds owned: 113ha *(279 acres)*
Chardonnay owned: 22ha *(54 acres)*
Chardonnay production: 240,000 bottles

As can be seen from the figures above, Chardonnay is an important part of the production at this Mudgee winery, now incorporated - along with the Wyndhams wineries in the Hunter Valley – into the giant Orlando group. Chardonnay is fermented in a mix of new French wood or in stainless steel at low temperatures, to make two wines. The basic Chardonnay has good wood tastes, the 86 was perfumed and softly elegant, the 87 lighter and more citric. The 89 Chardonnay, very rich, with weighty flavours, included fruit that would normally be used in the Reserve Chardonnay from the Stoney Creek Vineyard: the 86 Reserve was high in alcohol, peppery, needing four to five years' bottle ageing after wood fermentation.

MOSS WOOD ESTATE *→**
Metricup Road, Willyabrup, Western Australia

Total v'yds owned: 8.5ha *(21 acres)*
Chardonnay owned: 1.3ha *(3 acres)*
Chardonnay production: 4,200 bottles

This Margaret River winery, founded in 1969 and now owned by the Mugfords, aims for high quality, and certainly, with its reds, it succeeds. With its white Semillon, too, it makes some first-rate wines. However, Chardonnay has so far been more variable: the 86 seemed too oaky to support the fruit, while, conversely, the 87 was rather too thin and light, even raw. The fermentation of the wines is finished in cask, and they spend up to nine months in wood on the lees.

MOUNTADAM →***
High Eden Ridge, Eden Valley, South Australia

Total v'yds owned: 28ha *(69.18 acres)*
Chardonnay owned: 18ha *(44 acres)*

It shows how recently Chardonnay arrived in South Australia that this winery, founded in 1972, can claim to have been the first to plant the variety in the state. Owner Adam Wynn, of the family that used to own Wynn's in Coonawarra, trained in France and uses French vinification techniques, a minimum of filtration, barrel fermentation of Chardonnay, and maturation in Tronçais oak. In fact, two Chardonnays are produced:

Mountadam, which comes from the estate around the winery in the Adelaide Hills, and the less expensive "David Wynn" which is made from bought-in Eden Valley grapes.

ORLANDO   ** → ****

Rowland Flat, via Tanunda, South Australia

Orlando is big – 50 million litres of wine a year – but in the vast range of wines (which includes the top-selling Jacobs Creek range), it manages to make some of Australia's best Chardonnays. Now owned by the Pernod Ricard group of France, it has itself recently expanded in Australia by taking over Wyndham Estates in New South Wales. However, Orlando's production base is in the Barossa Valley, where much of its fruit comes from. The Chardonnay-based wines include the white Jacobs Creek, which is a blend of Semillon and Chardonnay, and is certainly one of the best value Australian wines around. Higher up the tree, are two wines which are blends of fruit from Victoria and South Australia: Rowland Flat (normally abbreviated to RF) is in a fresh, easy drinking style, without any obvious oak flavours (although with some oak fermentation). St Hilary, on the other hand, is classy stuff, the 86 (tasted in 1990) maturing well, full of lychees and tropical flavours, spicy, slightly nutty, ripe and enjoyably so. The top Chardonnay, Gramp's (named after the old name of the name, G. Gramp & Sons) uses Barossa fruit, a restrained, elegant wine, very stylish both in taste and bottle presentation, and right up at the top in the Australian Chardonnay league.

PENFOLDS   **

Nuriootpa, Barossa Valley, South Australia

The biggest wine company in Australia, owning Wynns (qv). Lindemans (qv), Kaiserstuhl, Tollana, Seaview and Tulloch. It also makes Australia's best red wine – Grange Hermitage (known in Europe simply as Grange), and a whole cluster of reds of high quality, as well as fortifieds which keep it in the top league in that area. In all this, whites tend to be forgotten, but Penfolds manages to produce some well regarded Chardonnays as well. The 86, made from a blend of Clare and Barossa fruit, was spicy, perhaps lacking a little acidity, but attractively drinkable; the 87, too, had a strong spicy element, and was rich and tropical in taste.

PETALUMA   → ****

Lot 6, Spring Gully Road, Piccadilly, South Australia

Total v'yds owned:	93ha (230 acres)
Chardonnay owned:	48ha (118 acres)

Brian Croser, managing director and shareholder in Petaluma winery, is one of the seminal influences in Australian Chardonnay production. Believing that wines are made in the vineyard *and* in the winery, and by using a mix of high tech and minimum interference with the juice (low sulphur levels through high degrees of cleanliness), he has shown other Australian producers how it can be done. It is obvious from the vineyard figures that Chardonnay features high in the list of wines made at Petaluma. And it has become even more important because of a joint venture with Bollinger to make a sparkling wine – called Croser Sparkling – made from Pinot Noir and Chardonnay. Still Chardonnays come from fruit grown in Clare Valley, in the Adelaide Hills and in Coonawarra. The 87, with half Clare and half Adelaide Hills fruit, is concentrated, homing in on very direct fruit tastes, hinting at baked apples, and needing time to mature. Earlier vintages have been bigger and more oaky: 85, oaky and citrusy, again needing time to mature; 83 appley and peachy using Coonawarra fruit; 82 much bigger and heavier using fruit from New South Wales as well as South Australia.

PETERSON   **→***
Mount View Road, Mount View, New South Wales

Total v'yds owned: 16ha (39 acres)

A small family winery in the Hunter Valley, making soft Chardonnay that matures well, and has well balanced citric tones. The 84 (tasted in 1987) was subtle, with a good degree of maturity; the 87 (tasted in 1990) suggested a longer maturation span, with firm fruit, hints of wood, and a weighty taste.

PIPERS BROOK   **
Pipers Brook, Tasmania

Total v'yds owned: 12ha (30 acres)
Chardonnay owned: 2.4ha (6 acres)
Chardonnay production: 12,000 bottles

The closely spaced vines of the Pipers Brook vineyard are more reminiscent of Europe than Australia. Come to that, so is the cool climate which lends itself to quite steely Chardonnays, with decently high acid levels, and good bottle ageing. A new plan is to create another vineyard for Chardonnay and Pinot Noir and sell the wines under the Pellion label: I have yet to taste the results.

ROSEMOUNT ESTATE   **→***
Rosemount Road, Denman, New South Wales

Total v'yds owned: 404ha (999 acres)

For many wine drinkers outside Australia, Rosemount was for quite a while the essential Australian Chardonnay, such was its marketing success (and the quality of the wines). Rosemount still is principally a Chardonnay producer, from its vineyards in the Upper Hunter Valley, while its Coonawarra (South Australia) vineyards are devoted to Cabernet Sauvignon. There is quite a range of Chardonnays produced. The basic wine is the Diamond Label which is mainly Semillon with a top-up of Chardonnay. The basic Chardonnay is in a fresh style, not for ageing, but with light, agreeable drinkability. The estate's reputation was built on its Show Reserves, which still have plenty of wood and warm tastes, even if they are more restrained than they used to be. Top of the range are the single estate Chardonnays, all from the Upper Hunter: the 87 Roxburgh, oaky rich, heavily ripe, but, for some, dominated too much by wood tastes; and the more restrained (and therefore more drinkable) Giants Creek, the 87 with quite high toast tastes, spicy, needing plenty of bottle age – unlike most of the Rosemount wines – but with good underlying fruit.

THE ROTHBURY ESTATE   ***→
Broke Road, Pokolbin, New South Wales

Total v'yds owned: 242ha (600 acres)

The Rothbury Estate was founded in 1969 by one of the greats of Australian wine, Len Evans, and a group of investors. It was originally designed as a red wine winery, but the collapse of the Australian red wine market in the late 1970s meant a rapid shift to white wines, for which it is almost more famous than for its reds. The winery owns a number of vineyards in the Hunter Valley and in the Upper Hunter at Denman, as well as a vineyard at Cowra, west of Sydney. Chardonnay comes from the Brokenback and Herlstone vineyards in the Lower Hunter, Denman Estate and Cowra. Both a standard Chardonnay and a reserve are made, the standard wine is made for immediate drinking, the Reserve, fermented and matured in new oak, gold in colour and spicy to taste, is designed for bottle ageing, and has gained a high reputation for the estate.

ROUGE HOMME   **→
Naracoorte Road, Coonawarra, South Australia

Total v'yds owned: 130ha (320 acres)

Founded by Bill Redman (hence the pun in the name) in 1908, this Coonawarra estate producer is now owned by the Lindeman group (qv) – and hence by Penfolds (qv). While chiefly renowned for its Coonawarra reds, a Chardonnay is also produced, the 87 (tasted in 1990) a soft, unobtrusive wine, with elegance and restrained acidity.

SALTRAM   ***→****
PO Box 321, Angaston, South Australia

Total v'yds owned: 28ha (69 acres)
Chardonnay owned: 7ha (17 acres)

Saltram, owned by the North American drinks giant Seagram, is one of the Barossa Valley's oldest producers, founded in 1859. It buys in the bulk of its grapes from a wide variety of sources - the Hunter Valley, Griffith, Coonawarra, Langhorne Creek, McLaren Vale and the Barossa itself. Its wines go from the inexpensive Hazelwood range, through Saltram varietals (wines named after a grape variety) and the top flight Pinnacle Range. However, Saltram quite rightly regards its Chardonnays as its finest wines: the South East Australian Chardonnay, a blend of Barossa and Riverina fruit with its attractive baked-apple nose, fresh and pleasantly weighty; and the top quality Mamre Brook Chardonnay, made from a blend of South Australian fruit, the

87 deep in colour, with a subtle, complex use of wood, creamy to taste, and with the ability to age well. One of the country's top Chardonnays.

TARRAWARRA VINEYARDS   ****
Healesville Road, Yarra Glen, Victoria

Total v'yds owned: 7.3ha (18 acres)
Chardonnay owned: 4.7ha (12 acres)
Chardonnay production: 50,000 bottles

This newcomer to the Yarra Valley made a spectacular start with its 1986 Chardonnay which has now been joined by the other success story of the region, a Pinot Noir. The estate (its name means meandering river) on the northern slopes of the Yarra, is run organically and, in the state-of-the-art winery, the wines are made with minimum interference or use of sulphur dioxide. The Chardonnay has little skin contact, barrel fermentation, extended contact on the lees for greater intensity of flavour, and a partial malolactic fermentation (a product of the cool climate conditions of the Yarra Valley). The results are superb: the 86, when first released in 88, was harmonious, rich, rounded, soft, with excellent wood balance, needing time in the bottle: later, in 89, it was revealing rich, creamy but delicate flavours in a classic, elegant style. The 87, tasted in cask in 1988, despite its obvious wood flavours, still showed great fruit balance and promised well.

TISDALL   **→
Cornelia Creek Road, Echuca, Victoria

Total v'yds owned: 130ha (321 acres)

For Victoria, this is large-scale winemaking. But the Tisdalls have rapidly established a reputation for quality as well as quantity since they released their first wines from the 1979 vintage. They have two vineyards, both of which grow Chardonnay: one, called Rosbercon, near the winery at Echuca in the Victorian Riverlands, the other, the Mount Helen Vineyard, in the ideal cool-climate growing conditions of the Strathbogie Ranges in Central Victoria. From the Mount Helen Vineyard comes the premium Chardonnay, the 83 a rich, buttery wine, using traditional French techniques, the 84 strongly toasty, with plenty of citric flavours, the 86 again oaky, both needing time to bring the fruit into balance.

TYRRELL'S   **→***
Broke Road, Pokolbin, New South Wales

Total v'yds owned: 152ha (375 acres)
Chardonnay owned: 31ha (77 acres)

The Tyrrells have been growing grapes in the Hunter Valley since 1858, and the current members of the family running the winery, Murray (known by himself and others as "the mouth of the Hunter") and his son Bruce, continue to work on traditional lines, making a range which includes the best-selling Long Flat red and white (from the vineyard of the same name), in the shadows of the Brokenback Range. Murray Tyrrell was among the first to plant Chardonnay in the Hunter Valley, and his Vat 47 Chardonnay continues to be one of the best whites they make. This is fermented in a mix of stainless steel and old oak casks, before being put into new French oak to finish fermentation and to mature for around six months. The less expensive unoaked Chardonnay is for easy drinking, floral and clean, without much excitement. The 87 Vat 47 Chardonnay was full of fat, toasty fruit and wood tastes, very ripe in a full-bodied style; the 84 was leaner, crisper, perhaps more elegant.

SIMON WHITLAM   ***→
Wollombi Brook Vineyard, Broke Road, Broke, New South Wales

Total v'yds owned: 8ha (20 acres)

This small Hunter Valley estate, founded only in 1982, has already made a big name for itself. The wines are blockbusters in the best sense, receiving rave reviews from day one. The 87 Chardonnay, ranking high in the league table of Australian Chardonnays, is full of very rich fruit and bags of wood tastes, a big wine with sufficient hugely ripe tropical fruit to stand up to the toasty, spicy wood.

WIRRA WIRRA   *→**
McMurtrie Road, McLaren Vale, South Australia

Total v'yds owned: 73ha (180 acres)

This winery, founded in 1969, using high-tech equipment inspired by Brian Croser at Petaluma (qv), makes Chardonnay from McLaren Vale grapes. The style tends to be rather too wood-dominated when young, the 86 Chardonnay definitely needing more fruit when tasted in 88, but promising to soften out to a more toasty/fruity taste given time in bottle (when tasted in 1990, it was well mature).

WOLF BLASS   **→***
Bilyara Vineyards, 97 Sturt Highway, Nuriootpa, South Australia

---

Total v'yds owned: 288ha (711 acres)

Wolf Blass, the man, is one of the most visible figures in the Australian wine industry. Sporting his motif of a bow tie, he has gone about marketing his wines with flair and skill. Until recently, all the wines were made from grapes and juice which were bought in and blended at the Barossa Valley winery. Now with estates in Clare Valley (the former Quelltaler) the company is able to source up to 30 percent of its needs from its own vineyards. It also has a majority share in Tim Knappstein (qv). Two premium Chardonnays are in the range: the 87, from Clare Valley fruit, was sweet both from new wood and very ripe fruit, and rather too heavy. The Barrel Fermented Chardonnay 84, from McLaren Vale fruit, is heavily spicy from its time in German and American wood, very smoky, and, to my mind, too much of a good thing. The wines are commercial and sell well in Australia.

WOODSTOCK   *→
Douglas Gully Road, McLaren Flat, South Australia

Total vineyards owned: 24ha (59 acres)
Chardonnay owned: 5ha (12 acres)

The original estate was founded in 1859, but the present
vineyards started life in 1974, with the first wines sold under the
Woodstock label in 1982. A Chardonnay is made from McLaren
Vale fruit. It is stainless-steel fermented and then matured in
new oak for three months. The 87 (tasted in 1990) was quite
citric, with few obvious wood tastes, coupled with a curious
linseed oil flavour which was slightly off-putting. I have heard
better reports than this, however.

WYNNS   ***→****
Memorial Drive, Coonawarra, South Australia
Although part of the Penfold group (qv), Wynns is still run as a
separate business, concentrating very much on its original
vineyards in the Coonawarra, of which Wynns was a pioneer.
The holdings amount to around one third of the total vineyards
on the famous *terra rossa* soil. I have always been a fan of Wynns
Chardonnays, very rich, very buttery, but always with the
balanced elegance that characterizes so much Coonawarra
fruit. The 87, for instance (tasted in 1989) had all the hallmarks,
with its big tropical fruit tastes, plenty of new wood, delightfully
over the top in some ways, and yet with a tinge of acidity and
class that stopped it being crude or clumsy. The 86 had a
cinnammon, spicy character, certainly fat, perhaps lacking a little
of the acid edge, but still bursting with rich fruit character.

CHATEAU XANADU   **→***
Off Wallcliffe Road, Margaret River, Western Australia

Total v'yds owned: 20ha (49 acres)

The name, of course, comes from Coleridge's poem of Kubla
Khan, and reveals considerable literary interests on the part of
the owners, both doctors. The Chardonnay from this southern
Margaret River vineyard is fermented in small oak barrels and
then matured in oak before bottling. Very tropical in flavour,
with peach and lychee tastes, the 86 was perhaps too fat, and
without the weight and style of the finer 87. But both are serious
wines which command respect.

YALUMBA   →***
Eden Valley Road, Angaston, South Australia

Total v'yds owned: 470ha (1,200 acres)

Under this heading are also included wines made under the Hill-
Smith Estate and Hill-Smith labels, as well as Heggies Vineyard
and Pewsey Vale. They are all part of S. Smith & Son, and are run
by the Hill-Smith family who own vineyards mainly in the South
Australian Riverlands, and in the Barossa and Eden Valleys of
South Australia, as well as some at high altitudes (such as
Heggies) in the nearby Adelaide Hills. The range of Chardon-

nays includes wines like the 87 Yalumba Chardonnay, all butterscotch and soft fruit, with a touch of wood. The 86 Hill-Smith Estate Chardonnay was more tropical/melony, again soft, with some toast from the new wood, but a gentle style of wine. Heggies Vineyard Chardonnay, grown at 500m (1,640 ft) above sea level, is a crisper style, green when young, with good wood flavours. The Hill-Smiths also own the Nautilus Vineyard in North Island, New Zealand: I have not had a chance to taste the Chardonnay produced there.

YARRA BURN →**
Settlement Road, Yarra Junction, Victoria

Total v'yds owned: 10ha (25 acres)
Chardonnay owned: 3.2ha (8 acres)

At the eastern end of the Yarra Valley, the view ringed by mountains, the Fyffes certainly have the most beautiful of the Yarra vineyards, along with a popular restaurant in which to taste the wines. While some of their Chardonnay comes from their own vineyard, other fruit is purchased from neighbouring properties. Their Chardonnay, fermented in stainless steel and matured in German oak, is in a cool, crisp style, the 87 very fragrant and citrusy, with only a slight peppery wood taste.

YARRA YERING **→
Briarty Road, via Coldstream, Victoria

Total v'yds owned: 16ha (39 acres)
Chardonnay owned: 1.2ha (3 acres)

Small production though it is, Yarra Yering's Chardonnay pioneered much of what has subsequently happened in the Yarra Valley. Founded in 1969, Dr Bailey Carrodus's vineyard led the revival of the valley as a cool-climate vineyard area of great importance. His Chardonnay, like all his wines, is fermented in small steel-lined mobile tanks, and then aged in new oak.

New Zealand

Probably because there is much greater international competition, Chardonnay from New Zealand has not had the instant worldwide media attention of Sauvignon Blanc. But producers are now making world class Chardonnays that reveal the same quality and direct tastes that characterize New Zealand Sauvignons. And because they are producing Chardonnay in most parts of the country – unlike Sauvignon Blanc whose main success has been restricted to the Marlborough area – there is a wide variety of styles that makes their study particularly worthwhile.

Chardonnay is now the second most widely planted vine in New Zealand (Müller-Thurgau is first, Cabernet Sauvignon is third). And despite a rapid increase in the decade from 1979 it is set to become even more dominant in the 1990s. Huge plantings, particularly in Marlborough, suggest that, from a distinct shortage in the late 1980s as worldwide demand outstripped supply, there is the real risk of a glut. While this should help consumers in the short term, by cutting prices, the long term is not necessarily good either for producers or wine drinkers. Many of the plantings are not being made by the wine companies but by contract growers, often without firm contracts, who are banking on an ever-increasing market.

THE CHARDONNAY ARRIVES

As with many of the classic varieties, the original clones of Chardonnay that arrived in New Zealand in the 1920s were quite unsuitable for the climate and growing conditions. They suffered from one of Chardonnay's principal enemies, the leaf-roll virus, and few plantings were made. The problem persisted right into the 1980s, and only from 1982 onward did new clones from Burgundy and California find their way into the vineyards. That means that a lot of Chardonnay in older vineyards is still causing problems, which will only be eradicated by their removal and replacement.

MAKING CHARDONNAY

Wood – generally French, and very often Nevers – is rarely far from New Zealand Chardonnays. While less expensive wines are generally stainless-steel fermented, many of the top reserve wines are barrel-fermented with long lees contact (to intensify flavour) and then have barrel maturation for anything up to a year. There is great controversy among producers about malolactic fermentation, some advocating it wholeheartedly, others wishing to preserve the acidity of the fruit. Of course, both styles are viable, and the pleasure is in seeing the results from each school of thought.

In fact, with its cooler climate vineyards and naturally higher acids and generally lighter styles, New Zealand Chardonnay is giving its firm rival, Australian Chardonnay, a very close run for its money. I would be hard put to say which I prefer. The

Australians have not yet started buying Chardonnay from New Zealand (they are buying Sauvignon Blanc), but they may easily decide that its qualities are just what their wines need.

CHARDONNAY VINEYARDS

While Chardonnay is found as far north as Kumeu and as far south as the Canterbury Plains, its main plantings are in three areas.

Gisborne. Until two years ago the largest viticultural area, the rich soils of Poverty Bay lend themselves to prolific Chardonnay production. Apart from one or two single vineyard wines, Gisborne tends to be the source of the less expensive Chardonnays, which have fatness without such great depth of character.

Hawke's Bay. This is the home of the rich, buttery, barrel-fermented, barrel-matured wines. At least two of New Zealand's best Chardonnays come from vineyards here, as do many of the top wines of the North Island wineries, either based in Hawke's Bay or in Auckland. Plantings have increased here, and have been pushed inland as good well-drained soil becomes scarce around the margins of the coastal plain.

Marlborough. First planted in 1973, Marlborough is now the source of the largest quantity of Chardonnay. From here come the piercingly fruit wines, generally not too heavily tempered with wood, that have been the success story of New Zealand in the past decade. Marlborough Chardonnays fit the bill perfectly, and invariably give the most glorious drinking pleasure. Vast new plantings, coming on stream from 1990 onward, will increase the importance of Chardonnay to the region.

Other areas. One of the smaller areas, Martinborough in the Wairarapa, has proved its potential for Chardonnay, and promises well.

North Island

PRODUCERS

BABICH   → ***
Babich Road, Henderson, Auckland, North Island

Total v'yds owned: 42ha (104 acres)
Chardonnay owned: 13ha (32 acres)

One (and one of the largest) of the group of wineries and vineyards founded by Dalmatian settlers in the early part of this century. It is still controlled by the Babich family, with Peter running vineyards and administration, and brother Joe running the winery. They have vineyards both in Henderson itself (one of the few areas still under vine in this suburb of Auckland) and a half share of the Irongate vineyard in Hawke's Bay. Other fruit is bought in from Gisborne and Hawke's Bay. They make three Chardonnays, all using Hawke's Bay fruit. The standard Chardonnay tends to softness, ripeness and is perhaps slightly unfocused, needing a little more acidity: certainly true of the 1988. The Stopbank Chardonnay 89, had good malo character

(28 percent goes through malolactic), was fermented in barrel (30 percent new wood) and matured in cask for four months. The flagship Chardonnay is from the Irongate vineyard, a big, toasty wine, full of flavour, full of ripe fruit, but with just the right amount of leanness to stop it going over the top.

COOPERS CREEK   ***
Main North Road, Huapai, Auckland, North Island

Total v'yds owned: 11ha (27 acres)
Chardonnay owned: 5ha (12 acres)
Chardonnay production: 3,000 bottles

Coopers Creek takes its name from a local river which flows near the winery north of Auckland. There is a small vineyard here, producing red wines, but the grapes for the Chardonnays are grown in Hawke's Bay. The winery, constructed in 1981 by owner Andrew Hendry and partner Randy Weaver, houses a restaurant as well as winery facilities. Of the white wine production here, Chardonnays are probably the stars. There are two: Hawke's Bay Chardonnay, fermented in stainless steel after extended skin contact, producing quite a dry, steely style of wine. And the single vineyard Swamp Road Chardonnay (named accurately enough, after the road that runs past the Hawke's Bay vineyard) is barrel-fermented in Nevers oak, and has lees contact before oak maturation. For many, this is classic New Zealand Chardonnay: rich, succulent, maturing well (the 87, drunk in 1990, was just softening nicely) and with mouthfilling fruit, coupled with a delicious cutting edge of acidity.

CORBANS & COOKS   **→
Henderson, Auckland, North Island

Total v'yds owned: 323ha (800 acres)

A series of complicated mergers in the mid-1980s left Corbans Wines as the owner of Cooks & McWilliams New Zealand. In turn, Corbans is owned by Australian financier Ron Brierley. The two main constituents in the group, Corbans and Cooks, found themselves with vineyards in Gisborne, Hawke's Bay and more recently in Marlborough, with the central winery in Auckland. The Cooks Chardonnay comes from Hawke's Bay fruit, and is one of the best of the middle-price Chardonnays coming out of New Zealand: flavoursome, not top heavy with wood, and with a good citric touch. Corbans' Stoneleigh Vineyard in Marlborough, on soil that resembles the huge pebbles of Châteauneuf-du-Pape in France, was first planted in 1980, using a narrow canopy method of training. It now makes a light, fresh, direct tasting Chardonnay which loses the character of heavy toast with a couple of years' bottle ageing. Stoneleigh also supplies fruit to Wolf Blass (qv) in Australia.

DELEGAT'S   ***→
Hepburn Road, Henderson, Auckland

Total v'yds owned and managed: 40ha (99 acres)

In the middle of suburban Auckland, the Delegat's winery harks back to the time when this was still countryside. Founded in 1923 by a Yugoslav immigrant, Nick Delegat, the firm is still run by the family, although local wine wholesaler Wilson Neill is now a substantial shareholder. Delegat's owns or manages land in Gisborne, Hawke's Bay and, from 1990, will also be taking fruit from Marlborough. The bulk of production is of white wines, and under the former winemaker John Hancock (now at Morton Estate – qv), the firm built a reputation for Chardonnays, which is being maintained by new winemaker Brent Marris. The two Chardonnays both come from Hawke's Bay fruit, and are a mix of stainless steel and barrel fermentation. The standard wine is full and fat, but without a dominant oak taste and with some softening from malolactic fermentation. The top of the range Proprietor's Reserve, of which only 2,000 cases are made each year, spends nine months in oak, giving a wine with a golden colour and a soft, rich, almost sweet style.

KUMEU RIVER ** → ****
2 Highway 16, Kumeu, Auckland, North Island

Total v'yds owned: 20ha (49 acres)
Chardonnay owned: 3.6ha (9 acres)

The Brajkovich family, headed by father Mate and eldest son Michael (who became New Zealand's first Master of Wine), run this winery north of Auckland. Unusually, they source all their fruit from the local Kumeu area (most other wineries in the Auckland region buy fruit mainly from other North Island vineyard areas). They make three ranges of wines: the San Marino is an inexpensive brand, sold mainly at the winery shop; Brajkovich is in the middle-price bracket and at the top is the Kumeu River label. There are Chardonnays under both the Brajkovich and Kumeu River names. The Kumeu River wine is gently pressed to break open the grapes (a technique used in champagne-making) before being fermented in a mix of stainless steel and barrels. There is 100 percent malolactic fermentation, and maturation in Nevers oak. The result, as in the 89, is a soft, creamy, spicy wine which has a very appetising flavour and delicious, if soft, fruit. The wines mature well.

MARTINBOROUGH VINEYARDS → ****
PO Box 85, Princess Street, Martinborough, North Island

Total v'yds owned: 16ha (39 acres)
Chardonnay owned: 7ha (17 acres)
Chardonnay production: 24,000 bottles

Only founded in 1980, Martinborough Vineyards has rapidly put itself and its region (technically named the Wairarapa, but generally called after the town of Martinborough) on the map, principally for Pinot Noir, but also for high-quality Chardonnay. Winemaker Larry McKenna, another Australian and Roseworthy graduate in the New Zealand industry, is experimenting with different styles and toasts of French wood, including Vosges and Allier, and working out the ideal blends. The wines, certainly the 89 tasted nine months after harvest, are broad, spicy, very ripe, with quite rich toasty tastes and excellent fruit flavours, plus a good streak of acidity to cut through the richness. They are big wines, but ones which will age.

MATUA VALLEY **
PO Box 100, Kumeu, Auckland, North Island

Total v'yds owned: 28ha (69 acres)

Founded and run by the Spence brothers, Ross and Bill, this winery has a growing reputation for its white wines. They source fruit for the Chardonnays from a number of different areas – in Marlborough, Hawke's Bay and Gisborne – as well as from the vineyard by the winery. The top Chardonnay is the Judd Estate, from a vineyard in Gisborne. The wine is fermented in Nevers oak barrels, and 25 percent goes through malolactic fermentation before wood maturation on its lees for two months. It is intended to be drunk comparatively young, and the 89, tasted at the end of that year, showed good richness and toast with well-developed fruit flavours. However, in keeping with the Spences' philosophy, this is designed very much as wine which can partner food – and which can be drunk in their vineyard restaurant. They also make a Gisborne Estate blend, which also sees Nevers oak, but is in a tighter, more austere style.

MONTANA ** →
PO Box 18293, Glen Innes, Auckland, North Island

Total v'yds owned: 808ha (2,000 acres)

The largest New Zealand wine producer, Montana was the pioneer of the Marlborough vineyards back in 1973, and is still by far the largest landowner in the region with 480ha (1,186 acres). But it also owns vineyards in Hawke's Bay (with greatly increased planting over the past two to three years) and in Gisborne. Despite this vast amount of land, it still needs to buy in two-thirds of its requirements from other growers. Subsidiary (if large) wineries in Gisborne and Marlborough make the wines which are finished and bottled in the group headquarters in Auckland. While Montana's size is certainly impressive, equally so is the quality of the wines it makes. The Marlborough Valley Chardonnay, which matures for 12 months in French oak, has long skin contact before fermentation, which gives an intense taste, and very keen, fresh fruit. With age, these wines take on some of the asparagus character of old Sauvignons – appropriately enough, given Marlborough's (and Montana's) reputation for this variety. Other Chardonnays come from Gisborne and from the single vineyard Kaituna Hills in Marlborough. While not in the very top league of Chardonnays, these are always reliable, light, fresh styles, which are most enjoyable to drink.

MORTON ESTATE ****
RD2, Kati Kati, Bay of Plenty, North Island

Total v'yds owned: 105ha (259 acres)
Chardonnay owned: 48ha (118 acres)

Chardonnay production: 174,000 bottles

The Morton Estate winery may be remote from most vineyard areas, but it is certainly not out of the way, situated on the main road between Tauranga and Auckland, and with the added attraction of a restaurant. The grapes come from vineyards in the Bay of Plenty and from Hawke's Bay. From the 1990 harvest, new plantations of 80ha (198 acres) in Hawke's Bay will be yielding for the first time. Winemaker John Hancock, like so many in the New Zealand industry an Australian, is a king of Chardonnay, and reckons he makes about 10 percent of the country's total Chardonnay production. What he makes is of world-class quality. Hancock enjoys the effects of wood on his Chardonnays, and makes up his final blends from a mix of wines with and without barrel fermentation and from a range of different French woods. He produces two Chardonnays. The White (actually grey/silver) Label is by far the larger production, mainly tank-fermented, with about 20 percent barrel fermentation, and then aged in wood for six months. The top Chardonnay is the Black Label, made from Hawke's Bay fruit with 100 percent barrel fermentation, 30 percent malolactic, giving a rich, golden-coloured wine, full of complexities from wood toasty tastes and very high-quality fruit. Chardonnay also forms part of the blend for a bottle-fermented sparkling wine.

NGATARAWA   →**

Ngatarawa Road, Bridge Pa, Hastings, Hawke's Bay, North Island

Total vineyard area: 12ha (30 acres)

Its name meaning, possibly – as winemaker Alwyn Corban puts it - between the ridge in Maori, Ngatarawa is a vineyard which is a small part of a 2,400ha (5,930 acres) sheep station owned by the Glazebrook family who are Corban's partners in this project. Given his pedigree as one of the Corban family who used to own one of New Zealand's largest wine companies, and his impressive academic record, people expect great things of Alwyn Corban's Ngatarawa wines. Possibly too much, because often they are correct rather than exciting. The Chardonnays, barrel-fermented, full of good fruit, seem just a little too lean for the weight of wood. They certainly take time to come round: the 86 tasted in 1989 was nowhere near mature, and left a strong acid/citrus aftertaste. The 88 Alwyn Chardonnay, made from "hand-picked" grapes (also tasted in 1989) was still too top-heavy with wood, and had sweeter fruit.

NOBILO VINTNERS   **→***

Station Road, Huapai, West Auckland, North Island

Total vineyards owned: 20ha (49 acres)
Chardonnay owned: 6ha (15 acres)
Chardonnay production: 180,000 bottles

As the figures above indicate, this is a large company owning only a small proportion of the vineyards it needs to cover its total production of 1.5 million bottles. Until the early 1980s, Nobilo made a huge range of wines, many Germanic in style, but it now concentrates its white wine production on the premium varieties of Sauvignon Blanc and Chardonnay. Much of the fruit for the Chardonnays comes from Gisborne, but fruit is also bought from Hawke's Bay and Marlborough, trucked up from South Island for crushing in the West Auckland winery. Nobilo make four Chardonnays, three of them from single vineyards. There is a straightforward blended Chardonnay. Two single vineyard wines, Tombleson and Tietjen, are partly barrel-fermented and matured, but the most prestigious Chardonnay is the Dixon Vineyard Chardonnay, from Gisborne. This spends eight months in wood after barrel-fermentation and a partial malolactic fermentation. It is a big, toasty, yellow/golden-coloured wine which has big flavours, and takes a while to mature.

C J PASK   →**
Korokipo Road, Hastings, Hawke's Bay, North Island

Total v'yds owned: 32ha (79 acres)

Although Chris Pask has been growing grapes for nearly 20 years, he only went into commercial winemaking very recently. His best known wines are reds, but he does make a Chardonnay from Hawke's Bay fruit which can lack acidity and become too soft and creamy, but it certainly has the rich, toasty, buttery character of many Hawke's Bay white wines.

SELAKS WINES   **→
Old North Road, Kumeu, Auckland, North Island

Total v'yds owned: 62ha (153 acres)
Chardonnay owned: 21.4ha (53 acres)

One of the many wineries founded by Dalmatian immigrants in the early years of this century, Selaks produced its first vintage in 1934. Today it is run by father Mate and sons Ivan and Michael, who have established a popular restaurant at the winery. As with most of the Auckland area wineries, although they have a small vineyard plantation at Kumeu near the winery and another near Brigham's Creek, much of the fruit comes from further south, in this case Gisborne. The company makes two Chardonnays, a wood-fermented standard wine, which matures quite quickly (the 1987 tasted in 1990 was already quite mature, with asparagus and cream tastes), although when young it has a very direct, rich tropical style. The top of the range Founders Chardonnay, adorned by a seal of the founder of the company, has around a year in Nevers oak, and is rich, complex, and quite toasty, needing three to four years before drinking.

TE KAIRANGA   **→
Martins Road, Martinborough, Wairarapa

Total v'yds owned: 32ha (79 acres)

The name means "the place where the soil is rich and the food plentiful" and this vineyard at the western end of the

Martinborough *appellation* (defined by its gravel soil ridge) is in the middle of rich sheep country. By the end of 1989, they had released only Chardonnays, with the first vintage being the 1986, although Pinot Noir is on the way. This wood-aged wine is tank-fermented, very clean tasting, still finding its character perhaps. More recent vintages, such as the 89, matured in Nevers oak, is richer, but still seems slightly undefined.

TE MATA ***→
Te Mata Road, Havelock North, Hawke's Bay, North Island

Total v'yds owned: 25ha (62 acres)
Chardonnay owned: 6ha (15 acres)
Chardonnay production: 36,000 bottles

Te Mata Vineyards, dominated by its spectacular hillside winery, has made great waves in the wine industry, due both to the quality of its red wines and the outspokenness of its managing director, John Buck. He and his partner, Michael Morris, acquired the winery (originally founded in 1892) in 1974, and from the start red wines were the predominant production. But one of their Hawke's Bay vineyards, Elston, is the regular source for their single vineyard Chardonnay. The vineyard soil is red metal gravel, topped by sandy loam. The Elston wines are fermented in French oak half new, half one-year-old, undergo malolactic fermentation and are then matured in wood. The style is one for ageing, the 88 (tasted in 1990) being full of wood tastes, spicy, but with the weight of fruit and citric acidity to give it a good life. Earlier vintages, too, have matured well.

VIDAL **→***
913 St Aubyns Street East, Hastings, Hawke's Bay, North Island

Total v'yds owned: none

Vidal, part of the Villa Maria group (qv), buys in fruit from Hawke's Bay and Gisborne to make wines in its Hastings winery, originally founded in 1905. Winemaker Kate Marris, trained in Australia at Roseworthy, is perhaps better known for her reds than whites, but she makes two Chardonnays from Hawke's Bay fruit. The straight 89 Private Bin Hawke's Bay Chardonnay seems a little dull, despite its barrel fermentation, but the Reserve Chardonnay is much richer, much more concentrated, with the taste of malolactic fermentation, and will mature well in bottle.

VILLA MARIA ***
5 Kirkbridge Road, Mangere, Auckland, North Island

Total v'yds owned: none

Villa Maria, which also owns Vidal (qv) in Hawke's Bay, has been concentrating on premium wines in the wake of financial problems, and has been winning awards and competitions, especially for its red wines. Australian winemaker Kym Milne has produced ranges of two wines, the Private Bin and the

Reserve, both of which include a Chardonnay. The 87 Private Bin, made with Gisborne fruit, is soft, with only slight hints of wood, and considerable elegance very Burgundian. The 89 Reserve, from Hawke's Bay, and the first vintage of this label, also has an elegance and a good acid balance. The barrique-fermented 87, 100 percent barrel-fermented, with 12 percent malolactic and long lees contact, is of richer stuff, but needs three to four years in bottle before giving its best.

South Island

PRODUCERS

CLOUDY BAY   ****
Jacksons Road, Blenheim, South Island

Total v'yds owned: 40ha (99 acres)

The worldwide success of Cloudy Bay's Sauvignon Blanc has slightly overshadowed the equal, possibly greater, success of its Chardonnays. The vineyard lies in the heart of the flat but well drained gravel soils of the Marlborough region of South Island. The Chardonnay vienyard is close planted, with a higher than usual number of vines per hectare. Until 1990 it was entirely owned by David Hohnen, owner of the Cape Mentelle winery in Western Australia, but the two wineries are now run in partnership with Veuve Clicquot Champagne. Hohnen came to Marlborough in 1985 because of the quality of the whites the region could produce, and Kevin Judd, a Roseworthy (Australia) trained winemaker, joined him. Together they have produced one of the top two New Zealand Chardonnays. The majority of the fruit goes through barrel fermentation (70 percent in the 88), and a varying percentage passes through the malolactic (30 percent in 88, 100 percent in 89). The 88 (tasted in 1990) although rich and with good wood tastes, scored well because of the sheer quality and taste of the fruit, piercing and fresh while obviously made for some ageing. The 89 will be richer, more honeyed, but (tasted in late 1989) will still have that directness of fruit which sets these wines apart.

GIESEN   *→**
Burnham, Christchurch, Canterbury, South Island

Total v'yds owned: 30ha (74 acres)

This is the most southerly vineyard in this book. The climate of the Canterbury plains is suitable for viticulture because of its lack of rain and therefore long growing seasons, rather than its high temperatures. Although Rhine Riesling is the best white variety, some Chardonnay is grown in the Giesen vineyards south east of Christchurch, although they also buy fruit from Marlborough. They use German oak (after all, the Giesen brothers came from the Rheinhessen in Germany), and some barrel fermentation, and allow a certain amount of malolactic fermentation, a necessary requirement given the high acid of some of the fruit. The main problem they seem to have is that the fruit is sometimes dominated by wood, but there is an attractive spiciness there which compensates.

HUNTERS ESTATE →***
Rapaura Road, RD3, Blenheim, South Island

Total v'yds owned: 18ha (44 acres)
Chardonnay owned: 7.2ha (17 acres)
Chardonnay produced: 18,000 bottles

This winery, with its charming and popular restaurant, is set in the middle of the Marlborough vineyards. Owner Jane Hunter and winemaker John Belsham, who trained in Bordeaux, are producing a range of wines with true varietal character from their own fruit and from fruit bought in from local growers. Their Chardonnay goes through a 40 percent barrel fermentation in Nevers oak, and prolonged lees contact, plus six to eight months maturation in wood. It has typical direct Marlborough fruit tastes, which lose their wood dominance once out of cask and balance out. As a one-off curiosity, Hunters made 300 litres of a botrytized Late Harvest Chardonnay in the 87 vintage, which has the true sweet and dry botrytis character, very floral, very intense.

MERLEN WINES **→
PO Box 8, Renwick, Marlborough, South Island

Total v'yds owned: 4ha (10 acres)
Chardonnay owned: 3ha (7 acres)
Chardonnay production: 15,000 bottles

A new, small winery, run by Almuth Lorenz, who started in the Marlborough area by making wine at Hunters (qv). The bulk of production is of Chardonnay. The fruit comes from local contract growers as well as the home vineyard. It is fermented in various woods, 15 percent goes through malolactic fermentation, and it is then matured for six to eight months in wood. The first release was the 87 vintage.

WEINGUT SEIFRIED *→**
PO Box 18, Upper Moutere, Nelson, South Island

Total v'yds owned: 35ha (86 acres)

By far the largest of Nelson's five wineries, Weingut Seifried, owned by German-trained Hermann Seifried, produces an almost bewildering range of wines, from sweet reds to sweet whites, with all styles in between. In this collection Chardonnay tends to be lost in favour of the more Germanic styles, but it should not be. Seifried makes early maturing wines (the 88, tasted in late 1989 was just at its peak), but is now employing more barrel fermentation and lees contact to give greater ageing potential.

Chile

Chardonnay was slow to take off in Chile, but it is catching up now. While most of the major *bodegas* have produced some for at least a decade, it was only in small quantities. In the early 1980s there were a mere 100ha (247 acres) recorded in the country, mainly in the Central Valley region, south of the capital Santiago. By 1985, this had supposedly reached 250ha (617 acres), and current estimates suggest about 1,000ha (2,470 acres) are planted. Obviously Chile sees the grape as the white wine source of the future, certainly one to rival the much better established Sauvignon Blanc.

Chile's style of Chardonnay is not so overtly New World as the Chardonnays of California or Australia. Producers are using much less new wood – perhaps because of cost – and are also fermenting much more in stainless steel, which has now been introduced at most of the major *bodegas*. This greater restraint probably also has as much to do with the influence of the local market, which traditionally has supposedly enjoyed oxidized white wines (perhaps because they had no choice) and certainly is not used to the overt fruit tastes of, say, Australian Chardonnay.

However, each vintage brings changes in the way Chardonnay is treated, and certainly the 1989 vintage wines were by far the best the country has made so far. As a rule, they are still light in style, with far fewer strongly wooded offerings and for this reason, perhaps, would make far better matches with delicate foods than some of the stronger, richer New World Chardonnays.

Whether the fact that all Chile's vineyards are planted on ungrafted roots – the phylloxera louse has never, for some reason, managed to take hold in this country – makes any difference to the wines is difficult to say. It certainly affects the vines, which have much greater vigour and sap than their European cousins because of their undiminished ability to draw nutrients direct from the ground. The quality of fruit in the naturally dry climate is normally first class – Miguel Torres, the Spanish wine producer who now has a vineyard in Chile has described the country as a "viticultural paradise".

PRODUCERS

CONCHA Y TORO   **→***
Fernando Lazcano 1220, Puente Alto

Total v'yds owned: 1,374ha (3,985 acres)
Chardonnays produced: Vineyard Chardonnay; Oak Aged Chardonnay.

Founded in 1882, this has always been one of the aristocrats of Chilean wines. It owns a large estate of vines, but still needs to buy in grapes for its 3.3 million-case production. There are two styles of Chardonnay – an unoaked and an oak-aged. The unoaked 88 was pleasingly citric, with a fresh clean, light touch.

The 89 Oak Aged Chardonnay is certainly more serious, with good toasty, nutty tastes, quite lean and dry, although even here the oak tastes are not too predominant.

COUSIÑO MACUL   **
Quilin con Canal San Carlos, Santiago

Total v'yds owned: 263ha (650 acres)
Chardonnay owned: 19ha (47 acres)

The old family estate – the oldest wine farm in the country – on the outskirts of Santiago is set in what appears to be almost a European park. The vineyards are around the *bodega* (where it is thought vines were first planted in 1554). The production is dominated by Cabernet Sauvignon, but an unoaked Chardonnay is made: the 89, fermented in stainless steel for the first time, is fresh, clean, perhaps slightly clinical, but with pleasing baked-apples and cream tastes. A good light wine.

ERRAZURIZ PANQUEHUE   →**
PO Box 2346, Santiago

Total v'yds owned: 168ha (415 acres)
Chardonnays produced: Vineyard Chardonnay; Reserve Chardonnay.

In 1870 this *bodega* pioneered enormous vine plantings of 1,000ha (2,470 acres) in the Aconcagua Valley desert, north of Santiago, but its vineyard holdings now only amount to 18ha (44 acres) in the north and 150ha (370 acres) elsewhere in the country. This means that most of its production is from purchased grapes. Two Chardonnays are made: a partially oaked regular wine and a fully oaked reserve. The regular 88 (tasted in 1990) was not an exciting wine, rather closed and tart, and with little sign of life. The 100 percent barrel-fermented Reserve 89 was much better, definitely tasting of new wood, with good, intense flavours which should improve with further bottle age: one of the most overtly wooded of the Chilean Chardonnays.

VIÑA LINDEROS   *
Vinedos Ortiz, Alameda 1370, Off 502, Santiago

Total v'yds owned: 81ha (200 acres)
Chardonnay owned: 21ha (52 acres)
Chardonnay produced: Linderos Chardonnay.

The 81ha (200 acres) of vines are all that remain of a much larger wine estate which was turned over to fruit farming during a crisis that the wine industry went through in the 1960s. From the 1990 vintage, white wines were fermented in stainless steel rather than the old-style wooden *cubas*. This fermentation would certainly explain the flat, dull taste of the Linderos Chardonnay 89, which was a great disappointment. Hopefully, things will improve.

VIÑA SAN PEDRO   **→
Aysen 115, Santiago

Total v'yds owned: 420ha (1.038 acres)
Chardonnay owned: 20ha (49.4 acres)
Chardonnays produced: Llave de Oro; Castillo de Molina.

One of the larger of the Chilean *bodegas*, Viña San Pedro has three farms in the Molina-Lontue region of the country, south of Santiago. The comparatively small planting of Chardonnay is being increased. From the 1990 vintage, stainless steel has been introduced, but the 89 Llave de Oro Chardonnay was cleanly made, with a firm taste of spicy American oak and good nutty, perfumed fruit. The Castillo de Molina Chardonnay 89, with partial fermentation in American oak is prettily balanced, with no overt or strong tastes of wood, and with light, perfumed fruit. The unoaked regular Chardonnay 89 was equally light, and rather lacking in personality.

VIÑA SANTA RITA   **→
Gertrudis Echenique 49, Santiago

Total v'yds owned: 225ha (555 acres)
Chardonnay owned: 17ha (42 acres)
Chardonnays produced: Medalla Real; Barrel Fermented Medalla Real.

With a *bodega* capacity of 9 million litres and 800,000 bottles, Santa Rita is big business in the Chilean wine industry. It is also one of the more advanced, with stainless steel vying with a huge capacity of American and French oak barrels. The two Chardonnays both see some wood: the Medalla Real regular Chardonnay 87 was attractively citrusy, with some hints of wood, but none too overt, while the 86, which spent between six and eight months in American oak, was gentle and smoky. The Barrel Fermented Medalla Real Chardonnay was first released in 1989: fermented in Vosges wood, it is quite a serious wine, somewhat austere with smoky wood tastes and restrained fruit, that should improve in bottle.

MIGUEL TORRES CHILE   **→***
Panamerica Sur Km 195, Curico

Total v'yds owned: 150ha (370.6 acres)
Chardonnay produced: Unoaked Chardonnay.

The Chilean end of the Torres family's wine business, based in Penédes in Spain, rapidly achieved a number of firsts for the country: the first stainless steel, the first small barrels, the first modern presses. The wines that have come from this operation, which has vineyards south of the main Central Valley vineyards, were spearheaded by a Sauvignon Blanc and then by a red, before Chardonnay came along. The Chardonnay is an unoaked wine, and relies on the top quality of the fruit to make its statement. On the 89, these are certainly ripe, vibrant, quite soft, but beautifully clean and fresh, making the wine a pleasure to drink.

South Africa

Chardonnay's success story in South Africa is only just beginning. Although it has been planted certainly since the 1960s, the clones that were used proved quite unsuitable and gave low yields and disease problems. This was partly due to the attitude of the government and the industry's governing body, the KWV, toward imports of vine cuttings and the long quarantine period they imposed.

CHARDONNAY VINEYARDS

Plantings of better clones of Chardonnay really only started in the mid-1980s. The search has been on in the Cape vineyards for the right location and, not suprisingly, the cooler areas are generally better.

Around Stellenbosch, a number of producers have taken advantage of either the cooling winds coming up from False Bay behind Cape Town, and the ocean itself, or have planted high up the slopes of the dramatic mountains which dominate so much of the area.

Another area of planting has been right down almost on the south coast at Hermanus, the most southerly point of the African continent.

MAKING CHARDONNAY

The Cape winemakers have learnt fast about the Chardonnay. They are using barrel fermentation in new wood from France (Nevers and Allier being preferred), and are maturing in wood to give the extra complexities modern Chardonnay-making demands. Some are using malolactic fermentation to produce rich, buttery tastes, although the risk of low acidity in the grapes makes other producers more cautious about this.

In a sense, therefore, Chardonnay producers have by-passed the stainless steel tank fermentation stage that hit Australia and California in the early 1980s, and have caught up with those other countries as they move into greater use of wood for fermenting as well as maturing.

In fact South African producers seem to take their cue much more from Europe – Burgundy in this case – than from other New World countries. Some of the top winemakers travel regularly to Burgundy for advice, training and to learn about new techniques.

Quantities are still small. With only 1,000ha (2,470 acres) under Chardonnay – and much of that new planting – it is very early days to judge the place of South Africa in the Chardonnay world. However, the results from the handful of wineries listed here show that the Cape vineyards are just as capable of producing world-class Chardonnay as the red wines for which they are already well known. Watch out for a rapid growth in the next few years.

PRODUCERS

BACKSBERG   ***
Paarl

Total v'yds owned: 180ha (444.7 acres)
Chardonnay owned: 15ha (37 acres)

Chardonnay is a relative newcomer to this family estate, more traditionally noted for its red wines. But Sydney Back, one of the perennial stars of the Cape wine industry with 54 vintages behind him, imported specially selected Chardonnay cuttings from France, and made his first vintage in the mid-1980s. The vineyards are on decomposed granite, on the slopes of the Simonsberg Mountain south of Paarl. Sydney's father bought them in 1916, and now Sydney himself has been joined by his son Michael. He was one of the pioneers of estate-bottling in the Cape, and the impressive Chardonnays are a worthy continuation of that tradition. There have been two star vintages so far: 86, toasty from new wood maturation, but not overblown, and 89, with good acidity to go with the ripe fruit a sure sign that the wine will last. The need for acidity in these wines means that malolactic fermentation is not encouraged, but barrel-fermentation helps give a good intensity of flavour.

BOSCHENDAL   **→***
Paarl

Total v'yds owned: 400ha (988 acres)
Chardonnay owned: 80ha (197.6 acres)

One of the oldest established estates in the Cape, the vast 4,000ha (9,883 acres) tract rolls beneath the Groot Drakenstein Mountain toward the Franshhoek Valley, east of Paarl. Now owned by the giant Anglo-American conglomerate, it was once owned by Cecil Rhodes, who set it up as a fruit farm when phylloxera blighted the Cape vineyards. Under the direction of extrovert Aachim von Arnim and, since 1988, Hilko Hegewisch, there has been a complete overhaul of the winery and a rationalization of the vineyard. Two Chardonnays are made from one of the largest plantings of the variety in the Cape. The still table wine is rapidly improved after a less than exciting first vintage in 1986: 89 is rich, full of fruit, and gathering good wood tastes. A sparkling Brut is now made a blend of Pinot Noir and Chardonnay.

DELAIRE VINEYARDS   →***
Helshoogte Pass, Stellenbosch

Perched on the crest of the Helshoogte Pass, between Stellenbosch and the Franshhoek Valley, this is cool vineyard country in Cape terms. The owners, Storm and Ruth Quinan have employed the winemaking talents of Stellenbosch University graduate Mike Dobrovic who, in the two vintages of Chardonnay I have tasted, is obviously making full use of the vineyard's location. He is on record as saying that he wants to make a Chardonnay in the style of New Zealand's Cloudy Bay, and there are similarities in the clean, fresh taste balanced by the taste of the new Nevers and Limousin wood. The 88 was the more woody, possibly because this was only the second crop from the vines, but 89 is lean, crisp, and has slightly fruit-salad ripeness, with a citrusy aftertaste.

DELHEIM →***
Simonsberg, Stellenbosch

Total v'yds owned: 118ha (291.5 acres)
Chardonnay owned: 4ha (10 acres)

Founded in 1899, this large estate came under its present ownership of Spatz Sperling in 1957. Since then it has elected to produce quality wines which include a late harvest. It also has a well-established reputation for its Cabernet-based blend, Grand Reserve. Chardonnay is a more recent development, spearheaded with a fruity 88 vintage, although it lacked the depth and wood tastes that came with the 89, which was partly barrel-fermented. According to Cape wine writer John Platter, Delheim uses the Burgundian clone 95, the only estate in South Africa to do so, which may account for the depth of flavour of the wine.

HAMILTON-RUSSELL VINEYARDS ***→
Hemel-en-Aarde Valley, Hermanus

Total v'yds owned: 40ha (99 acres)
Chardonnay owned: 25ha (62 acres)

This is one of the best known Chardonnays in South Africa – not just because owner Tim Hamilton-Russell is a very good promoter of his wines. It is expensive but it is also very good and one of the top two or three in the Cape. The vineyards are the most southerly in South Africa, in the Walker Bay Wine of Origin area, south-east of Cape Town. Set in a deep valley, they are less than a mile from the sea which sends cooling breezes through the gap the Onrus River makes in the coastal mountain range. The vineyards have no irrigation, except in drought conditions, and the vines, planted close together, have low yields which allow them to achieve considerable concentration. The Chardonnay is released a year after harvest, after a period of six months in French wood, and a further six months in bottle. The 84 vintage was rich in wood, broad, toasty and low in acidity; 86 was much greener, and the 87 was soft, floral, with less overt wood, and very ripe fruit. The best I've tasted is the 88, with excellent fruit acidity and wood balance smoky and creamy. The 89 was cooler, with fewer wood flavours, perhaps a little austere.

KLEIN CONSTANTIA ****
Constantia

Total v'yds owned: 70ha (173 acres)

Once part of the neighbouring Groot Constantia estate, Klein Constantia has recently been totally renovated, completely replanted with vineyards which stretch up the slopes of Table

Mountain, and a stunning new winery built. New Zealand-trained Ross Gower is the winemaker, and the combination of top-quality fruit and skilled winemaking has meant that Klein Constantia has rapidly gained a great reputation for itself. The first Chardonnay was the 88 vintage, and it exhibits overt fruit and wood in rich profusion, very New World in style. The 89 is even better, with 100 percent malolactic fermentation, big, rich, almost honeyed, and needing some time before drinking.

NEDERBURG ** → ***
Paarl

Total v'yds owned: 1,000ha (2,470 acres)

A famous name indeed, and not just for the annual auction which attracts a wide international audience. The estate, part of the giant Stellenbosch Farmers' Winery, is run independently, until recently under winemaker Gunter Brozel, now under Newald Marais. Like many Cape estates, the main reputation rests on its red wines – and, as a speciality here, on late harvest dessert wines. However, there are small quantities of Chardonnay made in the Private Bin range, and these rank high in the ratings of Cape Chardonnays. They tend to develop slowly, and to have not too-obvious oak characters. Of vintages tasted, 85 was the star, big and rich despite the lack of malolactic fermentation; 86 is lemony, very fruity, and developing well. The 84 had more wood and was generally softer, with less structure. A new development is a barrel-fermented Chardonnay/Sauvignon Blanc blend, called Prelude, released first in 1988.

OVERGAAUW ***
Stellenbosch

Total v'yds owned: 71ha (175 acres)
Chardonnay owned: 4ha (9.88 acres)

Overgaauw was created out of one of the early Cape estates in 1906 by the van Velden family who still own and run it, with Braam van Velden as winemaker. As with many estates, producing Chardonnay is a recent development, but the results have been very good, using some barrel fermentation and long lees contact, giving rich, oaky tastes and plenty of fruit. The best vintage so far is 88, although 89 promises well. The 86 was the first vintage; 87 soft; 88 full, oaky and honeyed.

RUSTENBERG → ***
Stellenbosch

Total v'yds owned: 80ha (197 acres)
Chardonnay owned: 5ha (12 acres)

A historic estate in one of the most beautiful settings in the Cape, in the shadow of the Simonsberg Mountain, where much of the land is used for cattle, fruit and sheep. A small proportion is given over to vines. Two estates, Schoongezicht and Rustenberg were combined in 1945, and from 1990 on, all the wines will be produced under the Rustenberg label. The

Chardonnay was first vinified, in tank, in 1986, and then matured in Nevers wood. The altitude of the vineyards and the cool growing season mean the wines have good acid balance will mature well. The 86 still tastes young, while 88 is quite lean with a strong wood presence. The 89 is richer, has barrel fermentation and lees contact, and is the most successful so far.

SIMONSIG →***
Stellenbosch

Total v'yds owned: 187ha (462 acres)
Chardonnay owned: 11ha (27 acres)

This estate, facing the Simonsberg Mountain is owned by the Malan family, and Johan, the youngest son of Frans, is now the winemaker. Much of the estate's reputation has rested on its bottle-fermented sparkling wine, Kaapse Vonkel, now made using a blend including Pinot Noir and Chardonnay. But still Chardonnay wines have been made since the early 1980s, and despite often being produced from poor-quality clonal material, have matured well. New clones have improved the wines immensely, and the 88 is rich, full of wood tastes, with a softness from the malolactic fermentation, and with tropical fruit overtones.

THELEMA MOUNTAIN VINEYARDS ***→
Stellenbosch

A relative newcomer to the list of wine estates, Thelema, formerly a fruit farm high up on the southern slopes of the Simonsberg Mountain is now owned by the Webb family. Gyles Webb, the winemaker, trained at the local Stellenbosch University, but also worked with the Heitz vineyards in California. He has made a spectacular start with white wines – and there is great promise for his reds. There is great flavour in the 89, which was barrel-fermented and barrel-matured in Nevers wood, and went through a malolactic fermentation. This combination gives the wine very ripe flavours, soft, honeyed, buttery and rich, very much in a New World style. The 88, the first vintage, was lighter and will mature faster.

VRIESENHOF →***
Stellenbosch

Total v'yds owned: 10ha (25 acres)
Chardonnay owned: 3ha (7 acres)

This small estate is the property of Jan Coetzee, who also acts as a consultant to other wine estates and has carved himself a reputation as one of the Cape's best winemakers. While the estate's main wines are red (including a Bordeaux blend), the quality of the Chardonnay is high, and is very much in a Burgundian mould, probably from his experience working in Burgundy in the early 1980s. The tiny quantity of the first vintage 86 has matured fast; 87 has remained rather light. The 88 also suffered from lack of weight, but 89 has good oak flavours, well balanced acidity and some tropical fruit flavours.

Italy

Italy has not long been associated with Chardonnay. Its white wines have tended to be of a Soave style, or else the rather non-descript efforts that come from the Trebbiano grape. A few odd-balls, like Gavi, or the white wines of Friuli, or wines made from the Muscat have completed a sometimes dismal line-up.

But it would be wrong to think of the whole of Italy as traditionally a non-Chardonnay country. Up in the far north, in the Sudtirol, they have been making Chardonnay since the early 19th century: admittedly that was Austria until 1919, but the sort of white Chardonnays that it makes now represent one very important Italian style. This style, light, fresh, clean, with not too much fragrance, is how Italians like their white wines. When presented with a really perfumed grape like Riesling, they will do their best to tone it down, because that way it goes better with their food. So it is with the Sudtirol (or Alto Adige, to give it its Italian name) Chardonnays. With a couple of exceptions they are clean, fresh and youthful, with few complications and much pleasure.

This style has also been associated with the Pinot Bianco grape, which is much more widely spread than the Chardonnay. In the old days, when the Chardonnay was thought to be Pinot Chardonnay, and there was considered to be a link with Pinot Blanc in France, definite confusion reigned in Italy between Chardonnay and Pinot Bianco – just as there is with the red grapes Cabernet Sauvignon and Cabernet Franc. But since the beginning of the 1980s a new style of Chardonnay has arrived in Italy: the fashionable, barrel-fermented, wood-aged, rich, creamy style of wines: in short the heading "the international style". Italy being a place where fashion is vital, all those producers with a reputation to maintain have leapt onto the bandwagon of producing one of these Chardonnays. And, in case that sounds somewhat cynical, the results have been very good, with a handful of world-class wines being produced, and a great many others of a very good standard.

Although producers right across north and central Italy have been turning to Chardonnay, certain areas – some obvious, some unexpected – are producing the largest amount of and, coincidentally, the best wines. Of the obvious areas, one is the Alto Adige which with its cool vineyards and tradition of Chardonnay is a natural selection; the other is Friuli, which already has an established reputation for quality white wines.

Less obvious choices include the Veneto, where local traditions of other white wines, such as Soave or Prosecco, are already strong; Tuscany, where producers are inveterate experimenters; and, Piedmont, the red wine heartland of Italy, which is now producing two of the best Chardonnays.

There are other Chardonnay areas, such as Franciacorta near Brescia, which already have established links with France, through red grape varieties. And there are even occasional sightings of Chardonnay further south (as in the Favonia wines of Simonini in Apulia), sometimes with astonishing results.

Not all the Chardonnay-makers are striving for this weighty, international style of wine with oak. There are those who are trying to compromise between the light, fresh Italian style and the rich, toasty international style. They are getting weight and richness by long maceration of the skins, which increases the intensity of the fruit. They argue that much of the white wine fruit grown in Italy does not lend itself to wood, simply because the fruit has a tendency to lack acidity.

THE LAW AND CHARDONNAY

Italian wine law has not been kind to the Chardonnay. Only in the Alto Adige does it receive DOC status, because of its traditional links with the region – and that status was only awarded in 1984. Otherwise all Italian Chardonnays go under the basic denomination of *vino da tavola*. Not that that bothers Italian producers who happily ignore the wine law if it contradicts the style of wine they want to make. It is quite possible to come across a Chardonnay *vino da tavola* with a hefty £20 price tag – just don't be surprised.

The wines

PIEDMONT

The home of Italy's most powerful red wines, Barolo and Barbaresco, certainly has an equally strong white wine tradition. But it is a tradition of sweet whites – in the form of Asti Spumante and the other myriad muscat-based wines – either still or sparkling. The amount of dry white wine is tiny by comparison – wines such as Gavi, or the Arneis-based wines are as far as it goes. So it is perhaps more understandable that Piedmont producers, given the international interest in white wine, should look for a style that they can produce. For the top producers, Chardonnay fits the bill. To my mind, the two best Italian Chardonnays are produced here, and their success would suggest that others might follow suit. They are very much in the big, bold toasty style – and it is most convincing. Some are labelled Chardonnay delle Langhe – which is the name for the area which covers both Barolo and Barbaresco.

PRODUCERS

FONTANAFREDDA, CHARDONNAY DELLE LANGHE   **
A large estate, noted for its Barolo and its Asti Spumante. The Chardonnay is a straight style of wine, without much obvious wood taste, the 89 (tasted in 1990) only needing a few more months in bottle before being ready to drink.

ANGELO GAJA, GAIA & REY   ***→****
The king of Barbaresco also, for many, makes the best Italian Chardonnay. The wine is beautifully shaped and structured, very Burgundian in approach, the 87 having an excellent

balance between wood and fresh fruit flavours, and the 85 (tasted in 1989) even better: soft, concentrated and intense. A fine wine by any standards.

MARCHESE DI GRESY, TENUTA CISA ASINARI   →***
The 87 (tasted in 1990) has a lovely champagne-like biscuity bouquet, with intense creamy fruit and wood in balance. The wine needs at least three years from vintage before drinking; when tasted in 1989, the wood was much too dominant.

PIO CESARE, PIODILEI   ***
One of the great traditionalists in Barolo, Pio Boffa of Pio Cesare has made an elegant Chardonnay, not as rich as some, with classic balance of fruit and light oak. On the 87, the fruit was concentrated rather than rich, giving a smooth, creamy wine with just a hint of acidity.

ROCCHE DI MANZONI, L'ANGELICA CHARDONNAY DELLE LANGHE   **→
The 88 of this wine was all apples and custard, with excellent acidity, some wood hints and rounded ripe fruit. In richer vintages it can be heavier, but the style always veers toward freshness.

TRENTINO/ALTO ADIGE (SUDTIROL)
This is the oldest home for Chardonnay in Italy, where it has long been the dominant white wine variety, and it is also where the light, fresh, clean, unoaked approach is most common. In the past, growers thought it was simply Pinot Bianco, and clones were planted for high yields and to make sparkling wine, without much thought given to high-quality still wine production. The quality of fruit is good here, but the problem remains the high yields which can produce dilute wines. A few producers are now making wine with some oak, and are obviously taking care to have low yields, from specific vineyards, because the approach works.

Most of the Chardonnay is planted on the gravelly plains along the Adige valley and, further south in Trentino, the best Chardonnay comes from the Sorni and Cembra Valley, while larger tracts in the Vallagarina are widely planted with the grape, much of it for sparkling wine.

PRODUCERS

BOLLINI, CHARDONNAY DELLA MEZZACORONA   **→
This merchant house buys wine from the Mezzacorona in the Trentino for its unoaked Chardonnay. The 88 was floral, fresh and aromatic, with sufficient acidity to keep the whole effect very cool and clean.

J HOFFSTATTER   **
A family winery in the village of Tramin making quite a crisp, appley style of wine, that, as in the 1988, needs time to lose some of its early acidity.

ALOIS LAGEDER ***
The best-regarded *cantina* in the Sudtirol, run by Alois Lageder who is also involved in the Portico dei Leoni project (qv). Two Chardonnays are made, using fruit from vineyards at Buchholz. One is unoaked – the 88 (tasted in 1989) had a delicious fresh touch, with good acidity. The other a *barrique*-aged wine, called Lowengang, has ten months on the lees, and 50 percent new barrels, which shows in its buttery, toasty taste. The 86 is a good crisp-tasting wine, which balances well with the softer fruit and oak.

JOSEF NIEDERMEYER **
The 88 from this *cantina* had good simple fruit flavours, richness and concentration, from low-yielding vines.

POJER E SANDRI ** →
One of the pioneer small private estates in the Trentino, with 12ha at Molini. The Chardonnays include a special bottling, called Faye, but the standard Chardonnay 88, was a straight-down-the-line wine with clean fruit, good concentration, no sign of wood.

PORTICO DEI LEONI → ****
A joint venture between Alois Lageder (qv) and Maurizio Castelli, a top oenologist based in Tuscany. This barrel-fermented Chardonnay is, for me, the finest Italian Chardonnay, if only because it does not go over the top in its use of wood. The balance of the 85 (tasted in 1988) was just right – creamy, yes, somewhat New World in style, but with a nice cool breeze of acidity across it. The 86 (tasted in 1990), fermented in a mix of Nevers and Tronçais wood, was a little leaner, more serious, but had the same fruit quality.

SAN MICHELE COOPERATIVE **
A range of Chardonnays are produced, of which the most attractive is the Chardonnay di Appiano. The 88 (tasted in 1990), without complexity but with decent weight and flavours, made very pleasant drinking.

TIEFENBRUNNER → ***
Herbert Tiefenbrunner, who owns among other things the highest vineyard in Italy (the Feldmarschall at 1,000m (3,280 ft), has made a name for himself with two Chardonnays, one *barrique*-aged, the other unoaked. The unoaked came first and is a deliciously ripe wine, with few complexities, that sometimes lacks acidity. The 85 *barrique*-aged vintage was toasty and perfumed, rich but with high acid, already mature in 1990, and only hinting at wood.

ROBERTO ZENI ** →
From a 4ha (9.8 acres) vineyard on the edge of the Rotaliano plain in Trentino, Roberto Zeni makes an estate Chardonnay Zaraosti, the 87 clean, fresh and soft, with piercingly direct fruit. The quality of the fruit shines through.

THE VENETO

Home of Soave, Valpolicella and Bardolino as well as sparkling Prosecco, the Veneto also finds plenty of room for lesser DOCs and wine regions, which is where the Chardonnay makes its appearance. Much of it is found in the central band of vineyards around Vicenza and to the north, where the vineyards of Breganze produce one of the best examples. On the flat plain of the Piave, near the Adriatic coast, Chardonnay is also found, here used as the base for sparkling wines. The Chardonnay has spread, along with red varieties like the two Cabernets, but is as yet unclassified with a DOC. While a number of the Veronese merchant houses and producers are now producing a Chardonnay, the three worth noting are listed below.

PRODUCERS

MACULAN FERRATA   ***

Fausto Maculan has almost single-handedly revived the fortunes of Breganze. Apart from making the classic wines of the region he has produced a *vino da tavola* Chardonnay, called Ferrata. The 87, elegant and restrained, with soft fruit characters, was deliciously balanced, well knit, and ready to drink by 1990, while both the 86 and 85 similarly showed this character of lightness and elegance, the 85 remaining still fresh in 1990.

VENEGAZZU-CONTE LOREDAN GASPARINI   →**

A surprisingly disappointing wine for such a prestigious house, merely fresh and clean, but without much character and with aromas muted.

CONTI GUERRIERI-RIZZARDI   **

An old estate which practises organic farming techniques and produces some of the top Valpolicellas and Soaves around. Their 1988 Chardonnay was a clean, citrusy wine, no wood overtones, but attractive appley fruit flavours, for ready drinking.

FRIULI–VENEZIA–GIULIA

The far north-eastern region of Italy has long been recognized as the home of some of the country's best white wines, made from Pinot Grigio, Tocai Friulano and the local Ribolla. In this scene, Chardonnay is a definite interloper, but a number of producers have been making this for the prestige it confers. They tend not to use much wood, if at all, and to emphasize the fruit quality of their wines. It is an interesting approach by producers whose main preoccupation until recently has been with the more aromatic grape varieties.

PRODUCERS

JOSKO GRAVNER   →***

Oaked Chardonnay from this small vineyard in Collio is certainly one of the most interesting from the region, and suggests a modicum of oak is no bad thing here.

SILVIO JERMANN   ***

Eschewing DOCs even for wines that could qualify for them, Silvio Jermann has created quite a stir with his two French-varietal white wines, a Sauvignon Blanc and a Chardonnay. The 88 Chardonnay was mature and earthy when tasted in 1990, the much better 87 was rich and concentrated, while the 85, with maturity, had achieved the character of a good unoaked white burgundy. He also made in 1986 and 1987 at least an oaked wine which was called inexplicably "Where the dreams have no end".

RUSSIZ SUPERIORE, MARCO FELLUGA   **

The vineyards at Russiz di Sopra are run by Marco Felluga and his son Roberto. Their 88 Chardonnay, from bought-in grapes, was unoaked but full of fruit with some appley acidity.

LOMBARDY

Chardonnay is widely used for sparkling wine in this region, notably in Oltrepo Pavese. The only still Chardonnay I have come across is also from one of those producers, Ca' del Bosco (**→), whose 1986 was big, rich, and oaky, full of tropical and melony flavours.

EMILIA-ROMAGNA

It may not be officially permitted in Emilia-Romagna, or even approved of, but at least two producers make some good Chardonnay. The best comes from Terre Rosse in the Colli Bolognese, where it is called Giovanni Vallania *vino da tavola*, the 88 (**→***) melony and biscuity, with broad but balanced fruit. Over in Romagna, the top producer of Sangiovese di Romagna, Fattoria Paradiso, also makes a Chardonnay called Jacopo (**), whose fresh flavours seem a far cry from the foggy, steamy Po Valley.

TUSCANY AND UMBRIA

This is the home of the super *vino da tavola*, the 100 percent Sangiovese blends which cannot be called Chianti, but which can cost twice as much as the same producer's DOCG Chianti Classico. So it is not surprising that the same producers should also be keen to experiment with Chardonnay. The best estates are mainly in Chianti Classico and Chianti Rufina. Again, as with Piedmont, the excitement and willingness to try is probably helped by the fact that there is no strong white wine tradition in the region (apart from localized wines like the Vernaccia di San Gimignano). In Umbria, it is the ever-resourceful Lungarotti family (qv) who make the one and only Chardonnay I have tasted.

PRODUCERS

CASTELLO DI AMA, COLLINE DI AMA   **→

This estate has created a whole range of *vini da tavola*, from Sauvignon, Merlot and Pinot Noir as well as Chardonnay, to go alongside their Chianti Classico. The Chardonnay 88 is an impressive wine, soft, perhaps lacking acidity, but with the compensation of excellent fruit quality and ripe, lightly vanilla flavours.

AVIGNONESI, IL MARZOCCO   ***
The top producer of Vino Nobile di Montepulciano also makes a *vino da tavola* Chardonnay, Il Marzocco. The 87 was a richly toasty, oaky wine of top quality, smooth and creamy, with bags of fruit, beginning to come into balance but really needing two more years in bottle.

VILLA BANFI, FONTANELLE   **→
This is the huge estate owned by the Italo-American firm Riunite, of Lambrusco fame. In southern Montalcino, it operates from a stupendous modern winery and a medieval castle. Despite the size of the operation, it is quite capable of making small quantities of the top wines, such as the Chardonnay Fontanelle. It is not designed for long ageing, but the 86 (tasted in 1989) showed excellent balance and poise, with its aromatic flavours and hints of vanilla-y oak.

TENUTA CAPARZO, LE GRANCE   **→***
This estate, in a splendid site high up on a ridge overlooking the Montalcino vineyards, makes this barrel-fermented Chardonnay to partner its Brunello and Rosso di Montalcino. It is a softly balanced wine, the 86 (tasted in 1988) was full of ripe flavours and balanced wood, which suggests it would still be very much alive for another three to four years.

TENUTA DI CAPEZZANA   **
The estate of Ugo Contini Bonacossi is famous for the way he pioneered the revival of the red wines of Carmignano in the Colli Fiorentini. His Chardonnay is made in an unoaked style, unlike some of its Tuscan rivals, but still gives big wines, like the 88, with its baked-apples fruit; the 87 is softer and lighter, with excellent acidity.

FRESCOBALDI, POMINO IL BENEFIZIO   →***
The merchant house and estate owner Frescobaldi can date its interest in wine back to the 13th century, and now has a considerable interest in Chianti Rufina and in the small DOC of Pomino which it virtually created. This was the first barrel-fermented Chardonnay to be made in Tuscany – and that was as recently as the early 1980s. For some years the style varied as experiments were made with more or less oak, but it now seems to have settled down into a well-made, lightly oaked wine, with good intense fruit character and great style.

ISOLE E OLENA, COLLEZIONE DE MARCHI   ***
Paolo de Marchi, young, intense, very talented, makes a few unusual wines alongside his superlative Chianti. They include probably the first Syrah in Tuscany, and this Chardonnay. The 88 (tasted in 1990) is a finely balanced wine, with ripe, soft fruit, tinges of acidity and no hint of wood.

LUNGAROTTI, CHARDONNAY DI MARADUOLO   **→***
In Umbria, the indefatigable Lungarotti family, progenitors of
Rubesco di Torgiano, make this single vineyard Chardonnay,
the 87, with its clean citric fruit character and freshness, has
only a hint of wood. I have also seen a Chardonnay called Vigna I
Palazzi, but I have not tasted it.

RUFFINO CABREO VIGNETO LA PIETRA   **→***
The big Chianti house of I L Ruffino produces this Chardonnay
from a single vineyard. The 86 (tasted in 1989) was a medium-
weight wine with some wood flavours, good open tropical fruit
and plenty of concentration.

CASTELLO VICCHIOMAGGIO,
RIPA DELLE MIMOSE   →***
John Matta, owner of this medieval castle, produces a finely
regarded Chianti Classico, as well as *riservas* such as Prima
Vigna. The Chardonnay, Ripa delle Mimosa is an excellent,
barrel-fermented wine, full of toasty qualities, but backed-up by
good fruit. The 88 (tasted in 1989) still in cask, promised well.

OTHER ITALIAN CHARDONNAYS
Further south, Chardonnay pops up in the most unusual
places. Probably the most curious of all is in the flat plains of
Puglia, down in the heel of Italy, where a few producers,
Simonini and Odoardi among them, are making very good
Chardonnays in a fresh, clean unoaked style. Tenuta di
Torrebianco, owned by the *spumante* producer Gancia, have
made a cool-climate Chardonnay, Preludio No 1, with fruit from
vineyards at a high altitude.

Spain

Chardonnay is hardly a widely planted variety in Spain. It has been restricted so far almost entirely to a few vineyards in Catalonia. But there it has produced a few world-class wines that suggest it could be used more widely. Elsewhere, notably in Navarra, in the Somontano region in the foothills of the Pyrenees and in Alella, north of Barcelona, there are experimental plantings.

PRODUCERS

JEAN LÉON
→ ***

C/Capitan Arenas 40, 08034 Barcelona

In 1967 an expatriate Los Angeles restaurant owner, Jean Léon, decided to produce two single varietal wines back in his native Spain. He chose the Penedés region of Catalonia, where he bought some land and set about planting Cabernet Sauvignon, to which he subsequently added Chardonnay, using cuttings supposedly derived from vines in Corton-Charlemagne in Burgundy. Since his aim was to sell the wines in his California restaurants, he deliberately chose to make them in a Californian, rather than Spanish style. Fermentation is in Limousin wood and the wine is aged for six to nine months before bottling. The result is a heavily oaked Chardonnay, which in a blind-tasting would be more likely to be placed in the Napa Valley than in Penedés. I have tasted the 87 Jean Léon Chardonnay twice recently, and found it ripely woody, perhaps a little too much so, but it is a convincing wine that gives off all the New World attributes of Chardonnay – spice, pepper and perfumed tropical fruit.

RAIMAT
** → ***

Ctra Nacional 340, 08758 Carvello, Barcelona

The Raimat estate is the long-term brainchild of the Raventos family, owners of the huge Cava sparkling-wine house of Codorniu. In semi-desert country in what is now the Costers del Segre region near Lerida well inland from the main Penedés vineyards, they bought an estate back in 1929, which is now producing excellent Cabernet Sauvignon and Chardonnay as well as sparkling wines under the Raimat label. The vineyards get little rain, so irrigation is allowed, the vines are trained on wires (unusual in Spain where most vines are simply bushes), and the wines are made in an outstanding winery which was designed by a pupil of the great architect Gaudí. The wines are getting better all the time, and the still Chardonnay – a blend of 82 percent Chardonnay, 9 percent Parellada and 9 percent Macabeo and which is unoaked – is now a good, middle-range wine, at a good, middle-range price. Even more interesting is the sparkling Chardonnay Cava which has aroused considerable critical acclaim.

VINEDOS MIGUEL TORRES

***→

08720 *Vilafranca de Penedés, Tarragona*

Total v'yds owned: 600ha (1,482 acres)
Chardonnay owned: 38ha (94 acres)

The innovations introduced by the Torres family are widely recorded. They have been the first to undertake any serious blending of local Spanish grape varieties with imported varieties. Their wines, ranging from relatively inexpensive to top-class world beaters, are always praised. They have promoted a new, modern image of Spanish table wines almost single-handed. Chardonnay has been planted in their vineyards in the Middle and High Penedés, inland from Vilafranca de Penedés, for some time and has been used in one of their most famous blends, along with the local Parellada grape: Gran Viña Sol has 30 per cent Chardonnay. With the 1985 vintage, Torres introduced a new 100 percent Chardonnay wine, called Milmanda. This is barrel-fermented in new wood: the 85 vintage in fact suffered from too much wood, but the 86 saw it come into better balance. By the 88 Milmanda, this was a world-class wine, surprisingly light, but perfectly balanced between some spicy wood and delicious clean fruit – definitely Old World in its comparative reticence despite the obvious wood overtones.

Other European Chardonnays

PORTUGAL

The Chardonnay craze has hardly hit Portugal, which continues to rely on its time-honoured local white varieties for its range of white wines, including Vinho Verde. However, there is one Chardonnay wine, which I have not tasted, made by the sparkling-wine firm of Raposeira in the Douro region in the north of the country. Called Quinta de Valprado, it is described by Charles Metcalfe and Kathryn McWhirter in their book *Wines of Spain and Portugal* (London 1988) as "buttery and honeyed" which would seem to suggest some oak in the maturing of the wine.

GERMANY

The Chardonnay is not a permitted grape variety in Germany, although there are a few experimental plantings under its German name of Weisser Clevner. It should not be confused with the Weissburgunder (meaning the white grape from Burgundy) which, despite its seeming similarity is, in fact, now shown to be the Pinot Blanc.

AUSTRIA

Nearly 100ha (247 acres) of Chardonnay are planted in Austria, putting it well down the list of officially permitted varieties. It needs the warmer regions such as Burgenland and Gumpolds-kirchen to produce wines of any depth or ripeness. It has been around for a while, submerged under local names such as Morillon and Feinburgunder. Only in the last few years has any serious attention been paid to it by a few producers. The best example I have tasted has been the *barrique*-fermented Chardonnay of Georg Stiegelmar in the Burgenland (   ) which, while a little too woody showed considerable varietal character, and could improve with bottle age.

BULGARIA

The growth of the Bulgarian wine industry in the few decades since the war is one of the perhaps few successes of the centralized economy under which the country was run until 1990. The target of providing cheap, well-made wine to Western Europe, particularly Britain, was set out clearly and exactly and succeeded to such an extent that, by 1989, the red Cabernet Sauvignon from Bulgaria was Britain's top selling red wine.

The development of Chardonnay is of much more recent origin. In 1983 I was shown "experimental" wines made from Chardonnay, and the wines only reached the export market with the 85 and 86 vintages. They have not had quite the success of Cabernet Sauvignon – the wines have not been quite so stylistically successful, and the market has turned more to the richer styles from the New World. However, what is made is of reasonable quality, considering the price, and it certainly stands comparison with some of the pricier offerings from the

Mâconnais in France. The Chardonnay vineyards are concentrated in the eastern wine region of the country in Silistria, Shumen, Varna and in Novi Pazar. Sparkling wine production using Chardonnay is also centred in this area. Modern stainless steel-fermentation is used, and currently none of the wine sees oak. There are four Chardonnays made from this region: a basic non-vintage Chardonnay; dry soft, perfumed, if lacking much varietal character; Novi Pazar Controliran (from a designated region), the 86 rather tart, a little sharp, but with a hint of the buttery character of the Chardonnay; best of all is the Khan Krum Chardonnay, another Controliran wine from a designated region ripe, with excellent balance. I thought I detected the hint of wood here, but certainly future examples of this wine will have some wood-ageing and possibly barrel fermentation, which should flesh out the wine. The fourth Chardonnay, a new Controliran wine from Varna, has just been released: I have not tasted this yet.

ENGLAND

Small amounts of Chardonnay have been planted in England with, as yet, few firm results. The risks of the climate are not so great as to rule out Chardonnay, provided adequate frost protection can be arranged. Ripening should present no more of a problem than it does with other varieties. At present the largest planting is at the Wellow Vineyard at Romsey, Hampshire, whose first wines were produced in 1988. The excellent 1989 harvest will have given a boost to this production, but I have not tasted the results. Other vineyards in Hampshire, Sussex, Avon, Devon and Somerset have small amounts of Chardonnay, and in the future it could lend itself to use in English sparkling wines which are now being produced.

The only English Chardonnay I have tasted was a 1986 produced at Yearlstone Vineyard in Devon, which was fermented in lightly toasted Limousin oak barrels and then bottled after six months in wood: it made a light, but well-knit slightly toasty wine, which had good smoky, buttery character (** →). It certainly suggested that Chardonnay has potential in the English vineyards.

Index